Third Party Politics since 1945
John Stevenson

British Science and Politics since 1945
Thomas Wilkie

British Public Opinion
Robert M. Worcester

Forthcoming:

British Industry since 1945
Margaret Ackrill

The Conservative Party since 1945
John Barnes

The British Monarchy
Robert Blackburn

The Labour Party since 1945
Brian Brivati and Andrew Thomas

Electoral Change since 1945
Ivor Crewe and Pippa Norris

Religion in Britain
Grace Davie

Foreign Policy since 1945
Anne Deighton

British Social Policy since 1945
Howard Glennerster

Sport in Britain since 1945
Richard Holt and Tony Mason

Parliament since 1945
Philip Norton

The Trade Union Question in British Politics
Robert Taylor

The Civil Service since 1945
Kevin Theakston

British Foreign Policy since 1945
Geoffrey Warner

Terrorism since 1945
Paul Wilkinson

The Politics of Immigration

Immigration, 'Race' and 'Race' Relations in Post-war Britain

Zig Layton-Henry

BLACKWELL
Oxford UK & Cambridge USA

First published 1992

Blackwell Publishers
108 Cowley Road
Oxford OX4 1JF
UK

238 Main Street, Suite 501,
Cambridge, Massachusetts 02142
USA

British Library Cataloguing-in-Publication Data

A CIP catalogue record for this book is available from
the British Library.

Library of Congress Cataloging-in-Publication Data

A CIP catalogue record for this book is available from the Library of Congress
ISBNs: 0 631 16743 9(hbk.); 0 631 16744 7 (pbk.)

Typeset in 10½ on 12½ pt Ehrhardt
by Setrite Typesetters Ltd.
Printed in Great Britain by T.J. Press (Padstow) Ltd, Padstow, Cornwall

This book is printed on acid-free paper

For Barbara

Contents

Tables

Figures

General Editor's Preface

The Institute of Contemporary British History's series *Making Contemporary Britain* is aimed directly at students and at others interested in learning more about topics in post-war British history. In the series, authors are less attempting to break new ground than presenting clear and balanced overviews of the state of knowledge on each of the topics.

The ICBH was founded in October 1986 with the objective of promoting the study of British history since 1945 at every level. To that end, it publishes books and a quarterly journal, *Contemporary Record*; it organizes seminars and conferences for school students, undergraduates, researchers and teachers of post-war history; and it runs a number of research programmes and other activities.

A central theme of the ICBH's work is that post-war history is too often neglected in British schools, institutes of higher education and beyond. The ICBH acknowledges the validity of the arguments against the study of recent history, notably the problems of bias, of overly subjective teaching and writing, and the difficulties of perspective. But it believes that the values of studying post-war history outweigh the drawbacks, and that the health and future of a liberal democracy require that its citizens know more about the most recent past of their country than the limited knowledge possessed by British citizens, young and old, today. Indeed, the ICBH believes that the dangers of political indoctrination are higher where the young are *not* informed of the recent past.

Of all the subjects covered in the series, few if any require more sensitive and dispassionate treatment, or are more important, than this volume on the post-war history of Britain's immigration. The book indeed makes most forcefully the case for the serious study of post-war history, as it tackles this most emotive of subjects with a rare blend of empirical data and mature analysis.

It is now twenty-four years since Enoch Powell's 'rivers of blood' speech, which so inflamed underlying passions on race. The speech occurred halfway through the period since 1945, which illustrates for how long the subject has been so prominent. Not that Powell's speech began the tension. As the author's text shows, racial tension predated 1968, and the unrest stemming from the African, Caribbean and Asian 'colonial' immigration from the 1940s. Serious unrest had earlier emanated from Jewish immigration from Eastern Europe and Russia from 1870–1914, and Irish immigration before that.

The topic of this book is no less than the transformation of Britain into a multicultural country, and the differing responses made by the various ethnic groups coming to this country, by the indigenous population and by Labour and Conservative governments. It is a book which all students of modern Britain and others with a serious concern about Britain's future should read.

Anthony Seldon

Preface and Acknowledgements

In 1984 when *The Politics of Race in Britain* was published, there were few general textbooks available for students which analysed the political consequences of New Commonwealth immigration to Britain in the post-war period. There were a number of excellent works such as Paul Foot's *Immigration and Race in British Politics*, Dilip Hiro's *Black British, White British*, Ira Katznelson's *Black Men, White Cities*, and Gary Freeman's *Immigrant Labor and Racial Conflict*. There was also the seminal study *Colour and Citizenship* by E. J. B. Rose, Nicholas Deakin and their associates. However, none of these quite covered the range of contemporary political issues, institutions and activities that I wished to address.

The neglect of 'race' issues by political scientists is much less significant now than it was even five years ago. There has been a large number of publications both of general texts and of more specialized studies which have given students and other interested readers a much wider choice of stimulating material. In particular, the diversity of the local politics of 'race' has been greatly enhanced by the publication of such books as J. Eade's *The Politics of Community: The Bangladeshi Community in East London*; M. FitzGerald's *Black People and Party Politics in Britain*; S. Shaggar's *Race and Public Policy*; P. Werbner and M. Anwar's edited collection, *Black and Ethnic Leaderships: The Cultural Dimensions of Political Action*, and W. Ball and J. Solomos' collection *The Local Politics of 'Race'*.

This book is a successor to *The Politics of Race in Britain*. It is substantially different from that work in terms both of its organization and of its coverage of material. It covers some of the same ground as its predecessor, but it has been substantially changed both in its content and in order to take account of new scholarship, contemporary developments and newly available archives. It has also been considerably updated.

There are a number of debts to be acknowledged. I am grateful to the Economic and Social Science Research Council for a personal research grant in 1989–90 which enabled me to start work on this book. I must thank Allen & Unwin for encouraging me to write *The Politics of Race in Britain*, and Anthony Seldon of the Institute of Contemporary British History and Blackwell Publishers for stimulating me to write this book. On occasion I have drawn on material first published in article or chapter form: in particular, 'Black electoral participation: an analysis of recent trends', published in H. Goulbourne (ed.), *Black Politics in Britain*, and which forms the basis for chapter 5 of the present book; I am grateful to Gower Publishing for permission to make use of the material here. I wish to thank the Macmillan Press for permission to use material from my chapter, 'Race and the Thatcher government', published in Zig Layton–Henry and Paul B. Rich (eds), *Race, Government and Politics in Britain*, 1986; and Mr Robert Waller of the Harris Research Centre for making polling data available and for granting permission to re-analyse the data. I am also grateful to Her Majesty's Stationery Office, the Macmillan Press, the National Association for the Care and Rehabilitation of Offenders and the Organization of Economic and Cultural Development for permission to publish the tables. The reports on immigration and race relations which have been published in *New Community* and, more recently, in *Contemporary Britain: An Annual Review*, edited by Peter Catterall for the Institute of Contemporary British History, have proved invaluable in encouraging me to keep up to date with new developments. I am indebted to the Commission for Racial Equality and Blackwell Publishers for providing the spur and for permission to make use of the material.

I have worked on this book in the stimulating environments of the Department of Politics and International Studies and the Centre for Research in Ethnic Relations, both at the University of Warwick. I am grateful to my colleagues for their support and am particularly indebted to Heather Lynn and Ann Shaw for their help as Librarians at the excellent resources centre which has been developed at CRER. I am grateful to Tomas Hammar,

Marian FitzGerald and Donley T. Studlar for their friendship and encouragement, and especially to Marian for reading and commenting on the first draft of the book. Her incisive comments have greatly helped to improve the manuscript. I am also grateful to Dr David Owen of the Centre for Research in Ethnic Relations for his help in preparing figures 1.1 and 1.2 and to Sue Phillpott for her excellent work as copy-editor. I must accept the blame for any errors or imperfections that remain. Finally, my thanks go to Dorothy Foster for her good humour and expertise in typing and correcting the manuscript, and to my family for their tolerance and support.

Zig Layton-Henry
Kenilworth

1 The transformation of British society

Britain has always been a country involved in migration, although in recent centuries emigration has been far more important than immigration. Since the eighteenth century large numbers of Britons have migrated overseas where they have helped to establish and populate the United States and the countries of the British Empire and Commonwealth. During the nineteenth century the majority of migrants went to the United States, but after 1900 most emigrated to Canada, Australia and other Commonwealth countries. By the beginning of the twentieth, emigration had become an important part of imperial policy. British governments believed that emigration would assist the economic development of the Empire, strengthen ties between the colonies or Dominions and the mother country, and increase the power of Britain in the world. Ties of kith and kin and language would foster British trade and influence.

The depression between the wars caused a change in the balance of migration, and the net flow became an inward one as many would-be emigrants returned home disillusioned after failing to establish themselves overseas. After the Second World War, however, emigration resumed at a high level, encouraged particularly by the policies of the Australian government, which was concerned to increase its population for economic and security reasons and also to maintain its British character. Between 1946 and 1950 some 720,000 people left Britain, an annual rate of 144,000. Most of these were relatively highly skilled.[1]

Britain experienced substantial emigration in most of the seventy years prior to the Second World War. The net migration between 1871 and 1941 was as follows:[2]

1871–80	−257,000
1881–90	−817,000
1891–1900	−122,000
1901–10	−756,000
1911–20	−857,000
1921–30	−565,000
1931–40	+650,000

The flow of emigration was reversed during the 1930s because of the world recession, and the balance of migration was reversed as many earlier emigrants, who had failed to establish themselves successfully, returned to Britain. The post-war shortage of labour and the resumption of traditional patterns of emigration to the Commonwealth, which had been interrupted by the war, were a source of concern to the Royal Commission on Population, which was established by the wartime coalition government in 1944 to assess post-war manpower requirements. They were worried about the disadvantages inherent in a falling population, but nevertheless thought that the government should continue to facilitate emigration for economic and political reasons. Both the government – which at this time was making strenuous efforts to recruit voluntary European workers from displaced persons camps in Germany, resettle Polish ex-servicemen and recruit migrant workers from Italy – and the Royal Commission on Population, failed to anticipate that labour shortages caused by post-war reconstruction and economic recovery would lead to spontaneous immigration from the Caribbean colonies and then from the Indian subcontinent.

Emigration has continued from Britain throughout the post-war period and has generally been at a higher rate than immigration. Most West European countries have gained considerable additions to their populations from immigration, but in Britain, in spite of considerable immigration, the net flow has continued to be an outward one:[3]

1951–61	+12,000
1961–71	−320,000
1971–81	−699,000
1981–8	−6,000

Immigration to Britain

Throughout its history Britain, especially England, has been a destination for immigrants and refugees. Early invaders, like the Angles, Jutes, Saxons, Danes, Norwegians and Normans, were attracted by hopes of booty and fertile land. Later immigrants, like the Flemings, Germans, Walloons and Dutch, were often invited by English monarchs or were fleeing religious or political persecution. It is estimated that after the Edict of Nantes in 1685 some 80,000 Huguenots fled to England to escape Catholic persecution in France. During the French Revolution French Catholics and aristocrats fled in large numbers to England for safety, but many returned after the Restoration.

The continuing presence of substantial numbers of foreigners in England and the ability of their children to integrate and assimilate has long been a cause of comment and satire, most notably by Daniel Defoe[4] in his poem, 'The True-born Englishman':

> Proudly they learn all men to condemn
> And all their race are true-born Englishmen
> Dutch, Walloons, Flemings, Irishmen and Scots,
> Vaudois, Valtelins and Huguenots ...
>
> Fate jumbled them together, God knows how;
> Whate'er they were, they're true-born English
> now.

Considerable migration has also taken place within the British Isles during the last two hundred years. This migration has largely been from the peripheral countries of the United Kingdom — Ireland, Scotland and Wales — to England.

Ireland in particular has been a major source of migrants. Between 1820 and 1910 nearly five million people left the island, mainly for the United States, but large numbers also settled in Britain. In 1861 the census recorded that there were 601,634 Irish born in England and Wales, about 3% of the population. In Scotland there were 204,083, some 7% of the Scottish population. This migration, caused by poverty and famine in Ireland and economic growth in Britain, was encouraged by Ireland's geographical proximity and the historic links between England and Ireland which go back to the twelfth century and beyond. In 1801 Britain and Ireland were formally united under one parliament, but the union was dissolved in 1921 with the creation of the Irish Free State. Despite the independence of most of Ireland, successive British governments have always allowed unrestricted movement between the two countries, and have never treated Irish citizens as aliens.[5] They are accorded full citizenship rights, including voting rights, and in practice are considered to be British. In 1965 Ireland granted local voting rights to foreign citizens who were permanently resident in Ireland. This mainly benefited British citizens and was the first step to full reciprocal voting rights between Britain and Ireland. In 1984 British citizens were accorded national voting rights in Eire. This was partly the result of a campaign in the Conservative party to restrict Irish voting rights, caused by frustration over the IRA campaign in Ulster. The initiative taken by the Irish government was successful in defusing the Tory campaign, and it completed the process of reciprocal voting rights for Irish citizens in Britain and for British citizens in the Republic of Ireland. Successive British governments and British employers have long regarded Ireland as a valuable source of additional workers, and every effort has been made to protect freedom of movement between the two countries.

The close ties between Britain and Ireland did not mean that Irish immigrants were welcomed by their fellow-citizens in nineteenth-century Britain. In both England and Scotland the Irish were faced with considerable hostility and violence. They were poor, and were willing to work long hours for lower wages than British workers. They were thus seen as direct competitors for jobs. They were also Catholic and therefore not regarded as properly British, as they owed allegiance to an alien Church. Religious antagonism was particularly strong in Scotland, where hostility to Catholicism was more intense than in England. The Irish were stereotyped as lazy, idolatrous, diseased and criminal – charges that were avidly propagated by the press, including *The Times*.[6]

Marx was very aware of the deep animosity between English and Irish workers. In 1870 he wrote:

Every industrial and commercial centre in England now possesses a working class divided into two hostile camps, English proletarians and Irish proletarians. The ordinary English worker hates the Irish worker as a competitor who lowers his standard of life. In relation to the Irish worker he feels himself a member of the ruling nation and so turns himself into a tool of the aristocrats and capitalists of his country against Ireland, thus strengthening their domination over himself. He cherishes religious, social, and national prejudices against the Irish worker. His attitude towards him is much the same as that of the 'poor whites' to the 'niggers' in the former slave states of the U.S.A. The Irishman pays him back with interest in his own money. He sees in the English worker at once the accomplice and the stupid tool of the English rule in Ireland.

This antagonism is artificially kept alive and intensified by the press, the pulpit, the comic papers, in short, by all the means at the disposal of the ruling classes. This antagonism is the secret of the impotence of the English working class, despite its organization. It is the secret by which the capitalist class maintains its power. And that class is fully aware of it.[7]

No attempt was made by the government to control Irish immigration as, in the period of greatest immigration-induced antagonism, Ireland was an integral part of the United Kingdom. Also, employers were only too pleased with the plentiful supply of cheap workers.

Immigrants, as Marx was clearly aware, are often perceived as foreign intruders, illegitimate competitors for scarce resources such as jobs, accommodation, health and welfare benefits. Large-scale immigration, in particular if it occurs over a short period, often results in resentment, hostility and violence, especially in those areas which become the focus for immigrant settlement. Between 1870 and 1914 a significant migration of Russian and Rumanian Jews to Britain occurred as a result of anti-Jewish pogroms in those countries. Most of these refugees settled in the East End of London. As had occurred with the Irish, anti-immigrant sentiments grew, and these were fanned by local Conservative politicians into considerable hostility. The frustrations and bitterness caused by poverty, unemployment, overcrowding and crime were projected on to the Jewish immigrants, who were blamed for causing the social problems which in fact already existed in profusion in the East End. About 120,000 Jews settled in Britain between 1875 and 1914, a relatively small number compared with Irish immigration but a similar number to the Polish settlement which took place during and after the Second World War and which caused relatively little agitation. Jewish immigration, though, became the target for a vicious political campaign aimed at imposing immigration controls on these 'undesirable aliens'. This campaign was, not surprisingly, focused on the East End of London.

Anti-Jewish agitation was led by a small number of Conservative back-benchers, notably Sir Howard Vincent from Sheffield and Major Evans-Gordon from Stepney. Evans-Gordon was particularly concerned to bolster his constituency support by whipping up and leading the anti-immigrant campaign in the East End. The campaign could rely on the diffuse anti-Semitism which already existed in British society.[8] Vincent and Evans-Gordon also knew they had support at the highest levels of the Conservative party as Lord Salisbury, the Prime Minister, had himself introduced a Bill to control immigration in 1894. Lord Hardwicke, a back-bench peer, introduced a similar Bill in 1898.[9] In 1889 a Select Committee of the House of Commons had investigated the immigration question. It had concluded that the number of aliens was not large enough to cause alarm, being lower than that of other European countries, and that their health was good. Concentrated settlement and overcrowding were a problem, but legislation to control immigration was not necessary — though it might become so in the future.

Evans-Gordon continued his campaign and in 1901 formed the British Brothers League, a militant anti-Jewish organization which arranged demonstrations and mass meetings in the East End. In 1902 the government responded to the pressure by setting up a Royal Commission on alien immigration which, like the Select Committee, found that the numbers of immigrants were small, that they were as clean and healthy as the host population and that there were very few criminals among them. Once language problems were overcome, their children adapted well to English schools and integrated well with local pupils. However, in spite of acquitting Jewish immigrants of the scurrilous charges made against them, the majority of the Commissioners, led by Evans-Gordon, supported the exclusionist position and recommended that certain categories of 'undesirable alien' should be refused entry to the country.[10]

The Aliens Act was passed in 1905. It gave the Home Secretary powers to refuse entry to those who could not support themselves and their dependants, to those whose infirmities were likely to lead them to become a charge on the rates, and to some known criminals. The principle of political asylum was reaffirmed, however, and an immigrant could not be refused entry if he could show he had been the subject of political or religious persecution. Foot argues that a bankrupt administration tried to exploit anti-alien sentiment in order to reverse its declining electoral fortunes. It passed legislation and set up an immigration control administration that was entirely unnecessary.[11] This was a precedent that was to be avidly followed by both Conservative and Labour administrations in their response to post-war New Commonwealth immigration.

The espousal of the anti-alien cause did not save the Conservatives from overwhelming electoral defeat at the hands of the Liberals in the general election of 1906. Major Evans-Gordon, though, saved his Stepney seat. The newly elected Liberal administration was able to use reports of violence against Jews in Russia to allow immigration to continue and resist pressure to enforce the Act vigorously. But they did not repeal the legislation. No further action was taken until, amid the outburst of chauvinism at the onset of the First World War, the government passed the Aliens Restriction Act 1914 which gave the Home Secretary complete power over foreign immigration and foreign residents in Britain. After the war the Aliens Restriction (Amendment) Act 1919 was passed; this repealed the 1905 Aliens Act and extended the 1914 legislation for a further year. In 1920 a new Aliens Order was passed and was then renewed every year, until superseded by the Immigration Act 1971; this 'temporary' legislation was renewed by the Expiring Laws Continuance Act. It was this legislation which gave the Home Secretary the power to deport any alien whose presence in Britain was not considered to be 'conducive to the public good'.

The results of the anti-aliens campaign were thus wholly negative. The agitation stirred up by Sir Howard Vincent and Major Evans-Gordon and acquiesced in by the Conservative leadership legitimized anti-Jewish hatred and violence in the East End. It made open anti-Semitism more respectable in British society — a respectability that was not dissipated until after the Second World War.[12] It prepared the ground for Mosley's British Union of Fascists who were also to focus their activities on the East End of London, where they hoped to harness the anti-Jewish sentiments fostered by the anti-aliens campaign. Much later, in the 1970s, the National Front also campaigned in the East End, hoping to mobilize support then based on an anti-immigrant tradition going back over eighty years. The anti-immigrant campaign contributed to a negative official attitude to Jewish refugees fleeing from Nazi Germany after Hitler's rise to power in 1933.[13]

The next major settlement of aliens occurred during and after the Second World War. The largest group were some 120,000 Poles who had been members of the Allied armies under British command. For the first time a British government took positive action to assist the integration and settlement of these alien residents. A Polish Resettlement Act was passed in 1947 and a Polish Resettlement Corps was established. The integration of the Polish ex-combatants and their families was achieved remarkably smoothly, despite some popular and trade union opposition. This integration was aided by the organizations established by the Polish government in exile during the war, which helped to arrange assistance, training and settlement. Public and elite sympathy for wartime allies who had lost their country facilitated government support. However, the main reason for the successful integration of the Polish ex-servicemen and their families was the acute shortage of labour at the end of the war, which resulted in their rapid absorption into the economy. Nevertheless, the positive measures taken by the government to settle the Poles and assist their integration was in marked contrast to the lack of assistance provided for most earlier and later groups, most of whom had to rely on themselves or on voluntary agencies.

The background to colonial immigration

The context within which the migration of colonial labour to Britain took place is very different from that of foreign or alien immigration, even though the response to alien and colonial immigrants has been remarkably similar. As subjects of the British Empire, colonial immigrants had the right of access to Britain and full rights of citizenship, including voting rights, the right to work in the civil service and the right to serve in the armed forces. In fact, many of the early migrants had seen service in the British forces during the war. Many had a good knowledge of the English language and of British history, and experience of the British education system. Many, especially those from the West Indies, felt themselves to be British and had high expectations of their reception, treatment and future in the 'mother country'.

However, their origins in colonies, or former colonies recently granted independence, carried disadvantages as well as advantages. The imperial legacy also involved the history of the conquest and enslavement of African, Indian and Caribbean people. The feeling and behaviour of native white British people, perhaps especially those of the political elite, towards Afro-Caribbean and Asian migrant workers, and their images of them, were influenced by the knowledge that these migrants had been subject peoples of the British Empire. In turn, colonial migrants were influenced in their attitudes, personality and culture by their legacy of subjection. They knew they had been badly treated in the past and hoped the victorious ending of the war and their contribution to the Allied Victory would herald a better future. In fact they expected it, so great was their confidence in British institutions and especially British notions of justice and fair play. For the large numbers of migrants who met with discrimination and disappointment, therefore, the disillusionment was so much greater, and for some the history of slavery, racism and exploitation in the Empire provided powerful explanations for their failure to realize their expectations as well as a justification for alienation, resentment and revolt.

British governments have traditionally favoured the free movement of capital and labour within the Empire, although by the turn of the century all the self-governing Dominions had acted to control immigration to their territories, largely because of concern over the potential extent of Indian immigration. Britain alone had no restrictions, a principle reaffirmed by the Nationality Acts of 1914 and 1948. In the debate on the Nationality Act of 1948 Sir David Maxwell Fyfe, the Conservative spokesman on home affairs, said, 'We are proud that we impose no colour bar restrictions making it difficult for them when they come here ... we must maintain our great metropolitan tradition of hospitality to everyone from every part of our Empire.'[14] A year later a Conservative party policy document stated that 'there must be freedom of movement amongst its members within the British Empire and Commonwealth. New opportunities will present themselves not only in the countries overseas but in the Mother Country, and must be open to all citizens.'[15] The assumption was, though, that the major population movement would continue to be emigration from the United Kingdom to the Empire and Commonwealth.

Before the Second World War there already existed small settlements of black[16] people in such ports as Liverpool and Cardiff, and in Manchester and London's East End. These had been established mainly by colonial seamen, especially during the First World War. The world depression in the inter-war years provided no incentive for immigration, and those who came to Britain were mainly returning emigrants unable to establish themselves in the Dominions because of the recession. There was some immigration of refugees from Central Europe as the Nazis consolidated their power.

An interdepartmental working party of civil servants, set up in January 1953 to consider a range of matters associated with colonial immigration, found there were no accurate estimates of the size and composition of the non-white community in Britain. They asked the police to provide such estimates for them, and the police estimated that at the beginning of 1953, a few years after the migration of colonial migrant workers had begun, there were about 40,000 non-white people living in Great Britain. The largest communities were in London (19,000), Liverpool (15,500), Birmingham (3,660), Manchester (3,000), Coventry (1,300), Cardiff (1,000) and Glasgow (850). The approximate composition by ethnic origin was as follows:[17]

West Africans	15,000
Indians and Pakistanis	9,300
West Indians	8,600
Arabs	1,600
Chinese	1,300
East Africans	700
Somalis	600

In addition, the Colonial Office estimated that there were 3,000 colonial students in London. There were no estimates of Indian, Pakistani or Ceylonese students.[18]

It was the outbreak of war in 1939 that had dramatically changed the situation and set in train the events that were to lead to the post-war migration of West Indian, African and Asian migrant workers and the transformation of Britain from a multinational state into a multiracial society as well. During the war colonial labour was recruited to work in forestry, munitions factories and the services. The major examples of official government recruitment were a group of 1,200 British Hondurans who were employed to fell timber in Scotland, about 1,000 West Indian technicians and trainees recruited to work in munitions factories in Merseyside and Lancashire, and 10,000 West Indians recruited for service in the Royal Air Force to work in Britain as ground crews. In addition, thousands of colonial seamen were either recruited or enlisted voluntarily in the merchant navy. Considerable numbers of West Indians, Asians and Africans served in the Allied forces during the war.

The war was a tremendously important catalyst and cause of post-war migration. Large numbers of colonial people were uprooted from their home communities; men serving abroad had their horizons widened and saw opportunities for work in Britain. Those colonial servicemen and workers who experienced war service in Britain did so under relatively favourable conditions. There was important work for them to do and every person was needed; they were participants in the struggle for national survival, and were reasonably well received by the British public. Racial prejudice and discrimination in housing and employment, which had been a serious factor blighting the lives of black people already settled in the seaport towns and confining them to particular areas, was now reduced.

After 1941 there was a substantial increase in the number of colonial stowaways who came mainly from West Africa and the West Indies, as well as bona fide colonial passengers and seamen, coming to Britain. And in 1942 it was made easier for colonial subjects to enter Britain, as restrictions on landing without documentary evidence of British nationality were lifted after representations from colonial governments. It was felt that since all British subjects were contributing equally to the war effort, there should be no restrictions on particular groups wishing to enter Britain. Given the shortage of labour caused by the war, these colonial migrants had little difficulty in finding employment. Then, after the war every effort was made to repatriate them, but many had got married and had decided to settle in Britain. In addition, many of those who had gone back to the West Indies were unable to find work, and so decided to return to Britain. The war had given many West Indians experience of British life, and the continuing shortage of labour meant that jobs were still easily available, especially for less skilled workers.

In 1948, because of the continuing labour shortage, the British government set up a working party on the employment in the United Kingdom of surplus colonial labour.[19] The committee noted the serious unemployment situation in Jamaica and the shortage of labour in the United Kingdom, but was concerned about the discrimination that 'coloured'[20] workers would face and the difficulties of assimilating them. It therefore recommended that no organized large-scale immigration of male colonial workers should be contemplated. The committee recognized, however, the importance of recruiting female colonial workers because of the huge shortage of nurses and domestic workers in the newly established Health Service.[21]

But the deliberations of the committee had already been overtaken by events, as the first immigrant ships began to arrive from the West Indies during 1948. A largely spontaneous movement of people from the Caribbean to Britain had begun, and this was soon to be followed by immigration from the Indian subcontinent. It is important to note that this migration was relatively unorganized and voluntary: the migrants decided themselves to migrate and paid their own costs – unlike the later migrant 'guest workers' to other European countries such as West Germany, who were recruited and financed by the respective governments. An estimation of net immigration from the New Commonwealth can be obtained from table 1.1.

Once migration from the Caribbean and the Indian subcontinent began, it quickly gained considerable momentum through the processes of chain migration. The early migrants encouraged friends and relatives to follow them, and employers desperate for the labour adapted their recruitment practices. The London

Table 1.1 Estimated net immigration from the New Commonwealth, 1953−62

	West Indies	India	Pakistan	Others	Total
1953	2,000				2,000
1954	11,000				11,000
1955	27,500	5,800	1,850	7,500	42,650
1956	29,800	5,600	2,050	9,350	46,800
1957	23,000	6,600	5,200	7,600	42,400
1958	15,000	6,200	4,700	3,950	29,850
1959	16,400	2,950	850	1,400	21,600
1960	49,650	5,900	2,500	−350	57,700
1961	66,300	23,750	25,100	21,250	136,400
1962[a]	31,800	19,050	25,080	18,970	94,900

[a] First six months up to introduction of controls.
Source: House of Commons, *Commonwealth Immigration to the United Kingdom from the 1950s to 1975: A Survey of Statistical Sources*, Library Research Paper no. 56, HMSO, 1976

Transport executive entered into an agreement with the Barbadian Immigrants' Liaison Service, as a result of which several thousand Barbadians were loaned their fare to Britain. In 1966 London Transport began to recruit workers in Trinidad and Jamaica. The British Hotels and Restaurants Association was also involved in recruiting workers from Barbados.[22] Woolf's rubber factory in Southall enlisted workers from the Punjab, and northern textile companies advertised for workers in the Indian and Pakistani press. The pre-war tradition of the Ministry of Health recruiting nurses and hospital domestic workers from the Caribbean continued after the war, including the period when Enoch Powell was Minister of Health. A considerable industry developed based on travel agents, shipping companies and airlines, which made substantial profits out of arranging the transport for migrant workers moving to Britain and other destinations in Western Europe.

Thus, New Commonwealth immigration occurred because post-war reconstruction and the expansion of the British economy in the 1950s and 1960s created shortages of labour which could not be filled by British, Irish or other European sources. The less profitable, often labour-intensive, sectors of the economy such as public transport, the Health Service, the textile industry and metal manufacture could not compete successfully for the labour of British workers with the more profitable sectors such as the car industry, telecommunications and insurance. The less successful employers were only too pleased to recruit New Commonwealth workers, who were attracted to and settled in those areas of the country where labour shortages were greatest, such as Greater London, Birmingham and Manchester. Afro-Caribbean workers settled predominantly in Greater London and the West Midlands; Indians mainly in Greater London and the West Midlands, with smaller settlements in West Yorkshire and Greater Manchester; Pakistanis mainly in the West Midlands, West Yorkshire, London and Manchester; Bangladeshis mainly in East London, but also in the West Midlands. Figure 1.1 shows the distribution of the non-white population as percentages of the total population in different parts of Great Britain in 1989: there is a considerable concentration in the English conurbations, especially in Greater London and the West Midlands metropolitan area.

Multiracial Britain

By 1988 the ethnic minority population of Britain, mainly of New Commonwealth descent, numbered 2,577,000 out of a total British population of 54,519,000, thus representing some 4.5% of that total. The major groups among the ethnic minority population are Indian, West Indian and Pakistani. The *Labour Force Survey* estimates for 1986–8 are set out in table 1.2. Because of the high sampling errors for ethnic minority groups in the survey, the survey average 1986–8 gives the best estimate of population size.

The relative sizes of the white and ethnic minority populations of Great Britain and the composition of the latter population are represented diagrammatically in figure 1.2.

A distinctive feature of the non-white population is its youthfulness compared with the total population. This is because most of the early migrants were young adults when they migrated to Britain. Most of them, forty years after the migration began, have not yet reached retirement age. In 1987 only 1% of non-whites

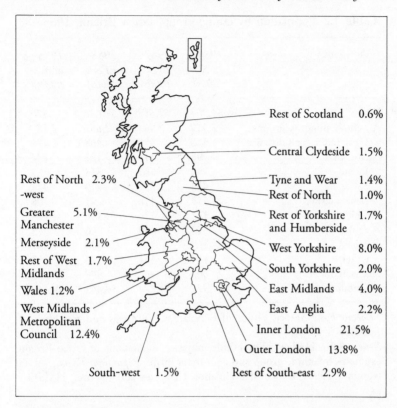

Fig. 1.1 Distribution of the non-white population of Great Britain as %s of total population, 1989 *Source: British Labour Force Surveys*, 1987–9, Office of Population, Censuses and Surveys, HMSO, 1991

were of retirement age, compared with 19% of the total population. In contrast, 34% of the non-white population were under sixteen years, compared with 20% of the white. Most people of both groups were of working age – namely, 61% of whites and 62% of non-whites. Gradually the age structure of the non-white population will become similar to that of the population as a whole, especially if the family size of recent Asian immigrant groups approaches the societal norm.

Another striking feature of the British ethnic minority population is its diversity. This can be seen in a rudimentary way in table 1.2, but the table gives little idea of the full diversity of European,

Table 1.2 Population by ethnic group, Great Britain, 1986—8

(Ethnic group	*1986 LFS[a] (000s)*	*1987 LFS (000s)*	*1988 LFS (000s)*	*1986—8 average (000s)*
White	*51,204*	*51,573*	*51,632*	*51,470*
All ethnic minority groups	*2,559*	*2,484*	*2,687*	*2,577*
West Indian or Guyanese	526	489	468	495
African	98	116	122	122
Indian	784	761	814	787
Pakistani	413	392	479	428
Bangladeshi	117	116	91	108
Chinese	113	126	136	125
Arab	73	79	66	73
Mixed	269	263	328	287
Other	164	141	184	163
Not stated	*607*	*467*	*343*	*472*
All groups	*54,370*	*54,524*	*54,662*	*54,519*

[a] *Labour Force Survey*, Office of Population, Censuses and Surveys, HMSO
Source: John Haskey, 'The ethnic minority populations of Great Britain: estimates by ethnic group and country of birth', *Population Trends*, vol. 60 (summer 1990), Office of Population Censuses and Surveys, HMSO

Caribbean, African and Asian people who have migrated to Britain in the post-war period. It is estimated, for example, that there are 800,000 Muslims in Britain, including Pakistanis, Kashmiris, Bangladeshis, Adenis, Yemenis, Somalis, Moroccans and Turkish Cypriots. Recently, Kurdish refugees have added yet another national group to the Muslim population. This diversity expresses itself not only in different territorial and national origins, but in religious affiliation and language too. Catholic Irish and Orthodox Cypriots mingle in a British context with Sikhs, Hindus and Muslims from the Indian subcontinent, alongside a largely secular non-practising Protestant majority. Similarly, in inner-city areas the English language, while predominant, is spoken together with Chinese, Creole, Urdu, Punjabi, Bengali, and a great many others. The now abolished Inner London Education Authority estimated that children in their schools spoke over a hundred different languages as their mother tongue.

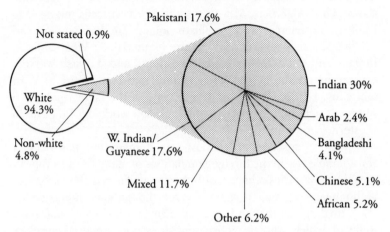

Entire population

Non-white population

Not stated 0.9%

Pakistani 17.6%

White 94.3%

Non-white 4.8%

W. Indian/ Guyanese 17.6%

Indian 30%

Arab 2.4%

Bangladeshi 4.1%

Mixed 11.7%

Chinese 5.1%

African 5.2%

Other 6.2%

Fig. 1.2 Population by ethnic group in Great Britain, 1990 (%) *Source*: *Population Trends*, vol. 67 (1992), Office of Population, Censuses and Surveys, HMSO

A European phenomenon

The migration of Third World people to Britain and the country's transformation from a predominantly Anglo-Saxon and Celtic to a multiracial society has been by no means a unique phenomenon. Similar processes have occurred in all the other advanced industrial societies of Western Europe. As these countries rebuilt their shattered economies and infrastructure after the war, labour shortages quickly developed. The gaps in their labour forces were initially filled by migrant workers from less developed neighbouring countries. Italian, Spanish and Portuguese workers migrated to France, Irish and Italians to Britain, Italians to Switzerland, Finns to Sweden. The Federal Republic of Germany not only absorbed huge numbers of refugees from Eastern Europe, particularly from former German territories lost after the war and from East Germany, but as its economic recovery progressed it recruited migrant workers from Italy, Spain, Yugoslavia, Greece and Turkey.

In the 1950s and more especially in the 1960s, the character of immigration into the major industrial states of Western Europe changed. The movement of workers from the periphery of Europe was supplemented and then overtaken by a movement from the Third World, often from the colonial territories of the receiving states. Thus Algerians, Moroccans and West Africans migrated to France; Surinamese and Antillians joined the Indonesians and Mediterranean people already in the Netherlands; West Indians, Indians and Pakistanis migrated to Britain, and Turkish workers became by far the largest foreign immigrant community in West Germany. France, Britain and Germany, as the largest industrial states, attracted three quarters of all migrant workers who came to Western Europe in the post-war period.

A major consequence of post-war immigration has been a considerable rise in the foreign populations of many West European societies. Countries which had hitherto considered themselves to be homogeneous nation states – even though such homogeneity was a myth, given that all European countries included minorities, some of which were even irredentist – now found themselves multiracial states with substantial non-European minorities. Table 1.3 gives an indication of the foreign populations of the seven major immigration countries in Western Europe. These figures do not reveal the full extent of immigration to Western Europe, because many immigrants to Britain, France and the Netherlands, as Commonwealth or colonial subjects, had the citizenship of the receiving country and so do not appear within the 'foreign population' statistics. Furthermore, in France, Sweden and Britain many foreign immigrants have become naturalized citizens of their new countries of work and residence.

Immigration has contributed hugely to the economic growth and rising standard of living in post-war Europe. West European countries have recruited millions of young, healthy and often relatively skilled people, while having avoided the costs of rearing and educating them. Immigrant workers have been prepared to work long hours, for less pay, in worse working conditions than native workers.[23] Generally they have contributed more in taxes than they have received in benefits. They have been law-abiding and cooperative residents. Many employers and governments have welcomed them as a hard-working, cheap and adaptable workforce.

However, especially when they have arrived in large numbers, immigrants have not been universally welcomed. They were welcomed as allies in the Second World War when every person

Table 1.3 Foreign populations of the seven major immigration countries of Western Europe, 1980s

	Foreign population	% total population
Belgium, 1988	868,800	8.8
France, 1985	3,752,200	6.8
Federal Republic of Germany, 1988	4,489,100	7.3
Netherlands, 1988	623,700	4.2
Sweden, 1988	421,000	5.0
Switzerland, 1988	1,006,500	15.3
United Kingdom, 1986	1,820,000	3.2

Source: OECD, *Continuous Reporting System on Migration*, 1989, Paris, 1990; *British Labour Force Surveys*, 1984–6, HMSO

was needed in the struggle for national survival; they were welcomed as doctors, nurses, drivers, conductors, cleaners and carpenters and in a huge range of other capacities during the 1950s and 1960s, when labour was scarce. But as people, as friends and neighbours or even as fellow church members, the welcome was very much less enthusiastic. Even when recruited as a replacement labour force to do the work that the natives rejected and to occupy inner-city accommodation that the natives wished to leave, they could still be seen by those who remained as competitors for jobs, housing and other scarce resources. Immigration has thus provided a stimulus for xenophobia and for campaigns for immigration control. When immigrants are non-European, latent feelings of racism may be stimulated and may have important consequences both among members of the political and economic elite and among the general population. Thus, foreign migrants may be welcomed by employers as workers but disliked and despised by them as foreigners and as non-Europeans. Governments may also welcome them as workers and subjects but be concerned about problems of housing and social integration. The general public may see little advantage in immigration at all, perceiving immigrants as just foreigners coming in to 'steal their food and jobs'. They may easily be incited into endorsing stereotypes of immigrants and supporting politicians demanding tough immigration controls.

However, these responses are not inevitable, and depend on the lead given by those in authority. It is therefore to the context of New Commonwealth immigration and especially to the reaction and responses of the government and the general public that we now turn.

Notes

1 J. Cheetham, 'Immigration', in A. H. Halsey (ed.), *Trends in British Society since 1900*, (Macmillan, 1972).

2 *Report of the Royal Commission on Population*, Cmnd 7695, HMSO, 1949.

3 Office of Population, Censuses and Surveys, *Annual Abstract of Statistics*, HMSO, 1990.

4 D. Defoe, 'The True-born Englishman', in H. Morley (ed.) *The Earlier Life and Chief Earlier Works of Daniel Defoe* (George Routledge & Sons, 1899), pp. 175–218.

5 When Eire formally withdrew from the Commonwealth in 1948 this raised a question mark over the political rights of Irish citizens in Britain as they no longer had the status of British subjects. The Labour government introduced the Ireland Act 1949 which allowed the political rights of Irish citizens in Britain to continue.

6 P. Foot, *Immigration and Race in British Politics* (Penguin Books, 1965).

7 D. McLellan (ed.), *Karl Marx: Selected Writings, Marx to Meyer and Vogt*, 9th edn April 1870 (Oxford University Press, 1977), pp. 591–2.

8 G. Lebzelter, *Political Anti-semitism in England* (Macmillan, 1978).

9 Foot, *Immigration and Race*.

10 B. Gainer, *The Alien Invasion: The Origins of the Aliens Act of 1905* (Heinemann, 1972).

11 Foot, *Immigration and Race*.

12 T. Kushner, *The Persistence of Prejudice: Anti-Semitism in British Society during the Second World War* (Manchester University Press, 1989).

13 S. Cohen, *From the Jews to the Tamils: Britain's Mistreatment of Refugees* (South Manchester Law Centre, 1988).

14 Parliamentary Debates, Commons (Hansard), vol. 453, col. 405, 7 July 1948.

15 Conservative Central Office, *The Right Road for Britain*, 1949.

16 The term 'black' will be used to include people of both Afro-Caribbean and South Asian descent, except when it is important to distinguish between the various ethnic minority communities.

17 Report of the Working Party on Coloured People Seeking Employ-
    ment in the United Kingdom, DO35/5216, Public Record Office,
    December 1953.
18 Z. Layton–Henry, 'The state and New Commonwealth immigration:
    1951–56', *New Community*, vol. 14 (1987), 64–75.
19 See p. 31.
20 The term 'coloured' is widely used in government documents of this
    period; it will be used only when quoting or reporting from these
    official documents.
21 Cabinet Papers, 'Coloured people from British colonial territories'.
22 C. Holmes, *John Bull's Island: Immigration and British Society,
    1871–1971* (Macmillan, 1988).
23 G. Wallraff, *Lowest of the Low* (Methuen, 1988).

2 The response to post-war immigration

It has already been argued in chapter 1 that immigration can provoke a hostile response from the political elite and the general population, even though immigrants may be fleeing persecution and poverty and be able to make a major contribution to the economic, cultural and social life of their new country. British history is replete with examples of the substantial contribution of immigrants such as the Flemings, the Huguenots and the Jews to the economic success and international reputation of the country. Many of the most successful companies in Britain have been developed and sustained by the energies and enterprise of immigrants, especially the Jews, who were so despised and reviled when they first arrived at the turn of the century. Many British Nobel prize winners and other men and women of distinction this century have been immigrants or the children of immigrants. However, despite the huge contribution that immigration can make to the skills, energy and enterprise of the nation, the usual response has been, at best, grudging acceptance and, at worst, outbursts of racism or xenophobia.

The impact of the Second World War

In many ways one would have expected the Second World War to have provided the ideal conditions for immigration to take place. As noted earlier, the huge demands for manpower caused by increased industrial activity and conscription to the armed forces meant that every man and woman was needed to contribute to feeding the nation, supplying its military and civilian needs and fighting for its survival. In Nazi Germany the pressures on man-power were so great that, as the war progressed, more and more extensive use was made of forced labour recruited from occupied countries. In Britain the recruitment of women workers filled part of the labour shortage, as did a substantial migration from Ireland. However, unlike Germany in 1939, Britain was the centre of a huge Empire and could rely on its imperial resources to help fight the war. Moreover, after war was declared a wave of loyalty and offers of help engulfed many colonies, and men and women volunteered to enlist or contribute to the war in other ways. In the West Indies in particular, British consulates were inundated with such offers.[1]

In such a national emergency one would have expected these offers to be accepted with alacrity and gratitude, but this was far from the case. It appears that imperial attitudes of racial superiority, and stereotypes of the unreliability, backwardness and inferiority of non-Europeans, were strong among members of the British government, the armed forces and civil service. At the beginning of the war all three branches of the armed forces in Britain restricted entry to people of pure European descent. Senior members of the forces wished to maintain this colour bar: for example, in July 1939 General Finlayson had recommended to the Army Council that:

1 commissions should be reserved for British subjects of British parents of *pure European descent*;
2 as the Royal Navy and the Royal Air Force did not need extra men, there was no need to change the rules barring men not of *pure European descent*; and
3 blacks resident in Britain should be registered but not called up for training once conscription was introduced.[2]

It is hard to imagine why the army was so adamant in wishing to maintain this colour bar, but there seems to have been a widespread feeling that black troops were less well disciplined than European troops, and there was considerable prejudice against allowing blacks to become officers. As late as 4 December 1944 the War Office informed the Colonial Office that the colour bar would be retained because 'British troops do not take kindly to being commanded by coloured officers and further ... the presence of coloured officers in a unit in peacetime is apt to be a source of embarrassment.'[3]

It was the Colonial Office whick took the lead in trying to remove the colour bar, both at home from the armed forces regulations and abroad in the administration of the colonies. It was well aware that, if the existence of the colour bar became widely known, it would provoke a furious response in the colonies, undermine the unity of the Empire and erode support for Britain in a war portrayed as the righteous struggle of democracy against Fascism. The support for the war in the West Indies, India and Africa would have been particularly affected. On 19 October 1939 the Colonial Office was successful in persuading the government to drop the colour bar, at least formally, and an announcement was made in both Houses of Parliament:

> During the present emergency, Indians, Anglo-Indians, Burmans, British subjects from the colonies and British protected persons who are in this country, including those who are not of pure European descent, are to be on the same footing as British subjects of pure European descent as regards voluntary enlistment in the armed forces and as regards eligibility to be considered for the grant of emergency commissions in those forces. This principle will apply in the case of all three services.[4]

This announcement appears to have been largely a public relations exercise for the benefit of the colonies, as, shortly after it was made, namely on 10 November 1939, the Foreign Office was advising its consular offices that 'only offers of service from white British subjects should be considered', and on 6 January 1940 the Colonial Office informed the Cabinet that 'colonial governments have already been informed that it is not desired that non-European British subjects should come for enlistment.'[5] Presumably the Colonial Office was acting under instructions, as during the war it was generally exerting pressure to get the colour bar in the services lifted, while the army and navy in particular were using every device and excuse to enforce it. It appears that only one black Briton, Arundel Moody, the son of Dr Harold Moody, President of the League of Coloured Peoples, received a commission in the British army during the war.

It was the Royal Air Force, presumably because the need for trained pilots was so great, that did accept black British subjects as officers, pilots and ground crews, and it was later widely acknowledged, even by the Cabinet, that they had given distinguished service during the war. But throughout the war the army and navy refused to drop the institutional racism[6] that they were enforcing. It was only in 1948 that the colour bar was finally removed from the army and navy recruiting instructions.

As regards the administration of the colonies, on 22 May 1941 Lord Moyne, Secretary of State for the Colonies, sent a circular to colonial governors stating: 'I trust that it will be possible in future to select for appointments to Executive Councils, persons of various sections of the community, and that no-one otherwise reasonably suitable, will be excluded because of social or racial reasons.'[7] The Duke of Windsor, then Governor of the Bahamas, was one of those who appeared to desire the maintenance of the colour bar, which then operated in the Bahamas, and he supported this position in a letter to the Colonial Secretary on 26 July. However, Lord Moyne continued to press for its removal.[8]

The arrival of black American troops in Britain in 1942 was a further test of official and public attitudes towards issues of 'race' and colour.[9] Segregation was rigidly enforced in the American armed forces, and this raised questions about whether segregation was to continue in Britain and how the British authorities and public would respond to the presence of black troops. The responses of the British authorities and those of the public seem to have been rather different. The government was against the stationing of black American troops in Britain and tried at first to exclude them or limit their numbers. When this was unsuccessful, it was willing to collude with white American policies of segregation and the subordination of blacks. A blatant example of British elite racism was contained in the 'Notes on relations with coloured troops' issued by Major-General Dowler to his district commanders in August 1942. Patronizing and highly offensive, these notes included the advice that white women should not associate with coloured men, that British soldiers should not befriend them and that white American troops should not be criticized for the way they treated their black compatriots.[10] One underlying concern which worried members of the government was the probability of sexual relations taking place between black troops and British women. Politicians such as Anthony Eden and Herbert Morrison were anxious to prevent this — for example, by restricting black troops to particular areas; but in practice they were powerless to prevent fraternization between American troops and members of the British public.

When black American troops began to arrive in Britain in 1942 they generally received a warm and friendly reception from local people in the areas where they were stationed, and there was much public criticism of their treatment at the hands of the American Army and of white American servicemen. However, there was a disapproval of black soldiers associating with British women that seems to have been quite widespread, and it was not confined to people of any particular class. The Duke of Marlborough, for example, complained to his cousin Winston Churchill, the Prime Minister, about sexual relations between black troops and English women[11]; and, in much the same way, the Duke of Buccleuch raised with Harold Macmillan the issue of the British Honduran lumbermen associating with local girls on his Scottish estate.[12] The offspring of the liaisons between black GIs and British women were widely regarded as a 'problem', and they were often taken into the care of the local authority as a matter of routine.[13] Smith concludes that racial prejudice against black GIs seemed to be greater among the middle and upper classes than in the lower and working classes.[14]

Racial prejudice and discrimination were already a factor constraining the lives of black people who had settled in Britain before the war. Certain places, like Tiger Bay in Cardiff, were well known as areas where colonial seamen had settled, and they, and their families, had suffered disproportionately high levels of unemployment and poverty. However, while black workers and servicemen in Britain during the war continued to experience and to have to fight racism, wartime conditions prompted greater expressions of goodwill and friendship and also forced the authorities to discourage blatant expressions of racism, even though they may have shared some of the underlying sentiments. The government was well aware of the vital contribution of the Imperial Indian Army and other colonial forces to the war in both Asia and Europe. This contribution, and Britain's post-war imperial role, would have been jeopardized by open support for racist policies. Its opposition to the racist policies of Fascist Germany might also have been brought into question.

The importance of the war in causing migration and settlement can be seen when we consider the winding-up of the special recruitment schemes. Most of the colonial men recruited under the schemes were eligible for gratuities and repatriation in 1945, but, although considerable efforts were made to encourage them to return home, many preferred to remain in Britain. Nearly half of the British Hondurans, for example, chose to settle in Scotland and the north of England. One fifth of the West Indians who were repatriated to Jamaica, finding themselves unemployed and with little prospect of finding jobs, spent part of their gratuities returning to Britain to seek further employment.[15] Black immigration and settlement were not welcomed by the British government or policy-makers after the war, in spite of concern about possible population decline, the needs of the labour market and the resumption of large-scale emigration from Britain. Policy-makers, whether politicians, civil servants or 'experts', were all concerned with how well immigrants would integrate and assimilate. They were also concerned about problems of crime and law and order which might be posed by their presence.[16] It was generally assumed that white European immigrants would be more skilled, valuable and assimilable as potential citizens than non-Europeans. This can be seen if we consider some of the initiatives taken by the government in the area of manpower planning after the war.

Post-war manpower requirements and population policy were matters of considerable concern to the wartime coalition government, which wished to maintain Britain's role as a great power and leader of the Commonwealth and Empire. In 1944 a Royal Commission was appointed to assess Britain's population needs. The Commission, which published its report in 1949, was particularly concerned with declining fertility and the disadvantages of a falling population, which it felt would reduce future economic growth, lead to an ageing population and result in an erosion of Britain's influence in the Commonwealth and the world. In particular, a low average family size would discourage emigration to other parts of the Commonwealth and the United States, and so reduce Britain's strong political and economic links with these countries.

The Royal Commission on Population did consider immigration as a means of combating the problems caused by declining fertility, an ageing population and the resumption of emigration after the war; but it concluded that large-scale immigration would probably be impracticable, as sources of supply of 'suitable' immigrants were meagre and colonial immigrants would be undesirable on account of the problems of training, housing and, above all, assimilation. It considered that 'immigration on a large scale into a fully established society like ours could only be welcomed without reserve if the immigrants were of good human stock [presumably European] and were not prevented by their religion or race from intermarrying with the host population and becoming merged with it.'[17]

This concern with the assimilability of immigrants was a matter which was to preoccupy politicians, civil servants and other policy-makers in the early post-war period. The independent research institute, Political and Economic Planning (PEP), published a report on population policy in 1948 which paralleled the concerns of the Royal Commission. It also assumed that European immigrants were superior to, and more suitable than, non-Europeans and stated that 'the absorption of large numbers of non-white immigrants would be extremely difficult.'[18]

The government's response to post-war immigration

The fact that some colonial governments, particularly in the West Indies, were anxious to reduce their own unemployment by encouraging emigration to Britain did not alter the British government's or the population experts' reluctance to recruit substantial numbers of colonial workers. However, in October 1948 an inter-departmental working party was established 'to enquire into the possibilities of employing in the United Kingdom surplus manpower of certain colonial territories in order to assist the manpower situation in this country and to relieve unemployment in those colonial territories'.[19] The committee noted the serious un-employment situation in Jamaica and the shortage of labour in the United Kingdom, but was uncertain whether there was much scope for further recruitment, as some 180,000 foreign workers, mainly Poles, Ukrainians and German ex-prisoners of war, had been allocated to vacancies in undermanned industries. (This was dissimulation, as the European workers could not fill the labour shortage.) The committee preferred European volunteer workers, it claimed, as they were subject to strict labour controls and could be prosecuted or deported if they broke their conditions of recruitment. In reality there was a considerable prejudice against recruiting black colonial workers. This can be seen in the committee's expressed fear that colonial workers might find unemployment benefits so generous compared with earnings in the West Indies that there would be little incentive for them to seek employment at all.[20]

The committee was more sympathetic to the recruitment of female colonial workers, noting the serious labour shortages in domestic employment, the textile industries and the Health Service, especially for nurses and hospital domestic workers. It also felt that accommodation could more easily be arranged for female workers. However, no action was taken on the committee's recommendations, and migration from the West Indies continued at a steady rate. In February 1950 the interdepartmental committee was reconvened, with representatives of the Colonial Office, the Home Office, the Ministries of Labour, Health and Transport and the National Assistance Board. Its recommendations were:

1 to press colonial governments to reduce the flow at source by making it known that jobs and accommodation in the United Kingdom are not too easily found, by not issuing passports to persons who cannot pay their passages or are obviously of the type who do not welcome regular employment and by imposing greater controls at the ports to prevent stowing away;
2 to stiffen up immigration practice at UK ports by a return to the pre-1942 practice of requiring all arrivals from any destination to produce satisfactory evidence of British nationality;
3 to set up a working party of representatives of the government departments concerned to tackle the problems of those colonials already here by dispersal, by finding employment and accommodation and by arranging for voluntary repatriation of the misfits.[21]

In March 1950 the Cabinet requested a memorandum from the Secretary of State for the Colonies on the immigration of 'coloured' people from the colonial territories. It was presented to the Cabinet on 18 May. Coloured immigration was seen as causing problems in the areas of accommodation, employment and law and order, and the remedy was seen to consist in discouraging migrants; but, since only three or four thousand people were involved at this early period of migration, the Labour government decided to take no action.

It is surprising, however, just how much interest and concern were aroused by the migration of a few thousand black people from the colonies. In June 1950 the Cabinet arranged a further review of the means by which the immigration of coloured people from British colonial territories might be checked and the implications of introducing control legislation.[22] This time a special committee was set up under the Home Secretary, and was much more positive in its conclusions. It recommended firmly that the numbers involved were so small and the issues of policy involved in control legislation so important and controversial that no action should be taken. Even legislation to control the entry of stowaways would mean a break in the traditional policy of giving all British subjects the right to enter the UK and enjoy the same rights and privileges as were given to UK citizens. It concluded that a very large increase in migration in the future might make legislation for control essential, but this was not justified at the present time.[23]

The discouraging attitude of the Labour government and its civil service advisers to colonial immigration is surprising, given the fact that the economy was being held back by a serious shortage of labour and the government was attempting to alleviate this by a number of schemes to recruit European workers. It can partly be explained by the fears of Labour politicians and trade union leaders that the boost in employment caused by post-war reconstruction and economic recovery might be short-lived, as happened after the First World War. This also explains the hostility among the unions to the employment of Poles and European volunteer workers immediately after the war, and their insistence on very stringent conditions for their employment. However, racial prejudice was clearly a powerful factor underlying this discouraging attitude and in the government's raising the consideration of immigration controls. If the immigrants had been of 'pure European descent' they would have been welcomed as a positive asset, contributing to economic growth, rectifying the labour shortage and compensating for post-war emigration. But while black immigrants were no less a positive asset in these ways, they were also seen as provoking racial prejudice (a classic example of blaming the victim) and thus likely to cause problems of law and order. Spurious reasons were therefore invented by civil servants to justify controls.

In public, the Conservative government elected to office in 1951 appeared little concerned with colonial immigration, but this was not true behind the scenes. Sir Winston Churchill reportedly told Ian Gilmour in 1954 that 'immigration is the most important subject facing this country but I cannot get any of my ministers to take any notice.'[24] Sir Winston's prejudices against black immigration were also revealed in a discussion with Sir Hugh Foot, Governor of Jamaica, when he said, 'We would have a magpie society: that would never do.'[25] In the House of Commons there had been a flurry of interest expressed in the form of questions to ministers when the first ships bringing significant numbers of West Indian immigrants, the *Empire Windrush* and the SS *Orbita*, arrived in 1948. However, the interest soon subsided. In 1954 concern about immigration revived as it became clear that a significant rise in West Indian immigration was taking place: this was due not only to the continuing labour shortage in Britain and the high levels of unemployment, particularly in Jamaica, but also to the partial halting of West Indian emigration to the USA caused by the McCarran–Walter Immigration Act of 1952.[26]

In December 1953 Brigadier Medlicott asked how many coloured persons had settled in the United Kingdom, only to be told by Sir David Maxwell Fyfe that the information was not available.[27] This did not deter members of parliament on both sides of the House from continuing to raise the issue and to lobby ministers informally. For example, in May 1954 Mr Erroll asked the Colonial Secretary whether he was aware that substantial numbers of people, mainly without adequate means of support, were arriving in Britain from abroad in search of work, and that this was causing public concern. What steps was he taking to deal with this social problem, and in particular to ensure that those who failed to find work were enabled to return home?[28] Mr Hopkinson replied that most immigrants had jobs to go to or relatives to stay with, and had adequate means. Erroll then raised the matter of reciprocal restrictions on immigration, to which Hopkinson replied, 'My Honourable Friend is certainly aware of the old tradition that British subjects from any colonial territory can come freely to this country. To change that would be to take a very drastic step, but I assure him that we are aware of the public concern that this matter is causing and that it is receiving very careful consideration.'[29]

During 1954 and 1955 the matter of immigration controls was raised by a number of MPs, both Labour and Conservative. Government ministers replied that they were considering the matter but could make no definite statement.[30] Finally in November 1955 the Prime Minister, Sir Anthony Eden, replying to a question from Cyril Osborne, stated that there was no question of any action being taken to control immigration and that in any case the largest immigration was from Eire.[31]

Behind the scenes, though, the government had been giving detailed consideration to the 'problem' of controlling coloured immigration, and the civil service interdepartmental working party, reconvened in January 1953, had spent months discussing proposals and how to justify them. Even though the settled coloured population was found to be very small and the police reports to the working party did not suggest they were responsible for a disproportionate amount of crime, the working party quickly decided it was in favour of controls, and that legislation was necessary as administrative measures were likely to be ineffective. The Ministry of Labour reported that black unemployment was higher than white on account of lack of relevant skills and discrimination by employers, and that employers complained of the high turnover of black workers, their quarrelsomeness and lack of discipline, and the objection to black workers raised by white employees. Black women were subject to particularly serious stereotyping: they were slow mentally, it was said, and the speed of work in modern factories was quite beyond their capacity. On the other hand, they were found to give reliable service as domestics in hospitals and elsewhere and were able to qualify as nurses.[32] That these reports were contradictory went unremarked.

The working party concluded that coloured immigrants were

law-abiding and willing to work but, because the fields in which they were suitable for employment were somewhat limited by their physique and the reluctance of some employers to take them on, their unemployment rate was higher than that for white workers. They were thus more likely to become a charge on National Assistance. Relations between black people and the rest of the community had been peaceful so far, but little assimilation was said to be taking place. Immigration was proceeding at around 3,000 per year and taking the form of permanent settlement. How far trouble between white and coloured people could be avoided in future if the coloured community continued to increase was, reported the committee, a matter of speculation.[33]

It is extraordinary that, at a time when Irish immigration was estimated to be 60,000 per year, immigration controls should have been considered in order to prevent the entry of a mere 3,000 people who, as colonial and Commonwealth citizens, were British subjects. However, the government took the matter very seriously. The opposition was consulted to ensure a bipartisan approach, and draft legislation was prepared and circulated to the Cabinet in October 1955. Regarding Irish immigration there was considerable discussion by the working party, who were united in wishing it to continue because of the labour shortage and its contribution to economic growth, and because of the fit young men and women being added to the population. The committee found that there had been complaints about overcrowding among the Irish and their tendency to live in condemned premises and, by so doing, to establish a prior claim on local authority accommodation; but it went on to argue:

> When all this has been said, however, it cannot be held that the same difficulties arise in the case of the Irish as in the case of coloured people. For instance an Irishman looking for lodgings is, generally speaking, not likely to have any more difficulty than an Englishman, whereas the coloured man is often turned away. In fact, the outstanding difference is that the Irish are not — whether they like it or not — a different race from the ordinary inhabitants of Great Britain, and indeed one of the difficulties in any attempt to estimate the economic and social consequences of the influx from the Republic would be to define who are the Irish.[34]

The Commonwealth Secretary, now the Earl of Home, warned his colleagues of the danger of giving the impression that citizens from India, Pakistan and Ceylon would be treated less favourably than citizens from the older Dominions, and of the dangers of retaliation. The British communities in the subcontinent, he argued, were not large but were of vital economic importance to us.[35] Nevertheless, at its meeting of 15 September 1955, the Cabinet invited the Home Secretary to circulate a draft Bill to control colonial immigration, and this was circulated on 27 October. At the Cabinet meeting on 3 November, Alan Lennox-Boyd strongly opposed legislation confined to colonial subjects. He argued that this would be open to the charge of racial discrimination and would have disastrous consequences for British relations with the West Indies and the future association of the proposed West Indian Federation with the Commonwealth.[36] The Cabinet was divided over whether to introduce legislation, and so decided that no action should be taken for the time being. This decision was announced by the Prime Minister in his reply to Cyril Osborne's question on 11 November.

The Prime Minister decided, however, that the matter could not rest there, and on 23 November he told his Cabinet colleagues that he was appointing a Committee of Ministers, consisting of the Lord Chancellor, the Lord President, the Home Secretary, the Commonwealth Secretary, the Colonial Secretary and the Attorney-General:

> to consider what form legislation should take, if it were to be decided that legislation to control the entry into the United Kingdom of British subjects from overseas should be introduced; to consider also the intended effect of such legislation upon actual immigration, how any such control would be justified to Parliament and to the public, and to the Commonwealth countries concerned; and to report to the Cabinet.[37]

The report from the Committee of Ministers had been circulated to the Cabinet in June 1956, and discussed at a Cabinet meeting on 10 July. The report noted the rise in coloured immigration from 3,000 in 1953 to 10,000 in 1954 and to 35,000 in 1955, but stated that coloured immigrants had little difficulty in finding work, were law-abiding and had met little public expression of 'race feeling'. Immigration was being stimulated by demand in Britain, especially in the transport industries and the Health Service; also, the Barbados government was encouraging emigration. The committee noted that there were housing problems, but that coloured immigrants had been making a valuable contribution to the labour force by filling low-paid manual jobs. Problems, they felt, were only likely to arise if there were a major recession in the economy. Ordinary people in Britain seemed by no means intolerant of coloured people in their midst, and there seemed to be little prospect of 'race' riots or colour-bar incidents. Public opinion seemed more accepting of immigration than had appeared to be the case two years earlier. If the government decided to legislate to control it, then legislation should be on the lines of the draft bill that had been prepared by the Home Secretary, Gwilym Lloyd-George, but entry should depend on the requirement and proven provision of accommodation rather than on the offer of a job, as this would be a more effective form of control. It should apply to all British Commonwealth and colonial subjects, and not just to West Indians. Nevertheless, while the committee felt coloured immigration was a problem, the majority decided that the balance of advantage was against imposing controls at the present time, though the situation should be kept under review and examined again, perhaps in a year's time. Lord Salisbury, the Lord Chancellor, dissented strongly from the majority view and was in favour of immediate action to control coloured immigration – action which he felt would command a strong body of public support. The Cabinet accepted the advice of the majority and decided to take no action for the time being.[38]

It is clear that there was widespread concern and even hostility among the political and social elite in Britain against black immigrants, whether they had come as colonial workers, black GIs or colonial volunteers during the war. They were not seen as valuable recruits to the labour force or to the armed services, but were accepted only reluctantly when pressures were irresistible, as in the case of recruits to the Royal Air Force or the black GIs. Black newcomers were seen as likely to 'provoke' problems of racial conflict and discrimination, and therefore as difficult to accommodate and assimilate. They were stereotyped as quarrelsome, lazy, unskilled and unenterprising. There was widespread prejudice against sexual relations and intermarriage between blacks and whites; and English women were not allowed to marry black GIs, though thousands married white American servicemen.[39]

The origins of racial prejudice are widely disputed; it exists in a great variety of societies with differing historical experiences. In Britain, involvement in the slave trade and the conquest and subordination of non-white people in the era of imperialism and colonialism influenced people from all classes and walks of life. One can hypothesize that members of the British upper class, whose rank was exalted even further by their belonging to an imperial power, were particularly influenced by the ideas and values that legitimized Britain's superior role in world affairs, and especially *vis-à-vis* non-European peoples. Part of the justification for considering immigration controls, though, was the assumed hostile reaction of the general population. 'We do not attempt to import blacks, coolies and Polynesians into Great Britain. The opposition of the working classes would be furious',[40] was the view of a liberal academic at the beginning of the century. It seems to have been a view widely shared by members of the political elite after the war. How much evidence is there to suggest that the public reaction was as hostile as anticipated?

The public response to post-war immigration

It is hard to gauge the early public reaction to immigration from the West Indies and the Indian subcontinent, perhaps because that response varied depending on local circumstances and the social context. Some writers have argued that the response was generally friendly and welcoming,[41] and even some Conservative politicians seem to have taken this view. For example, in a speech on the Race Relations Bill (1976) Winston Churchill said, 'Would the Home Secretary at the same time pay tribute to the wonderful way in which the British people have accepted for the greater part, the very substantial influx of alien culture and alien race into their midst without open conflict or prejudice.'[42]

This picture of tolerance and friendliness is, however, only partly correct and must be qualified in a number of respects.

First, there is considerable evidence that black immigrants faced discrimination in the employment sector not only from employers but also from local work groups and trade union branches, which tried to exclude them from certain occupations or confine them to the lowest grades.[43] Second, there was massive discrimination in the housing sector by landlords, estate agents and building societies, which forced black people into declining inner areas that were cheap and accessible. Access to council housing was initially difficult because of rules of residence and the points system which favoured local families in need. Renting rooms in ordinary suburban houses, which was a common practice for migrant Irish workers, was very difficult for black immigrants on account of widespread racial prejudice among landladies.[44]

There were also occasional incidents of violence when police action was needed to suppress disorder. In Liverpool there was anti-black rioting from 31 July to 2 August 1948, and another 'race' riot in Deptford, London, on 18 July 1949. In August 1954 there were two days of inter-racial violence in Camden Town, London.[45] There was a series of attacks on an industrial hostel housing Indian workers near Birmingham from 6 to 8 August 1949. Sporadic attacks by white youths on black men were not uncommon in the 1960s, and gave rise to the term 'Paki-bashing'. However, it appeared that all these were isolated incidents, and that New Commonwealth immigrants were being absorbed into the expanding British economy without too much difficulty.

It was in the area of housing that problems were most acute, with accusations, particularly in London, that landlords were using black tenants to push out local whites in controlled tenancies in order to realize higher rents and property values. In November 1957 a number of London Labour MPs raised these issues in an adjournment debate on housing led by Marcus Lipton, the MP for Brixton. He outlined some of the problems being experienced in his constituency – namely, the general difficulty of West Indian immigrants in finding accommodation, problems between neighbours, and the issue of controlled tenancies. Other London MPs raised similar problems. Lipton himself was coming under some pressure from his white working-class constituents, and he was worried that the local Conservatives might use the issue against him. The failure of central government to provide local authorities with additional funds to alleviate the shortage of accommodation in areas of immigrant settlement was a major factor contributing to inter-racial hostility. It encouraged the exploitation of black tenants by unscrupulous landlords; it fostered overcrowding and disputes between neighbours; and it fuelled resentment by black people of their treatment by white landlords and landladies who were openly discriminating against them.[46] These resentments and difficulties were allowed to build up until open conflict forced the issue on to the national political agenda.

It was the riots in Nottingham and Notting Hill in August and September 1958 that propelled the issue of black immigration on to the front pages of the newspapers and television, and made it a national rather than a series of independent local issues. Instead of the quiet though intense debates on the back benches and in civil service interdepartmental committees, the issue of immigration control became one of general public interest and debate. The first public opinion polls on popular attitudes towards immigrants, black—white relations and immigration control were carried out as a result of these riots, and their findings became important ammunition for those already advocating control. Although the 1958 disturbances did not last long, they involved many hundreds of people. Hostile crowds of 1,500 and 4,000 were reported to be involved in the Nottingham disturbances, and crowds of 200, 400 and 700 participated in some of the Notting Hill attacks. In London some 140 people were arrested during the four main days of the disturbances between 30 August and 3 September. Mr Norman Manley, Prime Minister of Jamaica, and Mr Carl Lacorbinière, Deputy Chief Minister of the West Indian Federation, flew to London for consultations and a tour of riot areas.

There were two immediate reactions to the riots. First, there was widespread condemnation of the violence — by politicians, by Church leaders and in editorials in the press. Young hooligans, often identified as Teddy boys, were blamed. Hugh Gaitskell, the leader of the Labour party, wrote in *The Times*: 'Whatever local difficulties there may be, nothing can justify the riots and hooliganism of the past few days.'[47] There was widespread satisfaction with Lord Justice Salmon's deterrant sentences on nine youths convicted of assault during the disturbances, and his forthright condemnation of their actions:

You are a minute and insignificant section of the population who have brought shame on the district in which you live and have filled the whole nation with horror, indignation and disgust. Everyone, irrespective of the colour of their skin, is entitled to walk our streets erect and free from fear. This is a right which these courts will always unfailingly uphold.[48]

The second reaction, and the one with the most far-reaching long-term consequences, was to analyse these attacks by young white men on black people as the response of local people who felt resentful against black immigration. A crude expression of this view was given by Mr George Rogers, the Labour MP for North Kensington, which included Notting Hill. He told the *Daily Sketch*: 'The government must introduce legislation quickly to end the tremendous influx of coloured people from the Commonwealth ... overcrowding has fostered vice, drugs, prostitution and the use of knives. For years the white people have been tolerant. Now their tempers are up.'[49] Mr Rogers was clearly justifying the vicious actions of the white thugs who belonged to families in his constituency and at the same time he was stereotyping the black people who were the victims of their criminal violence. While Rogers' reaction was a minority one on the left, it was influential not so much because he represented the area where the riots had taken place but because he was articulating racist views which many people held but had not dared to express openly. James Harrison, the Labour MP for Nottingham West, also supported controls, and had done so from the earliest days of post-war immigration.

The overwhelming reaction on the left was to condemn the riots as hooliganism and as illegitimate manifestations of racial prejudice. Gaitskell unequivocally condemned the riots, as did the National Executive Committee of the Labour party, which rushed out a statement on racial discrimination at the end of September, just in time for the party conference.[50] This statement, condemning all forms of racial prejudice, was endorsed by the party conference, which crystallized official Labour party policy to one of total opposition to immigration controls. Support for controls was condemned as capitulation to the worst excesses of racism.

Supporters of immigration controls were quick to seize on the riots as evidence of popular hostility to black immigration, and this view was given credence by a number of public opinion polls. A Gallup poll, taken immediately after the riots, found that 92% had read about them and, while 27% blamed whites for causing them and only 9% blamed blacks, the largest number, 35%, blamed both. A substantial majority of respondents favoured immigration controls, with only 1 in 5 opposing. The poll discovered that large numbers of people were prepared to admit to substantial levels of prejudice: 71% said they were opposed to mixed marriages, 61% said they might or would definitely move if large numbers of black people settled in their neighbourhood, and 54% opposed the view that black and white people should be subject to the same conditions for getting on to council house waiting lists. A poll in the *Daily Express*, quoted by Cyril Osborne, the notorious campaigner against black immigration, found that 79.1% of their national sample was in favour of controls, and in the London area it was as high as 81.5%.[51] The riots had moved the issue of immigration control away from the quiet discussions in Cabinet and government departments and occasional questions in the House of Commons, on to the front pages of the national press and into the public domain. The media seized on the sensationalist and news value of the issue: henceforth black immigration was to receive enormous publicity, particularly in the press.

The assumption that the British public welcomed, or was tolerant of, black immigration was considerably undermined by the riots and the subsequent polls. Major politicians began to speak in public as well as in private about the need for immigration controls. Norman Manley and Carl Lacorbinière were asked by officials if the West Indies would be willing to control immigration at source, as was done by the Indian and Pakistani governments. They rejected the suggestion, arguing that control was a matter for the UK government. More significant was the statement of Sir Alec Douglas-Home, Minister of State for Commonwealth Relations, who, speaking in Vancouver, said that curbs would have to be put on the unrestricted flow of immigrants from the West Indies. This was the first time a minister associated with Commonwealth affairs admitted that one of the cornerstones of Commonwealth policy would have to be abandoned. Later the same month the Conservative party conference passed a resolution in favour of immigration control. The Conservative government was not prepared to be rushed into breaking the time-honoured tradition of allowing free entry to Commonwealth and colonial subjects, but the proponents of control had received a huge boost to their campaign.

Notes

1 M. Sherwood, *Many Struggles: West Indian Workers and Service Personnel in Britain, 1939–45* (Karim Press, 1985).
2 Ibid., p. 4.
3 Ibid., p. 17.
4 Ibid., p. 5.
5 Ibid., pp. 5, 53.
6 Carmichael and Hamilton defined institutional racism as acts by the total white community against the black community. See S. Carmichael and C. V. Hamilton, *Black Power: The Politics of Liberation in America* (Penguin, 1967). Institutional racism may also be defined as racist practices inherent in the customs, conventions, rules and regulations of institutions in society, including the state.
7 *Independent*, 6 January 1992.
8 Ibid.
9 'Race': this term is often used to denote a group or category of persons connected by common origin. Scientists have proved there is no biological basis to the concept, though it is often used socially to denote people of different phenotypical characteristics. Some scholars do not feel the term should be used, as it gives credence to a term devoid of scientific meaning. It will therefore appear here in inverted commas to show that no biological distinction is intended. Racism can be understood as those ideologies and social processes which discriminate against groups of people on the basis of their assumed membership of a 'racial' group.
10 G. Smith, *When Jim Crow met John Bull* (I. B. Tauris, 1987), pp. 54–62.
11 Ibid., pp. 180–1.
12 Sherwood, *Many Struggles*, pp. 112–13.
13 Smith, *When Jim Crow met John Bull*, pp. 128–9.
14 Ibid.
15 Cabinet Papers, 'Coloured people from the British colonial territories', memorandum by the Secretary of State for the Colonies, (50) 113, 18 May 1950, Public Record Office.
16 See p. 31.
17 *Report of the Royal Commission on Population*, Cmnd 7695, HMSO, 1949, p. 124.
18 Political and Economic Planning, *Population Policy in Great Britain*,

1948.

19   Report of the Working Party on the Employment in the United Kingdom of Surplus Colonial Labour, Ministry of Labour Papers 26/226/7503, Public Record Office.

20   Ibid., para. 14.

21   Cabinet Papers, 'Coloured people from the British colonial territories', memorandum by the Secretary of State for the Colonies, (50) 113, 18 May 1950, Public Record Office.

22   Cabinet Papers, 'Immigration of British subjects into the United Kingdom', 128/44, February 1951, Public Record Office.

23   Ibid.

24   I. Bradley, 'Why Churchill's plan to limit immigration was shelved', *The Times*, 20 March 1978.

25   N. Deakin, 'The immigration issue in British politics', unpublished PhD thesis, University of Sussex, 1972.

26   This Act ended the system by which British West Indians could enter the United States under the generous quota available for British citizens.

27   Parliamentary Reports, Commons (Hansard), vol. 521, col. 257, 10 December 1953.

28   Parliamentary Reports, Commons (Hansard), vol. 527, col. 2092, 19 May 1954.

29   Ibid.

30   Mr John Hynd raised the question of Jamaican immigration at an adjournment debate on 5 November 1954. The issue was also raised in questions by a number of MPs, including Mr Reid, Mr Erroll, Mr Hynd, Mr Steward, Mr Lipton and Mr Robson Brown. In 1955 Mr Cyril Osborne and Mr Norman Pannell had begun their campaign on the issue, and raised the matter on several occasions.

31   Parliamentary Debates, Commons (Hansard), vol. 545, cols 2005–6, 10 November 1955.

32   Report of the Working Party on Coloured People Seeking Employment in the United Kingdom, DO35/5216, para 26, December 1953, Public Record Office.

33   Ibid., para. 51(8).

34   Report of the Committee on the Social and Economic Problems arising from the Growing Influx into the United Kingdom of Coloured Workers from Other Commonwealth Countries, Appendix 2, draft statement on colonial immigrants, para 3, 3 August 1955, CAB 129/77.

35   'Colonial immigrants', memorandum by the Secretary of State for Commonwealth Relations, 2 September 1955, CAB 127/77.

36   'Colonial immigrants', memorandum by the Secretary of State for the Colonies, 1 November 1955, CAB 129/78.

37   'Colonial immigrants', note by the Prime Minister 20 November

1955, CAB 129/78.
38 'Colonial immigrants', report of the Committee of Ministers, 22 June 1956, CAB 129/81.
39 Smith, *When Jim Crow met John Bull*.
40 G. Murray, 'The exploitation of inferior races in ancient and modern times', in W. Hirst, G. Murray and J. L. Hammond (eds), *Liberalism and the Empire* (Johnson, 1900).
41 P. Foot, *Immigration and Race in British Politics* (Penguin Books, 1965).
42 Parliamentary Debates, Commons (Hansard), vol. 906, cols 1550−2, 4 March 1976.
43 D. Beetham, *Transport and Turbans: A Comparative Study in Local Politics* (Oxford University Press, 1967).
44 J. Rex and R. Moore, *Race, Community and Conflict* (Oxford University Press, 1967).
45 R. Glass, *Newcomers: West Indians in London* (Allen & Unwin, 1960).
46 Rex and Moore, *Race, Community and Conflict*.
47 *The Times*, 4 September 1958.
48 E. J. B. Rose, N. Deakin, M. Abrams, V. Jackson, M. Peston, A. Vanags, B. Cohen, J. Gaitskell and P. Ward, *Colour and Citizenship* (Oxford University Press, 1969).
49 *Daily Sketch*, 2 September 1958.
50 Labour Party, *Racial Discrimination*, September 1958.
51 Parliamentary Debates, Commons (Hansard), vol. 906, col. 1563, 5 December 1958.

3 'Race', discrimination and class

The migrant workers from the Caribbean, Africa and the Indian subcontinent were attracted to Britain by the expanding economy in the 1950s and 1960s. The widespread availability of jobs raised hopes of a higher standard of living and better prospects for themselves and their families. They entered an urban, industrial society where political, economic and social relations were organized and constrained by a deeply embedded class structure. The migrants were young and often skilled, or with educational qualifications. Many from the Caribbean, for example, were skilled manual workers or young women coming to train as nurses. Most migrants, especially those from the Indian subcontinent, were male, though in the case of Caribbeans the gender balance was less uneven because of the substantial recruitment of women to fill vacancies for nurses, hospital domestics and workers in the catering industry.

Castles and Kosack[1] argue that Caribbean and Asian migrants to Britain were not entering a homogeneous, peaceful and friendly society but a class society where a small minority owns and controls the means of production and is able to dominate and exploit the vast majority. Social relationships are characterized by conflict and coercion, and not by harmony and free choice. Immigrants do not have to adapt to universally accepted norms and customs but, rather, they are assigned a place in the non-egalitarian social order. Relationships that immigrants make in their new society are with specific individuals and groups who are usually, though not always, more powerful than they are, such as employers, landlords, local government officials, doctors, policemen, shopkeepers, publicans, foremen, fellow-workers and neighbours.

The place assigned to immigrant workers in the post-war period of immigration, whether in the labour market, the housing market ← or other areas of social relations, was generally the lowest. While people from the Caribbean, Africa and the Indian subcontinent were attracted to Britain with high hopes of economic success and upward mobility, the demand was for relatively unskilled and semi-skilled workers. As noted earlier, the expansion of the British economy in the 1950s and 1960s created substantial shortages of labour, particularly in the relatively stagnant sectors of the economy − for example, textiles, metal manufacture, catering and transport − where low pay, long hours, shift work and job insecurity made employment unattractive to native workers. These industries were unable to compete with firms in the more bouyant sectors of the economy for native workers, who were in short supply. Immigrant workers thus filled this urgent need. In some cases, as noted in chapter 1, the pressure on employers was so strong that they recruited labour directly from overseas. Most migrants to Britain were not recruited directly, though, but came unaided as voluntary migrants.

In periods of economic expansion in early post-war Britain the more prosperous regions of the country, with growing industries, quickly developed labour shortages; these were partly filled by immigrants who settled in the major conurbations of Greater London, the West Midlands, Manchester, Merseyside and Yorkshire. Here the best employment opportunities were to be found. Immigrant workers obtained work mainly in unskilled or semi-skilled jobs, though a significant number were skilled men and women. Research in the mid-1970s revealed substantial variations in the type of employment taken up by migrant workers from different countries.[2] In the most extreme case, that of Pakistani men, 58% were found to be doing unskilled or semi-skilled work compared with 18% of white men, while 8% of Pakistani men, compared with 40% of whites, were doing non-manual jobs. For Indians and West Indians the contrast was less extreme, but still very large, with 36% of Indians and 32% of West Indians doing unskilled or semi-skilled manual work. All groups, especially West Indians (59%), were well represented in skilled manual occupations, but only Indians (20%) and Asians from East Africa (30%) were well represented among non-manual occupations.

New Commonwealth immigrants were found to be greatly over-represented in shipbuilding, vehicle manufacture, textiles, general manufacturing industry and transport. Afro-Caribbean women were heavily over-represented in the Health Service, both as nurses and domestic hospital staff, reflecting the long tradition of recruitment from the Caribbean, especially Barbados and Jamaica.[3] The Health Service also recruited large numbers of New Commonwealth doctors, especially from the Indian subcontinent. These were to form part of the non-white professional middle class which was to become more prominent in the 1990s.

Immigrant workers thus formed a replacement labour force, overwhelmingly occupying the unskilled, semi-skilled and skilled manual jobs vacated and rejected by the native workforce as they obtained better-paid and higher-status positions in the expanding economy. The acute labour shortage created by the war and the long post-war European boom was made more severe by the continuing willingness of Britons to emigrate overseas, particularly to North America and Australia. Thus, while the other major industrial countries of Western Europe were all recruiting substantial increments to their labour forces from Southern Europe, North Africa and Turkey, to man their industries and fuel economic growth and expansion, Britain's gains to her labour force were offset by her high levels of emigration.

Racial discrimination

The high levels of discrimination that immigrants from the Caribbean and the Indian subcontinent experienced in their search for employment and accommodation has been documented in a large number of studies, one of the first and most influential of which was carried out by Political and Economic Planning (PEP) in 1966–7. It was published in April 1967 as a report and subsequently in book form as *Racial Discrimination in England*.[4] This study not only included interviews with immigrants, employers, union officials, estate agents, people in accommodation bureaux and others involved in situations where discrimination might take place, but also employed black and white actors to apply for jobs, accommodation and motor insurance to test whether, and to what extent, discrimination was taking place. The actors used were English, Hungarian and Afro-Caribbean. These situational tests exposed very high levels of racial discrimination, much of which was not known to the persons being discriminated against, but was revealed subsequently.

In the interviews with different ethnic groups Daniel[5] found that 45% of West Indians claimed personal experience of discrimination, as did 34% of Pakistanis and 35% of Indians. Among Cypriots, however, only 6% did so. Not only did the researchers find the accounts convincing but, as a result of the situational tests with the black and white actors, they considered the claims to be substantial underestimates of the levels of discrimination that were actually taking place. Surprisingly, discrimination was highest against those with the best knowledge of the English language and the most qualifications – presumably, because they were competing for the better jobs. Employers often claimed, when interviewed by the researchers, that they only discriminated on grounds of ability, and justified their discriminatory actions on the grounds that Afro-Caribbeans and Asians had fewer qualifications and a poorer ⟵ knowledge of English. The situational tests proved that these excuses were inaccurate, and that blatant racial discrimination in employment was taking place on a massive scale. Employers were found to stereotype black workers and to employ them only when suitable white workers were not available.

The role of the trade unions was found to be ambiguous in the workplace. National officials and union policies were opposed to discrimination and many individual union officials fought hard against discriminatory practices, but many union members shared the prejudices of their employers and managers with regard to employing and promoting black people, and so aided and abetted discriminatory practices in the workplace. This collusion between unions and management was reported to be widespread in some industries where many black people were employed, such as transport and textiles.[6]

In the housing market the situation was even worse. The three main ways for people to find accommodation were by privately renting a room, flat or house, buying a house or flat, or renting from the local authority. All three options were very difficult for black immigrants. Before racist advertising was banned by the

1968 Race Relations Act, there was widespread use of phrases like 'Europeans Only', 'No Coloureds', and even 'Sorry, No Coloureds', aimed at excluding black people from applying for rooms or flats to let. The PEP study found that, even when racial discrimination was not openly admitted in advertisements for private lettings, it still occurred in two thirds of the cases, revealing a massive overall level of discrimination.[7] In the situational tests used to estimate the amount of discrimination, there was found to be hardly any against the Hungarian actor, compared to the huge amount against the Afro-Caribbean. However, there was no difference in discrimination by class. Professional Afro-Caribbeans received just as many discriminatory refusals as manual workers. And once again, reported experiences of racial discrimination by Indians and Afro-Caribbeans who had sought rented accommodation, which was claimed by two out of three, underestimated actual levels of discrimination because they could not always know that they were being discriminated against.

In trying to purchase houses and flats, black immigrants were discriminated against by vendors and estate agents anxious to maintain the prices of property in residential areas. Building societies often considered black applicants to be bad risks and refused mortgages or imposed higher charges and rates of interest.[8] In the council house sector the normal criteria for allocating local authority housing – giving priority to those with long periods of local residence, to those who had been longest on the waiting list, as well as to those with the most urgent need – meant that new immigrants had to wait years just to get on the list, let alone qualify for housing, in this very important sector of the housing market for working-class people. The exclusion of single people from qualifying for council accommodation at this time also meant that many immigrants were forced to seek private rented accommodation or to buy. Daniel also found that, when black people were housed by local councils, they often dispersed them or placed them in inconspicuous areas because of the hostility of white tenants who were unwilling to accept them as neighbours. Many councils purchased inner-city accommodation to house black people, in order to avoid these problems.[9]

The result of these discriminatory policies and practices is well known. Afro-Caribbean and Asian immigrants became residentially concentrated in inner-city areas, where housing was relatively cheap and available to them because nobody else wanted it. Once again, black people accepted accommodation rejected by everybody else, replacing the white working-class inner-city population which was already involved in the drift to suburbia, moving out to new council estates or private residential housing being built on the outskirts of towns and cities.

The result of the research by PEP was to expose the complete inadequacy of the 1965 Race Relations Act. This Act outlawed discrimination in public places and incitement to racial hatred in speech or written material, but it completely omitted the vitally important areas of housing and employment. The origins of the first Race Relations Act and its weakness can be explained by the internal and external pressures on the Labour government that introduced and passed the legislation. The Labour party had committed itself to legislation outlawing racial discrimination in 1958, after the anti-black riots in Nottingham and Notting Hill. A number of Labour MPs, notably Fenner Brockway and Reg Sorenson, had been campaigning for such legislation but had been unable to persuade the Conservative government that anti-discrimination legislation was the best way of preventing discrimination and prejudice in individuals' private dealings with black people. Some Conservatives argued that race relations legislation could cause popular resentment, as it might be interpreted as favouring blacks over whites.

However, the Labour party leadership was so shocked by the 1958 riots that the National Executive Committee was persuaded to oppose immigration controls and to support race relations legislation. The NEC statement after the riots included the following commitment: 'Although we believe that the fundamental and long-term solution of this problem is educational, nevertheless there are public manifestations of racial prejudice so serious that they must be dealt with by legislation.'[10]

When the Labour party was returned to office in 1964 it was reeling from the narrowness of its overall majority of five and appalled at the racist victory of the new Conservative member for Smethwick, Mr Peter Griffiths. The defeat of Patrick Gordon Walker, the presumptive Foreign Secretary, at the Leyton by-election in January 1965 further stunned the government and reduced its majority to a mere hair's breadth of three seats overall. Determined to accede to the powerful tide in favour of immigration control but at the same time needing to maintain something of its anti-racist credentials, it decided to push ahead with its proposed race relations legislation. However, in order to minimize any political unpopularity that might accrue, the government decided to do its best to obtain opposition support for its anti-racial-discrimination legislation. The Conservative leadership was willing to accept a Bill based on conciliation but not one based on criminal sanctions, and the Labour Home Secretary, Frank Soskice, was happy to concede this on behalf of the government in order to achieve bipartisan consensus in an area where the Labour government felt electorally vulnerable. The 1965 Race Relations Act was thus declaratory rather than effective or efficient. The major emphasis of the Bill was on conciliation rather than on criminal sanctions: it urged people to do what was right without penalizing them for doing what was unfair and unjust. The Labour government was relieved and pleased that the Conservatives had accepted the principle of anti-discrimination legislation, and also that it could claim a small positive achievement in appeasing its critical supporters, some of whom were very angry at the total reverse of its immigration policy.

The Race Relations Board, responsible for enforcing the legislation, was hamstrung with neither political backing nor public support. It quickly found that most of the complaints it received were outside its jurisdiction,[11] and even those it could deal with it had little power to enforce. The Board quickly decided that strengthening the legislation was a major priority and, together with the National Committee for Commonwealth Immigrants, sponsored the independent research carried out by PEP which provided the scientific evidence necessary to convince policymakers that racial discrimination was occurring on a large scale and that stronger action was necessary to reduce it.

The report on racial discrimination gave powerful support to those who wished to strengthen the Race Relations Act. Its publication also occurred at a propitious time, after Labour had secured itself in office with its handsome victory in the general election of 1966.[12] Roy Jenkins, who succeeded Frank Soskice as Home Secretary in November 1965 and continued in this office after the general election, was a strong supporter of tougher legislation. He was determined to extend the provisions of the Act to employment and housing, and to include criminal sanctions. He worked hard to convince vested interests like the CBI and the TUC of the need for new legislation, and also to persuade the wider public of the value of a new, strengthened, Race Relations Bill. The campaign that Jenkins and the Race Relations Board had promoted appeared to have every change of success, and the Cabinet agreed to introduce new legislation covering housing and employment and including enforcement provisions.

The positive political climate, so carefully constructed with the help of Labour's secure majority and the favourable reception of the PEP report, was destroyed in a few short months. In the summer of 1967 the press gave considerable publicity to the landings of small numbers of illegal Asian immigrants on beaches in South-East England. In the autumn Asian immigration from Kenya began to rise, as the Kenyan government vigorously pursued labour market policies favouring Kenyan nationals at the expense of non-nationals, especially Asians who had retained their British citizenship at independence. Large numbers of these British Asians were dismissed from their jobs and forced to close their businesses. Duncan Sandys and Enoch Powell started a campaign to control this new source of immigration, as a result of which press and public attention began to shift away from the issue of the injustices of racial discrimination within Britain to the question of immigration from abroad. In November 1967 Roy Jenkins was moved from the Home Office to the Treasury and was replaced by Jim Callaghan, who was less strongly committed to 'race' relations legislation.

These events reduced the priority of anti-discrimination legislation and raised to prominence the opposite issue – the spectre of discriminatory legislation against non-white British citizens. Callaghan's first issue as Home Secretary was how to react to the increasingly vociferous campaign pursued by Powell and Sandys. In February 1968 the pressure increased with speeches by Powell and Sandys and a back-bench motion sponsored by Sandys and supported by several prominent Conservative MPs. On 18 February the government dispatched Malcolm MacDonald to Kenya for discussions with the Kenyan government, which, predictably, refused to ease its policy against non-citizens. The growing support among Conservatives for immigration control, and the absence of a firm government response, caused anxiety among British Asians in Kenya and a rush to Britain before restrictions were imposed. On 20 February Sandys tabled another motion requesting legislation, and ninety Conservative MPs signed it. More surprisingly, fifteen Labour MPs signed an amendment agreeing that some kind of legislation was necessary.[13] On the 22nd the Cabinet met and decided to impose a quota on the number of British Asians allowed to enter the United Kingdom from Kenya each year. Richard Crossman in his *Diaries* is vividly honest about the reasons for this openly discriminatory legislation:

> A few years ago everyone there would have regarded the denial of entry to British nationals with British passports as the most appalling violation of our deepest principles. Now they were quite happy reading aloud their departmental briefs in favour of doing just that. Mainly because I am an M. P. for a constituency in the Midlands, where racialism is a powerful force, I was on the side of Jim Callaghan.[14]

The Bill was introduced on 27 February and rushed through its main stages in three days. The major provision was that unconditional rights of entry to the UK were restricted to those with close ties to the country by birth, naturalization or descent. This was the first immigration control Bill to include an element of 'patriality',[15] which was to become a keystone of the 1971 Immigration Act. While the leading government and opposition spokesmen denied the Bill was racist, it was clearly designed to restrict the entry of British citizens without close ties to the UK, the vast majority of whom were non-white.

In the House, the Liberals led the opposition to the Bill, which was also opposed by some Conservative and Labour members – notably, Iain Macleod who, as Colonial Secretary, had guided Kenya to independence. Outside the House, the Bill was widely condemned by the voluntary organizations concerned with 'race' relations, the quality press and the Churches. *The Times* thundered: 'The Labour party has a new ideology. It does not any longer profess to believe in the equality of man. It does not even believe in the equality of British citizens. It believes in the equality of white British citizens.'[16] Auberon Waugh, writing in the *Spectator*, described the Act as 'one of the most immoral pieces of legislation to have emerged from any British Parliament'.[17] Nevertheless, because of the support of both government and opposition, it achieved a majority on second reading of 310 (372 to 62). In the Lords the Archbishop of Canterbury, Chairman of the National Committee for Commonwealth Immigrants, condemned the Bill.

The capitulation of the government to the Sandys – Powell agitation against the immigration of British Asians from Kenya was a disastrous betrayal of principle, and exposed the political weakness of the government on this issue. The result was a racially discriminatory Bill which devalued British citizenship by creating two classes of citizens: one subject to immigration controls and the other not. It was a clear breach of faith with people who had kept British citizenship for their own protection in a situation where they felt insecure, and they were betrayed at the hour of their greatest need. Moreover, the Kenyan Asians were relatively well qualified and well educated people with a good knowledge of English who, if they had been white, could have expected a warm welcome. The Act was a major erosion of the grand expansive ideal of British imperial citizenship subsumed in the phrase 'Civis Britannicus Sum', and was a step towards the narrower definition of British citizenship based on those people with a close connection with the territory of the United Kingdom, which was eventually to be embodied in the Nationality Act of 1981.

The Race Relations Act 1968

The government pressed ahead with its 'race' relations legislation, which had become even more necessary to its prestige and reputation after its unprincipled capitulation to anti-immigrant pressure over the Kenyan Asians Bill. The second Race Relations Act was passed in October 1968. It made it unlawful to discriminate on grounds of colour, 'race', ethnic or national origins, in employment, housing and the provision of commercial and other services. The publication or display of discriminatory notices or advertisements was also banned. The Act reconstituted and expanded the Race Relations Board and gave it the duty to secure compliance with its provisions by investigating complaints of racial discrimination, by instituting conciliation procedures and, if these failed, by legal proceedings. However, as in the earlier Act, considerable emphasis was placed on conciliation procedures, and legal proceedings were seen as a last resort. The Act also created the Community Relations Commission, to act in an advisory capacity on behalf of the Home Secretary, performing as a statutory body the duties and functions previously carried out by the National Committee for Commonwealth Immigrants.

The reconstituted Race Relations Board was much happier with the new legislation, particularly its wider scope. There were, however, still some loopholes in the law, such as the allowance of discrimination in order to maintain a racial balance.[18] Also, some important areas remained outside the scope of the legislation – notably, complaints against the police. The first report of the new Board did express concerns at a complaints-based procedure, arguing that the number of complaints could well be limited because victims might not realize they had been discriminated against; they might accept discrimination and not complain to the Board; and as there was often little financial loss, they might be deterred by the low level of compensation.[19]

The concerns of the Board were well founded. Despite the widespread evidence of discrimination, the number of complaints the Board received was relatively small and in a high proportion of these it formed the opinion that discrimination had not occurred, or at least could not be proved to have occurred. Between 1 April 1969 and 31 March 1970 the Board investigated 982 complaints, and formed an opinion of no discrimination in 734 cases (75%). In the 248 cases where it did form an opinion of discrimination, over half (143) concerned advertisements, an area of the Act where violations could easily be proved, and the Board was completely successful in eliminating this form of discrimination. In other areas, such as employment and housing, it was much harder to prove that discrimination had taken place, and the high proportion of complaints where the Board formed an opinion of no discrimination was a continuing feature of its annual reports. The problems of proof and political prudence also made it extremely reluctant to take cases to court, and great efforts were made to achieve results by conciliation. By 31 March 1972 the Board had investigated 2,967 cases, of which it had taken court action in only seven. Even when it went to court, it usually only asked for nominal damages. Not surprisingly, the number of complaints received remained at a low level, averaging around 1,000 per year.[20]

The impact of the Board was thus minimal, given the massive levels of discrimination that were known to exist. It quickly became clear that it needed far stronger powers to make a significant impact, including subpoena powers and discretion to initiate strategic investigations.

The Community Relations Commission, also created by the 1968 Race Relations Act, had an even less precise purpose: namely, 'to encourage the establishment of harmonious community relations and to co-ordinate on a national basis the measures adopted for that purpose by others and to advise the Secretary of State'.[21] The CRC saw its functions as being to combat racial prejudice by persuasion and education, and by explaining and interpreting the cultures and backgrounds of the different ethnic groups to the host community, and vice versa.[22]

In practice the Community Relations Commission gave a high priority to expanding the network of voluntary Liaison Committees, which were renamed Community Relations Councils, and to providing them with professional staff. By 1975 there were 85 Community Relations Councils with 144 Community Relations Officers (CROs) and assistant CROs. The Community Relations Councils were under similar constraints as the earlier local Liaison Committees. Substantial participation by local authorities was a precondition for grant aid from the Commission, and there was, on occasion, intense conflict between campaigning activists at the local level who felt they were representing the members of the ethnic minorities in their communities and the cautious non-partisan approach of the national officers of the Commission.[23]

The CRC continued with the NCCI's expert advisory panels on employment, education, housing, children, information and training. These provided information and training to a wide range of professionals such as teachers, social workers, trade union officials, police, local government officers and magistrates. However, it is always hard to measure the national impact of this kind of promotional and educational work, and the CRC constantly felt that its work was undermined by the fact that successive governments continued to link progressive community relations with increased restrictions on immigration. Alex Lyon put this argument to the House of Commons during the second reading of the Bill: 'One cannot say to a man who is black "we shall treat you as an equal member of this society, as a full citizen of this community", and say to him at the same time, "we shall keep your wife and children waiting seven years before they can come and live with you."'[24] The promotion of harmonious 'race' relations was almost impossible against a background of public and political opinion which was hostile to New Commonwealth immigration.

The second PEP report

Between 1972 and 1975 Political and Economic Planning carried out another series of surveys and situation tests to examine the extent of racial disadvantage in Britain. They found that members of non-white minority groups continued to be concentrated in the worst jobs, to receive lower earnings, to do disproportionate shiftwork, to be concentrated in particular plants and to be more vulnerable to unemployment.[25] The situation tests proved that discrimination was occurring on a large scale despite the 1968 Race Relations Act, and that this was greatest for unskilled jobs (46%) and less for skilled jobs (20%). Lack of qualifications was not the explanation for discrimination as, while 79% of white men with degree-standard qualifications were in professional or managerial jobs, only 31% of similarly qualified non-whites were in such jobs. Similarly, 83% of white men with 'A' levels were in non-manual jobs, compared with 55% of non-whites.[26] Discrimination was clearly based on colour prejudice and not on prejudice against foreigners: the Greek actor used in the situation test as the control 'foreigner' suffered very little discrimination.[27] Victims were generally not aware that discrimination was taking place, and this revealed a major weakness in the 1968 Race Relations Act, which required the victims to make formal complaints. This, together with the difficulty of substantiating such complaints, the fear of reprisals and the derisory compensation awarded in these cases, explained the small number of complaints received by the Race Relations Board.

The researchers also found that significant discrimination was taking place in the housing sector, although there appeared to have been a substantial decline in such discrimination since the 1967 study. Large proportions of Asians (76%) and Afro-Caribbeans (50%) had been forced to buy small inner-city terraced housing of poor quality. In contrast to the majority population, where owner-occupiers came disproportionately from the wealthier groups, among Asians the poorest groups were the most likely to have bought their own homes because of their inability to gain access to other types of accommodation. Naturally, they could only afford the cheapest properties available. Few Asians occupied council property (only 4%) though a quarter of Afro-Caribbeans did (26%), but generally they had been allocated the inferior council properties, for which they received no reduction in rent. The researchers found strong evidence to suggest that local authority housing policies were racially discriminatory, at least in their effects.[28]

In the privately rented sector, which was used by 24% of Afro-Caribbeans and 19% of Asians, there was still considerable discrimination in spite of the 1968 anti-discrimination legislation. It occurred in 27% of cases. However, this did represent a substantial decline since the 1967 survey. But patterns of discrimination that existed at the time of post-war immigration had already determined the residential distribution of most Afro-Caribbean and Asian settlers. As these communities expand, due to natural increase, future residential concentrations in inner-city areas will grow, even though some social and residential mobility will take place.

By the mid-1970s the optimism which lay behind the Race Relations Act 1968 and its statutory bodies, the Race Relations Board and the Community Relations Commission, had faded, and there was considerable support for new legislation. The return of a Labour government in 1974 committed to legislation to counter sex discrimination and strengthen the Race Relations Act augured well for new initiatives, as did the appointment of Roy Jenkins as Home Secretary once again. Both the Board and the Commission were arguing that existing legislation was insufficient to tackle racial discrimination, and that their work lacked credibility among the black communities. This was dramatically confirmed in October 1974 when, in the case of the Preston dockers' club, the House of Lords decided, in effect, that working men's clubs were outside the scope of the Race Relations Act.[29] This was a major setback to the Race Relations Board, especially as it was already clear that the number of cases being dealt with in no way reflected the widespread extent of racial discrimination.

The Select Committee on Race and Immigration, established in 1968, had also criticized the government for failing to devise effective 'race' relations policies, and it now recommended a clear and demonstrable government commitment to equal rights, the provision of greater resources and the strengthening of 'race' relations administration, including a Minister of Equal Rights attached to the Home Office. It also recommended the merging of the Race Relations Board and the Community Relations Commission.[30]

The government issued its own White Paper on racial discrimination in September 1975, which argued:

> The problems with which we have to deal if we are to see genuine equality of opportunity for coloured youngsters born and educated in this country may be larger in scale and more complex than had been initially supposed ... the government is convinced, as a result of its review of race relations generally, that a fuller strategy to deal with racial disadvantage will have to be deployed than has been attempted so far.[31]

The government shrewdly took action on sex discrimination first: Roy Jenkins was determined to link the disadvantages suffered by women and ethnic minorities, so that a coherent rationale would justify sex and 'race' legislation and increase support for both. The Conservatives were sympathetic to legislation against sex discrimination, and in fact had themselves drafted a Sex Discrimination Bill. Since government and opposition were united on this issue, Jenkins was able to use the Sex Discrimination Act to smooth the path for his new Race Relations Act and secure opposition support for that legislation as well.

The new Race Relations Bill, representing a considerable advance on previous legislation, was published on 3 February 1976. It extended the definition of 'discrimination' to include not only direct but also indirect discrimination, where unjustifiable practices and procedures, which apply to everyone have the effect of putting people of a particular racial group at a disadvantage. It allowed individuals who felt they had been discriminated against on racial grounds to take their complaints to the Country Court in all cases except in employment, where they could go to industrial tribunals. The Act followed the recommendations of the Select Committee and abolished the Race Relations Board and the Community Relations Commission, creating instead the Commission for Racial Equality, with greatly enhanced powers of investigation and enforcement to enable it to make wider strategic use of the law in the public interest.[32]

The Bill was supported by the Labour and Liberal parties, and was not opposed by the Conservatives. Roy Jenkins, introducing the Bill, stated that the growing black population born and bred in Britain was entitled to full rights and equal treatment, and that racial discrimination was not only morally repugnant but a social and economic waste. He added that the success of the legislation depended on the leadership of government and parliament, and on the response of society as a whole.[33]

Mr William Whitelaw, for the opposition, argued that it was because of the Conservative party's clear commitment to the principle of non-discrimination and to the interests of racial harmony that he advised his honourable friends not to oppose the Bill.[34] Only a few Conservatives did oppose it, but most Conservatives who spoke on the second reading argued that strong immigration controls were the quid pro quo for strong anti-discrimination legislation, and the present controls, they felt, were not strong enough. There was, however, recognition among many Conservatives that discrimination remained at a high level and that it was necessary to assuage the growing alienation of black youth by adopting stronger measures to combat it. Mr Dudley Smith, a strong support of controls, was one such, although his views on anti-discrimination legislation may have been influenced by his membership of the Select Committee. He said in the debate that there was 'a need for a crusade to overcome racial discrimination and to give our fellow Britons who are in the minority a new confidence which they have significantly lacked in recent years'.[35] Strenuous efforts were made by the Conservatives to amend the Bill in committee, to restrict its scope, but these were unsuccessful, and it received its third reading virtually unopposed.

The major innovation of the Race Relations Act 1976 was to

outlaw not only intentional direct discrimination — where a person treats another person less favourably on racial grounds than he treats, or would treat, someone else — but also indirect discrimination. Indirect discrimination was defined as applying an unjustifiable requirement or condition, which appeared to apply equally to people of different racial groups but which in practice was discriminatory. For example, a firm might refuse to employ any workers from inner-city areas, and the result of this requirement might be to greatly reduce the chances of employment for black people while having relatively little effect on the employment opportunities of whites.

The Commission for Racial Equality was thus a much more powerful body than its predecessors, with much greater scope and powers for strategic initiatives in enforcing the law. The extension of the law to cover indirect discrimination was a huge advance, and suggested that parliament was willing to allow a serious attack on the legacy of institutional discrimination which permeated British society.

It was perhaps inevitable that the high expectations generated by the new Commission and the stronger legislation have not been fulfilled. The Commission had only limited resources, and had difficulty deciding whether to prioritize its law enforcement or its promotional work. Enforcing anti-discrimination legislation proved to be a slow process, calling for formal investigations to obtain the high standards of evidence required. By the end of 1979 some 39 investigations had been started, but only four had been completed. This slow start did not enhance the credibility of the Commission. The return of the Conservatives in June 1979 created a less favourable environment for the Commission's work, as the Conservative party was now much less favourable to positive 'race' relations initiatives than it had been three years earlier.[36]

The Commission was engaged in a huge range of other activities, apart from its enforcement work. These included drafting codes of practice, monitoring legislation, helping individuals pursuing cases of discrimination under the Act, funding and assisting local Community Relations Councils, advising government, industry and local authorities. It has been expected to advise and assist whenever a 'race'-related crisis arises. Gradually the Commission has become more effective, but it is hard to assess what impact it has made on the huge levels of discrimination that persist. It has achieved some notable successes, such as the acceptance by parliament in 1984 of its code of practice on employment, the widespread and growing use of ethnic monitoring in the public and private sectors, and the completion of a significant number of formal investigations which include the reports on immigration control procedures, on Hackney's housing procedures, on Massey Ferguson Perkins Ltd, on Oaklawn Developments Ltd, on the National Bus Company and on St George's Hospital Medical School. In 1990 the CRE scored a notable success when Police Constable S. Singh won his case of racial discrimination against the Nottinghamshire Police Authority. The CRE has become very concerned about discrimination in the criminal justice system, and has sponsored research by the Institute of Criminology at Oxford University to investigate this.

In a society where racial prejudice is a normal rather than an exceptional aspect of culture,[37] there is an overwhelming case for tough anti-discrimination legislation and a strong enforcement agency. The CRE has been able to make only a small impact on racial discrimination in Britain, and has requested more resources and even tougher legislation. In 1985 it submitted detailed proposals for changes in the Race Relations Act, but failed to gain a positive response even though the government did strengthen fair employment legislation in Northern Ireland to reduce discrimination on religious grounds. The vital ingredient for a successful crusade against racial discrimination is active government commitment and support for CRE enforcement of anti-discrimination legislation. So far this has been only half-hearted.

Immigration and class structure

The post-war immigration of black migrant workers to Britain has had profound effects on class relations and on the class structure in British society, including class-consciousness and class conflict. Other recent migrations, such as those by the Irish, Jews and Poles, have had less effect, as the discrimination faced by these migrants, while initially severe, has not prevented them from becoming integrated into the class structure and into British society.

In the case of the Irish, for example, the huge antagonism between British and Irish workers noted by Marx in the last century did not prevent Irish workers from becoming an integrated part of the British working class and achieving mobility into the middle class. There now seems to be relatively little anti-Irish discrimination in the labour, housing and education markets, even though recent Irish migrants, especially seasonal workers, are often poor, badly housed and, like their black neighbours, concentrated in inner-city areas.[38] The political situation in Northern Ireland, especially the campaign by the Irish Republican Army, may cause anti-Irish sentiment in Britain to increase. Irish groups in Britain argue that anti-Irish discrimination does exist, but any examples of it appear to be directly related to the IRA campaign, such as the anti-terrorist legislation or police actions against suspected Irish terrorists – those convicted of the Birmingham pub bombings, for instance. There is little evidence of systematic discrimination against Irish people.

Black workers, however, face extensive discrimination in all aspects of their social lives, particularly in employment and housing but also in education and in relations with the police and other branches of the criminal justice system. Moreover, the Select Committee on Home Affairs found in 1980–1 continuing extensive racial discrimination against second- and third-generation black people born and educated in Britain which was preventing their integration into British society on the basis of equality and justice.[39] Some black parents believe there is something like a white conspiracy aimed at preventing young blacks achieving success in British society.

The persistent levels of discrimination faced by black people, both from members of the middle class with power over their lives – such as employers, managers, central and local government officials – and from fellow-workers and neighbours, have caused some analysts to argue that black people form a separate class formation in British society: namely, an underclass. This view is most strongly associated with John Rex who argues that, because of racism, black people are forced into a situation of defensive confrontation with white society, and are obliged to defend themselves through their own organizations, in conflict with white workers as well as with the white middle class. Rex maintains that there is a structural break between black immigrants and the main body of the white working class, and that black Britons form, at least potentially, a revolutionary underclass. This argument is justified not only because of the poverty and the poor housing, the lack of jobs or the occupation of low-paid jobs, the failure of black children in the schools and the criminalization of young black people — which puts them disproportionately at the bottom of society — but because of racism, including working-class racism. Racism prevents black people from moving into the better council estates for fear of intimidation and harassment. It denies them fair representation by the trade unions and the Labour party, the institutions of the working class. It is a bar to promotion and economic security, and to educational success and upward social mobility. Rex argues:

> What is being expressed in immigrant politics is not the politics of the simple and straightforward class struggle within capitalism either in its reformist or its marxist version. What we are considering is the political formation of an immigrant underclass. It is that class which is cut off from the main class structure of the society, not merely in quantitative but in structural or qualitative terms and for the moment at least cannot be construed as merely the under-privileged part of the British labour movement.[40]

Black people are therefore seen as constituting a class beneath the working class by virtue of their inferior economic and social circumstances, and because they and their children, as a result of racism, face inferior life chances compared with other people in similar circumstances.

Most theorists, in contrast to Rex, regard immigrant workers as part of the working class, sharing common disadvantages with other workers. Racial disadvantages merely increase these shared handicaps. Black workers are thus part of a basically united working class, a class united by the necessity to sell its labour to earn a decent standard of living.[41] Other theorists, however, do believe that racism is such a powerful force that it divides people who otherwise would be united by their common economic circumstances. The best-known proponents of the divided working class thesis are Castles and Kosack, who argue that racism is such an important component of working-class consciousness that it becomes entrenched, dividing white workers from non-white immigrant workers, who are seen as both cheap competitors for work and as culturally inferior because of their Third World origins. In addition, they are regarded as foreigners, even though they may be British citizens, and because of this they are seen as not having equal rights to economic and state benefits. Racism is high in the working class, according to Castles and Kosack: fearful of competition for jobs, workers are economically insecure; they experience a repressive socialization which has inculcated in them middle-class aspirations for a good life and standard of living, but has denied them the chance of achieving these aspirations. Their frustrations and aggression become directed at their black fellow-workers and black neighbours, who are regarded as illegitimate competitors for jobs, houses and the social benefits of the welfare state.[42]

The result is that, although both immigrant workers and indigenous workers belong to the same class by virtue of their non-ownership of the means of production, they are divided, both by the generally inferior economic situation of immigrant workers and by indigenous racism, into two distinct strata.[43] A variation of this argument is proposed by Castells, who emphasizes the lack of political rights of foreign workers in many West European countries. He maintains that this lack of political rights is a major factor contributing to the greater exploitation of foreign migrant workers. Lack of citizenship cuts them off from indigenous workers and encourages them to think of themselves as part of their homeland's proletariat rather than that of their country of residence. Insecurity about their rights of residence and employment makes them willing to accept lower wages and worse working conditions than native workers, and fearful of participating in trade union activities, including strikes. They are thus vulnerable to increased exploitation by employers and landlords.[44]

Another model used to describe the class relations that have resulted from the post-war migration of Third World workers is the notion of class fraction. This is argued most powerfully by Miles and Phizacklea, who state that classes are not homogeneous entities but are divided by economic and ideological factors.[45] Women, they maintain, constitute a good example of a class fraction. They are discriminated against in the labour market and allocated a subordinate position because of their assumed role as (actual or potential) wife and mother. Women tend to be confined to particular jobs in a largely segmented labour market, and are denied opportunities for training and promotion on the same basis as men. If they do break their careers to look after their children when they are very young, as they are encouraged to do, they lose for ever the chances of promotion that they have forgone. They are thus generally confined to subordinate positions in the middle and working classes. The beliefs that set women apart as inferior members of the labour market can be described as sexism, which attributes significance to biological or other inherent characteristics which women possess in order to legitimize treating them differently from men.

Miles and Phizacklea argue in a similar way that black workers can be said to constitute a class fraction. Racism within classes to some extent sets black people apart from fellow-workers and professional colleagues. Black migrant workers, like women, are ascribed negative characteristics because of the widespread racist beliefs that pervade all areas and sections of British society. These racist beliefs result in actions that confine black people to subordinate positions in employment and reduce their chances of promotion, confine them to the least desirable sectors of the housing market, and cause their children to fail in the schools and to be criminalized by the criminal justice system. Black workers are not fully integrated into the working class, nor are black professionals fully integrated into the middle class. They can therefore be described as belonging to class fractions.[46]

It is hard to adjudicate between these different descriptions of the impact that immigration has had on the class structure and class relations in Britain. Ideal types or models of the class structure simplify the complex reality of social relations in order to capture the key elements that the authors wish to emphasize. The impact of post-war immigration on the class structure is complicated by the wide variety of sources of that immigration and by the differing positions that Afro-Caribbeans, African Asians, Pakistanis, Indians and Bangladeshis have come to occupy in the labour and housing markets. Generalizations can be drawn but there are numerous exceptions, and the different communities adopt different strategies to avoid discrimination and combat racism. Social scientists are attempting to analyse a dynamic situation; descriptions of the class structure will change over time — depending for example, on the relative success or failure of the economy, the impact of anti-discrimination legislation, and the relative success of the strategies adopted by black people to secure economic security and success.

It is true, as Rex and Tomlinson argue, that black workers disproportionately occupy the worst jobs and the worst housing in British society and their children generally go to schools which are the least well resourced, but what emerges from their survey of Afro-Caribbean and Asian people is the relatively low levels of dissatisfaction with their situation. Even if the answers they gave to Rex and Tomlinson do not reflect their true feelings, they seem far removed from developing, even potentially, into a revolutionary underclass.[47] It is also clear that the various Afro-Caribbean and Asian communities are not in the same position in the employment, housing and education markets: while most experience racism and racial discrimination, this does not have uniform consequences for these communities. The anti-police riots in 1981 and 1985 appeared to give some credence to the notion of a revolutionary underclass, but this is a mistaken view. The limited nature of the riots and the focus of the violence suggest that they were an intensely violent response, to oppressive policing, by predominantly black but also white young people in specific inner-city locations.[48] It is worth adding that organized or partially organized violence against members of other ethnic groups is almost wholly perpetrated by whites on blacks and is fostered by extreme right-wing groups.[49]

Surveys suggest that most black people do identify themselves as working-class and support the major institutions of the working class, such as trade unions and the Labour party.[50] At the same time they are very concerned by issues which affect them as black people, such as discrimination — especially in employment and education — policing policies, and the failure of all parties and of the trade unions to challenge racism and change racist practices. Even black people who occupy middle-class positions and are economically more successful than other members of their communities tend to identify more with their communities than with their class. Thus large majorities of the Afro-Caribbean and Asian middle classes support the Labour party, presumably because of the perceived racism of the Conservatives as expressed in their tough immigration control policies and the frequent pronouncements by prominent politicians attacking the size of the immigrant communities and advocating ever more stringent immigration controls,[51] even though they are already so strict that human rights are routinely abused and people with the legal right to enter Britain are frequently turned away.[52] There therefore appears to be more truth in the view that the classes are segmented, fractionalized or pluralistic, and that black people occupy a distinct position, like women, as segments or fractions of the particular class they objectively belong to by virtue of their occupational status. This distinct position is caused by additional subordination due to the operation of discriminatory practices against them, through racism.

The political consequences of post-war immigration

One point on which almost all commentators are in agreement is that the political consequences of post-war immigration have been profoundly conservative. Immigration has contributed to economic growth and prosperity. It has acted as a check on inflation, as migrant workers have been prepared to work long hours for low wages. They have also assisted the upward social and economic mobility of indigenous British workers because, as a replacement labour force, they have been assigned the lowest positions in the labour and housing markets. Indigenous workers have been able, because of post-war economic growth, to achieve higher-status jobs and better housing, and have sometimes been able to sell their inferior housing to migrant workers. However, far from being welcomed as valuable economic assets, migrant workers have been considered a necessary evil and stereotyped as inferior, lazy, poorly qualified and even as criminal. Indigenous workers, practising the innate snobbery that native inhabitants often manifest towards newcomers, have been able to look down upon their new neighbours and feel superior. Racial prejudice could be, and has been, exploited by some politicians to attract indigenous workers to parties of the right. The working class has thus become more sharply divided between a more privileged indigenous sector and a less privileged non-indigenous sector based on migrant workers and their families. The results may be an increased propensity for indigenous workers to be less conscious of the issues and causes which unite them with fellow-members of the working class; and even their identifying with those parties which are hostile to, and attack, migrant workers.

Notes

1   S. Castles and G. Kosack, *Immigrant Workers and Class Structure in Western Europe* (Oxford University Press, 1973).
2   D. Smith, *Racial Disadvantage in Britain: The PEP Report* (Penguin Books, 1977).
3   Ibid.
4   W. W. Daniel, *Racial Discrimination in England* (Penguin Books, 1968).
5   Ibid., p. 65.
6   Ibid., pp. 132–40. See also D. Beetham, *Transport and Turbans: A Comparative Study in Local Politics* (Oxford University Press, 1970); D. Brookes, *Race and Labour in London Transport* (Oxford University Press, 1975).
7   Daniel, *Racial Discrimination*, pp. 154–7.
8   Ibid., pp. 170–6.
9   Ibid., pp. 177–8, 190. See also P. Ratcliffe, *Racism and Reaction: A Profile of Handsworth* (Routledge & Kegan Paul, 1981).
10 Labour party, *Racial Discrimination*, September 1958.
11 Race Relations Board, *Annual Report, 1967*, para. 15.
12 In the general election of 1966 the Labour party secured an overall majority of 96, which ensured that it would have a full term in office.
13 D. Steel, *No Entry* (C. Hurst, 1969).
14 R. Crossman, *Diaries of a Cabinet Minister*, vol. 2 (Hamish Hamilton and Jonathan Cape, 1977), p. 679.
15 Patriality: in the provisions of the Immigration Act 1971 the term 'patrial' is used of persons having the right of abode in the UK. It includes UK citizens and Commonwealth citizens born to, or adopted by, a parent who, at the time of the birth or adoption, had UK citizenship by virtue of their own birth in the UK. See Home Office, *Immigration Act 1971*, HMSO, 1971, clause 2.
16 *The Times*, 1 March 1968.
17 *Spectator*, 1 March 1968.
18 Home Office, *Race Relations Act 1968*, section 8(2), HMSO, 1968.
19 Race Relations Board, *Annual Report, 1970*, p. 5.

20 Ibid., para. 42.
21 *Race Relations Act 1968*, section 25.
22 *Community Relations Commission Annual Report, 1970*, p. 5.
23 C. Mullard, *Black Britain* (Allen & Unwin, 1973).
24 Parliamentary Debates, Commons (Hansard), vol. 912, col. 57, 24 May 1976.
25 Smith, *Racial Disadvantage*.
26 Ibid., p. 67.
27 Ibid., p. 111.
28 Ibid., pp. 243–84.
29 P. N. Sooben, *The Origins of the Race Relations Act*, Research Paper in Ethnic Relations no. 12, Centre for Research in Ethnic Relations, University of Warwick, September 1990.
30 House of Commons, *The Organisation of Race Relations Administration*, second special report from the Select Committee on Race Relations and Immigration, Session 1974–6, vol. 1, HMSO, 1975.
31 Home Office, *Racial Discrimination*, Cmnd 6234, HMSO, 1975.
32 Home Office, *Race Relations Act 1976*, HMSO, 1976.
33 Parliamentary Debates, Commons (Hansard), vol. 906, cols 1547–67, 4 March 1976.
34 Parliamentary Debates, Commons (Hansard), vol. 906, cols 1568–77, 4 March 1976.
35 Parliamentary Debates, Commons (Hansard), vol. 906, col. 1594, 4 March 1976.
36 The reasons for this are discussed in more detail in ch. 8.
37 D. Lawrence, *Black Migrants, White Natives* (Cambridge University Press, 1974), p. 46.
38 J. Rex and S. Tomlinson, *Colonial Immigrants in a British City: A Class Analysis* (Routledge & Kegan Paul, 1979).
39 House of Commons, *Racial Disadvantage*, fifth report from the Home Affairs Committee, Session 1980–1, HMSO, 1981.
40 Rex and Tomlinson, *Colonial Immigrants*; J. Rex, 'Black militancy and class conflict', in R. Miles and A. Phizacklea (eds), *Racism and Political Action* (Routledge & Kegan Paul, 1979).
41 J. Westergaard and H. Resler, *Class in a Capitalist Society* (Penguin Books, 1976).
42 Castles and Kosack, *Immigrant Workers and Class Structure*.
43 Ibid.
44 M. Castells, 'Immigrant workers and class struggles in advanced capitalism: the West European experience', *Politics and Society*, vol. 5, no. 1 (1975), pp. 33–66.
45 A. Phizacklea and R. Miles, *Labour and Racism* (Routledge & Kegan Paul, 1980), pp. 6–9.
46 Ibid.
47 Rex and Tomlinson, *Colonial Immigrants*.
48 Lord Scarman, *The Brixton Disorders, 10–12 April 1981*, report of

an inquiry, Cmnd 8427, HMSO, 1981; J. Benyon (ed.), *Scarman and After* (Pergamon Press, 1984); J. Benyon and J. Solomos (eds), *The Roots of Urban Unrest* (Pergamon Press, 1987).
49   For additional information, see pp. 144–6.
50   Rex and Tomlinson, *Colonial Immigrants*; M. FitzGerald, *Black People and Party Politics in Britain*, Runnymede Trust, 1987.
51   Mrs Thatcher's 'swamping' speech on 30 January 1978 (see p. 184) would be a classic example of such a statement.
52   See, for example, Joint Council for the Welfare of Immigrants, *Target Caribbean: The Rise in Visitor Refusals from the Caribbean*, July 1990.

4 The politicization of 'race'

The widespread racial prejudice against and disdain for black people remained prevalent in elite circles after the war, and partly explains the immediate opposition to the immigration of small numbers of colonial and post-colonial workers who came to Britain in the early 1950s. However, elite opposition in this early period of migration continued to make little impact on public opinion. It was confined to informal lobbying of ministers by members of parliament, quiet discussions between Cabinet ministers and between members of the government and the opposition, and civil servants' deliberations in the various interdepartmental committees. To some extent, members of the political elite were responding to anxieties expressed by their constituents, but much of their own concern was concealed from the public and the mass media.

Thus in the early post-war period the issue of immigration control was not high on the public political agenda, and ministers had strong reasons for wishing to exclude it from public debate. Not least of these was the controversy and embarrassment that would arise if immigration controls were introduced against British subjects, breaking with a long imperial tradition and arousing suspicions of racism so soon after a world war partly waged against the racial genocide of the Hitler regime. Immigration controls against Commonwealth and colonial subjects would not only have been highly controversial at home, but would also have resulted in damaging international criticism and would have jeopardized relations with colonial Commonwealth governments at a time when Britain was extolling the virtues of its multiracial Commonwealth. In the 1950s the Commonwealth was an important cornerstone of British foreign policy, and Commonwealth trade and support were of vital importance. In the background, but not unimportant, were the considerable economic advantages of colonial immigration and the acute shortage of workers which recruitment from Ireland and Southern Europe were unable to remedy.

In contrast to elite anxieties about black immigration from the West Indies and the Indian subcontinent, which were partly fuelled by the American race relations experience, public concern appeared to be muted and confined to areas of immigrant settlement. Here it was often linked to competition for housing. It may be useful to contrast this with the reception of the Polish forces after the war. Anti-Polish feeling had been quite high in the latter part of the war because of Polish hostility towards Britain's Russian allies and the significant number of Polish troops stationed in Britain. But this hostility and suspicion declined and dissipated after the war, despite an increase in Polish troops and their families arriving in Britain to settle. The Polish Resettlement Act (1947) assisted the settlement of Polish ex-servicemen and their families, and played a major role in their smooth integration into the housing and labour markets. Immigrants from the West Indies, India and Pakistan were not assisted in this way. They were regarded as voluntary migrants who should fend for themselves. Racial discrimination made it particularly difficult for them to find suitable accommodation. Local authorities in areas like Lambeth and Birmingham made urgent requests for extra resources to assist immigrants, but the government refused to help.

In parliament a small number of Conservative and Labour MPs, pressing for controls to be introduced, asked questions about the incidence of disease and crime among immigrants.[1] Cyril Osborne (Louth) was the first and most active Conservative campaigner on this issue, beginning as early as 1952, but his was a lone voice for some years and his questions and lobbying were treated with disdain by government ministers, who publicly paid tribute to the contribution of West Indians, in particular, to the Health Service and to public transport. After 1955 Osborne was joined in his efforts by Norman Pannell (Kirkdale), Martin Lindsey (Solihull) and Harold Gurden (Selly Oak). He also received growing support among Conservative activists in the constituency associations.[2] On the Labour side also there was a small group of MPs who were strong supporters of controls: these included John

Hynd (Attercliffe), Harry Hyne (Accrington), George Rogers (N. Kensington), Albert Evans (S. W. Islington) and James Harrison (Nottingham W.). However, they did not command significant support in the party.

It was the anti-black riots in Nottingham and Notting Hill in August and September 1958 and the huge publicity these events received in the press that put black immigration on the national political agenda, and the public opinion polls taken in the aftermath of the riots revealed widespread support for controls. A poll in the *Daily Express*, cited by Cyril Osborne in parliament[3] in support of his campaign, found overwhelming public support:

Nationally	*In the London area*
79.1% for control	81.5% for control
14.2% for no action	11.2% for no action
6.7% didn't know	7.3% didn't know

It was also during this period that 'immigration' became associated in the public mind with non-white immigration, and an 'immigrant' in popular discourse came to mean a non-white person − usually an Afro-Caribbean or Asian. This misuse of language became so prevalent and enduring that even black people born in Britain were assumed to be immigrants. Such descriptions, setting non-whites apart from the rest of the population, were never applied to second-generation Irish, Italians or Poles, and showed the depth of racial prejudice and the political potential of the issue. The racist nature of the opposition to black immigration was made clear by Martin Lindsey when, in a private motion in December 1958, he emphasized that it was coloured immigration and not immigration as such that should be controlled: 'We all know perfectly well that the core of the problem is coloured migration. We must ask ourselves to what extent we want Great Britain to become a multi-racial community ... a question which affects the future of our own race and breed is not one we should merely leave to chance.'[4]

The extent and seriousness of the 1958 riots shocked Labour politicians and forced them for the first time to take immigration seriously as a political issue. As noted earlier, the overwhelming reaction in the party was to condemn the riots as racist hooliganism.

Gaitskell was fierce in his condemnation, as was the National Executive Committee, whose statement not only condemned the violence and expressed abhorrence at all manifestations of racial prejudice, but emphasized the importance of the multiracial Commonwealth as a means of building racial understanding, confidence and cooperation in the world. Most significantly it argued that, if Britain were to remain the centre of the Commonwealth, the welcome to Commonwealth citizens coming to Britain should be wholehearted and unreserved.[5] The NEC statement was overwhelmingly endorsed by the party conference. The Labour party had not formulated a policy on immigration before 1958. In principle it was opposed to racial discrimination both in Britain and in the colonies, but it had not developed coherent or consistent policies to tackle the problem. The riots forced the rapid formulation of party policy, which emerged as total opposition to immigration controls for Commonwealth subjects, strong support for the ideal of a multiracial Commonwealth, and support for legislation to combat racial discrimination. The riots were regarded as ugly, isolated incidents of racism to which no concessions should be made.

The response in the Conservative party and among senior civil servants was very different.[6] The riots were interpreted as part of a rising trend of public concern about, and opposition to, black immigration. The proponents of control, especially Cyril Osborne, were encouraged to step up their campaign, in the knowledge that they had considerable public support as well as support in the grassroots organizations of the Conservative party. However, the Cabinet remained divided and was unwilling to take such a controversial initiative so soon before a general election, which they were confident they had every chance of winning, given the strength of the economy. When the election was duly held in October 1959 the Conservatives won easily, with a majority of 100.

After the election the tide of events ran strongly in favour of the advocates of control in the Conservative party. The pre-election boom and the increasingly public debate about the introduction of controls contributed to a huge rise in immigration from the West Indies and the Indian subcontinent. Many of the newly elected Conservative MPs favoured controls, especially those from the West Midlands, where in October 1960 the Birmingham

Immigration Control Association was formed. In 1960 the informal efforts of the government to restrict the flow by persuading colonial and Commonwealth governments to restrict the issue of passports collapsed, when the Indian Supreme Court ruled that it was unconstitutional for the Indian government to refuse to issue passports to its nationals. This raised the possibility of a dramatic increase in migration from a virtually unlimited source.

However, it was pressure from within the Conservative party that made the Cabinet decide to do what had been discussed and deferred so often since 1948. Thirty-nine resolutions demanding control were sent in by constituency associations for debate at the 1961 annual conference, and while R. A. Butler, the Home Secretary, made no commitment to introduce a Bill, the strength of feeling at the conference and the dramatic rise in numbers coming in decided the issue. A Bill was hurriedly prepared, the decision to legislate was announced in the Queen's speech on 31 October, and the Bill was published the following day.

The government hoped that its Bill would be widely accepted. Control of Commonwealth immigration had been under discussion for a considerable time, and draft legislation had been prepared in 1955. The Bill appeared to have widespread public support. Moreover, it was a modest measure, controlling the immigration of all holders of Commonwealth passports except (1) those born in the UK, (2) those holding UK passports issued by the UK government, and (3) those included on the passport of a person exempt from immigration control under (1) or (2). Other Commonwealth citizens wishing to immigrate had to have a Ministry of Labour voucher before they could enter the UK. These vouchers were to be issued under three categories: category A for those migrants with a specific job to come to; B for those with special skills in short supply; and C for all other intending migrants, who would be dealt with in order of application, with priority being given to those with war service.

The Bill was poorly prepared, however, and in the rush to introduce it there was no opportunity for proper consultations with Commonwealth governments. The decisive change in British government policy and the break with the long tradition of treating all Commonwealth and colonial people as British subjects with equal rights of citizenship, including access to the UK as native

Britons,[7] were factors that many Conservative ministers and MPs were unhappy with − which provided an opportunity for the opposition to launch a furious onslaught on the government. Gaitskell, attacking the Bill as cruel and brutal anti-colour legislation, exploited its ambiguities and the mishandling of the Irish provisions by Macmillan.[8] The charge that Commonwealth governments had not been properly consulted was very damaging, and the Bill was condemned by Commonwealth leaders.[9]

However, Labour's furious opposition on the second reading, which was supported by the Liberals, the Churches and much of the quality press, was not sustained. Patrick Gordon Walker, who had supported Gaitskell with a powerful speech summarizing the opposition's case in the debate on the second reading, was attacked in his constituency for opposing controls and withdrew from combating the Bill. Already, a few months before the second reading, he had exposed the divisions within the Labour leadership over the Bill. In reply to a question on immigration on the radio programme 'Listeners Answer Back', he said:

> I think there is a case for restricting or controlling immigration in certain circumstances when it gets too big ... I don't think that at the moment the rate of immigration of coloured people, which is, I think, what most people are worried about, has reached the point where there should be this sort of control. But I would not reject the idea of control as such.[10]

The government made some concessions, such as permitting annual renewal of the Bill, and it easily passed, becoming law on 1 July 1962. Later in the year Labour's uncertain position was again emphasized, when Denis Healey repudiated a statement made in Accra by John Strachey that 'the Labour Party would repeal the Act when returned to power'.[11]

Public concern had by now become thoroughly roused both by the 1958 riots and by the angry debate over the Commonwealth Immigrants Bill. Moreover, the press and some local Conservative politicians were responding to, and exploiting, these fears. In September 1963 the Southall Residents' Association was formed to protest at the increasing number of Indians settling in the borough and at the growing number of Asian children in local schools. Less widely reported was the successful exploitation to the issue by local Conservatives in Patrick Gordon Walker's constituency of Smethwick.[12] In the months before the general election of 1964 the Labour party became more defensive on the issue. In October 1963 the new leader of the Labour party, Harold Wilson,[13] modified Labour's policy of total opposition to controls and announced in the debate on the Expiring Laws Continuance Bill that the Labour party 'do not contest the need for immigration control'.[14] In the manifesto for the general election the Labour party's compromise was announced: Labour would legislate against racial discrimination and incitement to racial hatred in public places, but would retain immigration control pending an agreement with Commonwealth governments limiting immigration.[15] This compromise – that there should be voluntary control by the Commonwealth countries themselves – had already been tried by the government, and its failure had been a major reason for the introduction of controls.

Smethwick and the general election of 1964

The politicization of black immigration was intensified during the general election of 1964. In election speeches in Bradford and Birmingham, Sir Alec Douglas-Home claimed credit for the Conservative government for excluding nearly a million people by means of the Commonwealth Immigrants Act, while Wilson accused the Conservatives of using immigration as an excuse for failing to redress the problems of housing slums, inadequate schools and poor education.[16] The great shock of the election was the Smethwick result where, against the national trend, the Conservative candidate, Peter Griffiths, achieved a stunning victory over Patrick Gordon Walker, the shadow Foreign Secretary. In the previous year Griffiths had refused to condemn those who used the slogan, 'If you want a nigger neighbour, vote Labour', and was accused of 'running an openly anti-immigration campaign'.[17] It was shockingly successful. Griffiths captured the seat with a 7.5% swing to the Conservative in the midst of a national swing to Labour of 3.2%.

The result confirmed the views of the anti-immigration lobby that the public was behind them, and suggested more widely that the exploitation of racism could reap electoral dividends. It struck fear into many Labour politicians who were worried that the electorate was deeply racially prejudiced.[18] They noted that anti-immigrant candidates had also done well in Southall and Birmingham Perry Bar and that Fenner Brockway, the tireless campaigner for anti-discrimination legislation, had lost his seat at Eton and Slough. The vulnerability of the new Labour government, with its majority of five, was increased when, as noted earlier, Patrick Gordon Walker lost the Leyton by-election in January 1965, reducing its majority to only three. It seemed that another general election would quickly be forced on the government before it was prepared. The government rapidly adopted the policy of appeasing the Conservatives on both race relations legislation, where they removed criminal sanctions from the Bill and narrowed its scope, and immigration controls, which they tightened in August 1965.[19] Moreover, there was no pretence of adopting non-racist immigration controls by including the Irish or other aliens in the legislation; the controls that Labour imposed in 1965 were clearly intended to curb New Commonwealth immigration.[20] They were successful in creating a bipartisan consensus on these issues, which saw them safely through the general election of 1966.

The successful exploitation of racism in Smethwick by Peter Griffiths and by other Conservative candidates created a precedent for others to follow, when similar opportunities arose. Despite Wilson's attack on Griffiths, who, he said, 'would serve his term as a parliamentary leper',[21] Griffiths was never repudiated by the Conservative party leadership and, after losing his Smethwick seat in 1966, was selected and returned to parliament in 1979 as the member for Portsmouth North.

The Kenyan Asian crisis

The tough immigration controls that Labour had imposed in 1965 and the bipartisan consensus that had been so carefully constructed had only a short-term effect in keeping immigration off the political agenda. By 1967 non-white immigration was becoming an issue once again, as British Asians from Kenya began migrating to Britain in increasing numbers. Fearing discrimination by the Kenyan government, these Asians had decided to retain their

British citizenship even though the Kenyan government refused to allow dual nationality. As British passport-holders, they were not covered by the Commonwealth Immigrants Act and so were not subject to immigration controls. The Kenyan government, as noted in chapter 3, was determined to give preference in employment to Kenyan citizens, and so Asians who had retained British citizenship were losing their jobs and being forced to leave the country. As Enoch Powell's and Duncan Sandys' campaign to control the new source of non-white immigration intensified, immigration from Kenya rose and the media became more hysterical, fuelling Asian fears of controls.[22] The numbers rose to 13,000 Asian immigrants from Kenya in the first two months of 1968, as they rushed to beat the anticipated controls.

The second Commonwealth Immigrants Act, which became law on 1 March 1968, proposed that any citizen of the UK or colonies, who was the holder of a passport issued by the UK government, would be subject to immigration control unless they, or at least one parent or grandparent, had been born, adopted or naturalized in the UK, or registered as a citizen of the UK and colonies. The Act was the logical outcome of the policy of appeasement that the Labour government had adopted in order to achieve the bipartisan consensus with the Conservatives and to reduce the electoral salience of the issue. It represented a major intensification of the politicization of racism in Britain, and both major parties had cooperated in its implementation. The political consequences, however, were more damaging for the Labour government. They had shown that they were so afraid of the electoral consequences of appearing weaker than the Conservatives on the issue of immigration controls that both in 1965 and 1968 they had introduced tougher measures than even the Conservatives, if they had been in government, would probably have introduced. The supporters of immigration control now knew that they had the upper hand and that they could dictate the political agenda. The temptation to escalate the issue proved irresistible.

The rise of Powellism

It was Enoch Powell who became the populist leader and spokesman for those concerned about non-white immigration and the perceived threat to British national identity and culture. Public concern had remained at a high level since 1958, but had been stifled between 1965 and early 1968 by the bipartisan consensus. It was an issue that was constantly raised at MPs' surgeries, and the response to the Asian immigration from Kenya showed the parties were well aware of its high political potential. Powell was concerned with what he regarded as a preventable evil.[23] He argued that the number of immigrants and their geographical concentration would prove an insuperable barrier to assimilation, and would lead to similar 'race' problems in Britain as existed in the United States. These concerns led him to demand a net immigration of nil, and to advocate a programme of voluntary repatriation to offset the natural increase of black immigrants already settled here.[24]

On 20 April 1968, two days before the second Race Relations Bill was introduced, Powell made his apocalyptic 'river of blood' speech, which made him a national figure overnight, the focal expression of anti-immigrant resentment and a challenger for the leadership of the Conservative party. The speech was not a major departure from his previous ones, though its language was more colourful. However, its reception in the media made it a cataclysmic event in the remorseless process by which the 'race' issue has been politicized in Britain.

Powell used reported incidents and conversations to raise fears of immigrant invasion and take-over of streets and whole areas, fears of harassment of old people and even fears of prosecution under the forthcoming Race Relations Bill. He warned about the future of Britain if immigration was allowed to continue: 'We must be mad, literally mad, as a nation, to be permitting the annual inflow of some 50,000 dependants who are for the most part the material of the future growth of the immigrant-descended population. It is like watching a nation busily engaged in heaping up its own funeral pyre.' The most dramatic, best-remembered part of his speech came at the end, when he attacked the forthcoming Race Relations Bill and its supporters:[25]

> For these dangerous and divisive elements the legislation proposed in the Race Relations Bill is the very pabulum they need to flourish. Here is the means of showing that the immigrant communities can organize to consolidate their members to agitate and

campaign against their fellow citizens, and to overawe and dominate the rest with legal weapons which the ignorant and the ill-informed have provided. As I look ahead I am filled with foreboding. Like the Roman, I seem to see 'the River Tiber foaming with much blood!' That tragic and intractable phenomenon which we watch with horror on the other side of the Atlantic but which there is interwoven with the history and existence of the States itself, is coming upon us here by our own volition and our own neglect.

Powell's speech gained tremendous publicity and popular support. Overnight, he became the best-known and most popular Conservative politician. His support could be measured in four opinion polls, which recorded percentages from 67 to 82 in his favour, the deluge of letters he received[26] and the public demonstrations of support, notably by the dockers. The polls also indicated that large majorities were against his dismissal from the shadow cabinet. His words had tapped the widespread popular frustration with the bipartisan approach to immigration and 'race' relations issues.[27] There was also considerable dissatisfaction with the anti-discrimination legislation, which many people did not understand and did not support. Many felt it gave black immigrants a privileged position.

The 'river of blood' speech enraged the Labour government, which saw its carefully constructed bipartisan policy smashed to smithereens; but it also infuriated many of Powell's colleagues in the shadow cabinet, notably Edward Boyle and Quintin Hogg, who felt the speech was offensive and racialist. Hogg was particularly furious, as he felt that Powell had trespassed into his area of shadow cabinet responsibility. Heath and Whitelaw also felt the speech was offensive, and Heath quickly decided to sack Powell from the shadow cabinet. However, Powell was reflecting the frustrations not only of those who felt threatened by New Commonwealth immigration, but also of those angered by Britain's imperial decline and of those who felt the major parties and politicians in general were ignoring their interests. He proved unable to translate the immense public support he gained on the immigration issue into other areas of politics, nor did he try to build a personal following in the Conservative party, but his April speech stimulated eighty constituency resolutions on immigration at the annual conference, where he received a standing ovation for a speech advocating tighter controls. Powell had too much support within both the party and the country for Heath to ignore: in September, before the party conference, he had already announced that tougher immigration controls would be introduced.

Powell returned to the attack with another hard-hitting speech at Eastbourne in November. He warned of the dangerous gap that had developed between the overwhelming majority of the people in the country and the tiny minority with a monopoly on the channels of communication, who seemed determined not to know the facts nor to face the realities. He predicted a minimum immigrant population of 4.5 million by the year 2,000, and advocated large-scale voluntary, but organized, financed and subsidized, repatriation. He even advocated the establishment of a Ministry of Repatriation.[28] He argued: 'The West Indian or Indian does not, by being born in England, become an Englishman. In law he becomes a United Kingdom citizen by birth; in fact he is a West Indian or Asian still.'[29]

The campaign launched by Powell and the publicity that his emotive language generated raised enormously the salience of 'race' and immigration issues. They legitimized the expression of deep prejudices and racial hostility which many people thought embarrassing, immoral and even illegal, given popular confusion over the Race Relations Act and the incitement to racial hatred provisions of the Public Order Act. In Powell, popular hostility and prejudice against black immigrants found a national political leader, highly respected for his ability and oratory, willing to raise issues and articulate fears that the major parties had preferred to keep off the agenda.

The Eastbourne speech was widely condemned in the press and by leading politicians of all parties, who felt that this time Powell had gone well beyond the bounds of acceptable conduct. Heath described his speech as 'character assassination of one racial group' and added, 'That way lies tyranny.' He also said that the Conservative party would never accept a total ban on coloured immigration.[30] Powell, of course, had moved on from immigration controls as a solution to racial problems to the idea of voluntary repatriation, but this commanded little support in the shadow cabinet. However, in spite of the distance and hostility between

Heath and Powell, the latter's popularity remained high both among the public and in the Conservative constituency associations. In December the Conservative Political Centre carried out a survey of its 412 constituency groups, and found that 327 wanted all immigration stopped indefinitely and a further 55 favoured strictly limited immigration of dependants combined with a five-year ban on new immigration.[31] Party officials and leaders were horrified by these results, and their response contributed to the decision by the leadership to include in the 1970 election manifesto the promise of a new immigration Act and assistance for voluntary repatriation.[32]

The general election of 1970

The most extraordinary feature of the 1970 general election was the role of Enoch Powell who, though a Conservative candidate, acted as a political force in his own right. His election address, issued early in the campaign, was treated by the press as a manifesto and, on the issues of immigration and entry into the EEC, was at variance with party policy and a challenge to Heath and the shadow cabinet. He demanded a complete halt to new immigration, a new citizenship law to distinguish UK citizens from everyone else, and voluntary repatriation. Otherwise – and he gave his oft-repeated warning – 'the immigration problem could bring a "threat of division, violence and bloodshed of American dimensions".'[33] It was widely believed that, if the Tories lost the election, as was widely expected, Powell would attempt to gain the leadership.

The election campaign began quietly, with Conservative leaders attempting to ignore Powell. However, on 3 June Tony Benn dramatically attacked him, accusing him of 'raising the flag of racialism over Wolverhampton – a flag which was beginning to look suspiciously like the one that fluttered over Dachau and Belsen.[34] Benn's attack received enormous publicity and made Powell the centre of attention once again. Benn's extravagant rhetoric enabled Heath to condemn his language while disassociating himself from Powell's views on immigration. On 11 June Powell himself raised the temperature when he returned to an old theme of his, accusing the authorities of misleading the public about the numbers of immigrants coming into the country to the point 'where one begins to wonder if the Foreign Office was the only Department of State into which enemies of this country were infiltrated'.[35] This speech was widely criticized, but Heath refused to disown Powell as a Conservative candidate and contented himself with saying, 'I will never use actions or words or support actions which exploit or intensify divisions within our society.'[36] The violence of the language used by Benn against Powell distracted attention from the hostility that existed between Heath and Powell. The latter realized that he would have no chance of serving in a Conservative administration under Heath but, hoping to succeed him after the likely defeat, he called on his supporters to vote Conservative.

The unexpected victory at the general election, when the Conservatives gained 77 seats and achieved a comfortable overall majority of 43, greatly strengthened Heath's position as leader and led to Powell's increasing isolation in the party and finally to his departure to the Ulster Unionists. Paradoxically, Powell was a major contributory factor in the Conservative party's victory and in his own political downfall. It is clear that his anti-immigration campaign had a significant effect on the result of the election. At the time of the general election of 1966 a majority of the electorate could perceive no difference in the positions of the major parties on immigration control, but, as is shown in Table 4.1, by 1970 a majority saw the Conservative party as being the toughest. It was Powell's campaign that had had the decisive effect. Furthermore, immigration was considered the fourth most important issue in the campaign. Academic studies of the impact of immigration on the election result, while coming to different conclusions about the size of that impact, agree that there was a national effect which con- tributed very substantially to the Conservative electoral success.[37]

The new Conservative government acted swiftly to fulfil its commitments on immigration, which Powell had forced it to include in the election manifesto. It introduced the Immigration Act of 1971 which consolidated and extended existing legislation and came into force on 1 January 1973. The main provisions of the Act were that employment vouchers would be replaced by work permits, which would not carry the right of permanent residence or the right of entry for dependants; and that patrials − that is,

Table 4.1 Perceived positions of the parties on control of immigration, 1964−70: Which party is more likely to keep immigrants out? Responses in %

Responses	Autumn 1964	Spring 1966	Summer 1969	Summer 1970
Conservatives	26	26	50	57
Labour	19	13	6	4
No difference	41	53	36	33
Don't know	14	8	8	6

Source: D. Butler and D. Stokes, *Political Change in Britain*, Macmillan, 1974, p. 306

people with close connections with the United Kingdom through birth or descent − would be free from all controls. There were also provisions to strengthen the powers to prevent illegal immigration; and, finally, voluntary repatriation was to receive some modest financial assistance.[38] These provisions gave the government complete control over the immigration of non-patrials, and ended the rights of non-white Commonwealth citizens to immigrate and settle in the United Kingdom. The legislation did not, however, end the controversy over black immigration, and it proved to be only another major milestone in the process of erecting racist immigration controls.

Powell continued his campaign on immigration in 1971, with speeches that brought increasing condemnation upon him from the press and other politicians. His continued accusations of deliberate fraud in the presentation of immigration statistics and his warnings of racial civil war made him appear to be more and more a fomenter of racial strife than a credible politician and prophet of the future. In parliament his actions in committee on the Immigration Bill helped to get the patriality clause restricted to anyone who had British nationality at the time of birth, thus restricting the right of abode in Britain to the first generation born abroad.

The Ugandan Asian crisis

If the Conservative party leadership hoped that the Immigration

Act 1971 would finally end the immigration debate and deprive Powell of his most popular and widely known issue, then they were to be brutally disappointed. On 4 August 1972 General Idi Amin, President of Uganda, announced the expulsion of all Asians from his country. Most of the 50,000 Asians in Uganda were British passport-holders, though a small minority were Ugandan citizens, and many were of uncertain citizenship. As most were British citizens, it was clear that Britain would be primarily responsible for them.

The announcement that Britain might receive some 50,000 Asian immigrants from Uganda all at once was greeted with shock and horror in the media and by some politicians, particularly Powell, who claimed that Britain was not responsible for the Asians in East Africa and that they should be returned to India or Pakistan. There was considerable lobbying of MPs, and the Home Office received substantial mail on the issue. Some local authorities, like Leicester, indicated that they did not wish to receive any more Asian immigrants.[39] However, the government decided that Britain would have to accept them, and established the Ugandan Resettlement Board to assist their reception, dispersal and integration. Strenuous diplomatic efforts were made to get other countries to assist by admitting some of these Asians, particularly the stateless ones, and substantial numbers were accepted by India, Canada and other countries. Britain finally accepted 27,000.

The Ugandan Asian crisis received considerable publicity in the media and was a major boost to anti-immigrant organizations, both those within the Conservative party, like the Monday Club, and those on the extreme right, like the National Front. It was tremendously embarrassing to the Conservative party leadership, which had been elected on a tough immigration platform but which now appeared powerless to prevent an influx of Asians caused by an African dictator. The Monday Club, a right-wing group originally formed to oppose decolonization in Africa, started a 'Halt Immigration Now' campaign. It was hostile to many of Heath's policies and generally sympathetic to Powell. However, many in the Conservative party agreed with Heath and the Cabinet that Britain had a moral obligation to the Ugandan Asians. The supporters of the Conservative leadership rallied at the annual party conference and Powell's motion condemning the government's action was successfully amended by the Young Conservatives, who defeated the Powellites by 1,721 votes to 736. This was a rare victory on an immigration issue for liberal Conservatives. It infuriated Conservative right-wingers in the constituency associations, some of whom left the party to join the National Front. In some ways the major beneficiary of this crisis was the National Front: it began a period of growth and electoral advance which was not decisively rebutted until the general election of 1979.

The Labour party's response to electoral defeat

The unexpected defeat at the general election of 1970 was a major blow to the Labour party, but it provided an opportunity for a complete reassessment of its race relations and immigration policies. The initial reaction to defeat was to blame Powellism, and this was reflected in many of the speeches at the annual conference following the election. The motion on racialism and discrimination emphasized this view: 'This conference condemns discrimination on the grounds of race, creed or colour. It is concerned that the pernicious and reactionary ideology of Powellism has, with the help of the Tory party and press, gained a hold with many electors who have been frightened into support through not having enough facts to counter the argument.'[40]

The considered response came from the National Executive Committee's study group on immigration, which in March 1972 produced an opposition Green Paper on citizenship, immigration and integration.[41] This document was the first detailed study of race relations and immigration policy ever produced by the Labour party. It provided a careful examination of the development of immigration policy, and outlined how it considered immigration and 'race' relations policy should be developed in the future. The study group argued that it was possible to devise a coherent and acceptable immigration policy which was not based on the colour or 'race' of the prospective migrant; that a discriminatory policy makes integration more difficult and contributes to racial hostility; and that the notion that increasingly severe restrictions on coloured immigration would play a major part in reducing racial hostility had proved to be false, since each move towards stricter controls had led to a demand for even narrower exclusiveness or for a complete ban on coloured immigration. This was an admission that Labour's bipartisan policy of appeasing the Conservatives was a failure, and that a new, more combative, policy had to be tried.

The report also called for a major review of the citizenship laws, as it argued that a logical immigration policy must be based on a logical concept of citizenship. Since 1962 colonial citizenship had had much of the positive content, such as free access to the mother country, removed. The report argued that a government inquiry should be set up to examine all aspects of citizenship of the United Kingdom and colonies. It needed to be decided, for example, whether to retain colonial citizenship, or to abandon it and allow the remaining colonies to enact their own citizenship provisions. British citizens of overseas origins with no colonial, dual or other citizenship should be allowed free entry to the United Kingdom on the same basis as other UK citizens. The report also demanded that free movement within the EEC should be extended to all citizens of the UK, and not be restricted to the narrow concept of UK national as presently defined in the Treaty of Accession. Immigration controls, once the citizenship laws had been redefined, would apply only to non-citizens, and this would be the logical basis of a non-discriminatory policy.[42]

On integration, the report called for more aid to inner-city areas on the basis of social need generally and not primarily for the welfare of immigrants. Also, since the proportion of immigrants among the black population was declining and the proportion of British-born black citizens was rising, the study groups recommended that responsibility for integration policies, including the responsibility for the Community Relations Commission and the Urban Aid Programme, should be transferred from the Home Office to the Department of Health and Social Security, this being the department most concerned with overall social policy. The Home Office would retain responsibility for the enforcement provisions of the Race Relations Act and the Race Relations Board. The debate within the Labour movement, which the Green Paper was meant to provoke, was largely pre-empted by the Ugandan Asian crisis, but even so the careful work of the study group was to provide the basis for the policy statements on immigration in Labour's *Programme 1973* and the Labour party manifesto in 1974.[43]

In parliament the Labour opposition was in a more embarrassing position in developing its response to Conservative immigration policy, as it was saddled with the legacy of its own stringent immigration policy of 1964–70. The blatantly racist aspects of the patriality clauses of the Immigration Act of 1971 were foreshadowed in Labour's own Commonwealth Immigrants Act of 1968. The opposition's strategy in opposing the 1971 Act was largely based on stressing the need for a review of the citizenship laws in order to resolve the anomalies of immigration legislation. The Ugandan Asian crisis in 1972 provoked comparisons with the Kenyan Asian crisis in 1968, and the relatively generous response of the Heath administration compared well with the treatment of the Kenyan Asians by the previous Labour government. This was particularly so as the Heath government had substantially increased the number of entry vouchers available for Kenyan Asians.[44]

Outside parliament, both the TUC and the NEC made positive statements accepting Britain's obligations to the victims of Amin's expulsion order. The Home Policy and International Committees of the NEC issued a joint statement:

> The Labour Party fully accepts this country's moral and legal obligations towards the Asian UK citizens and passport holders who are being expelled from Uganda ... we therefore welcome the decision of the government to accept their responsibilities to receive the UK citizens from Uganda and we will give our support to measures introduced by them which will positively assist the resettlement and integration of those expelled.[45]

The annual Labour party conference in 1972 endorsed the NEC statement and condemned the actions of President Idi Amin.[46]

The National Front

One of the major beneficiaries of Enoch Powell's anti-immigration campaign was the extreme right, especially the National Front. The Second World War and the revelations of the holocaust had discredited the far right in the period immediately after the war; Mosley's attempts to rebuild his Union Movement fizzled out, and he went into voluntary exile in 1951. In the late 1950s there was a flurry of activity by a new-wing movement, the League of Empire Loyalists, formed in 1954 to protest against the dissolution of the Empire and especially against the Conservative party's move to grant independence to the African colonies. The League made little impact, and its more militant members quickly left to join more aggressive groups such as the White Defence League and the National Labour Party, which in 1960 merged to form the British National Party.

In 1966 the National Front was founded, as a result of a merger between the League of Empire Loyalists and the British National Party. Some other esoteric groups also joined, or dissolved themselves and urged their members to join. These included such organizations as the English National Party, the Anglo-Rhodesian Society, the Racial Preservation Society and the neo-Nazi Greater Britain Movement led by John Tyndall.[47]

The formation of the National Front took place shortly before the Powell–Sandys campaign against the immigration of Kenyan Asians, which the National Front fully supported. But it was Powell's 'river of blood' speech in April 1968 that provided a massive boost to the fortunes of the Front. Paul Foot was told by a leading Front official at this time in Huddersfield:

> We held a march in support of what Powell had said and we signed eight people up as members of the branch that afternoon. Powell's speeches gave our membership and morale a tremendous boost. Before Powell spoke we were getting only cranks and perverts. After his speeches we started to attract, in a secret sort of way, the right-wing members of the Tory organisations.[48]

Powell's campaign thus gave tremendous publicity to the 'race' issue, which was the National Front's major *raison d'être*; it legitimized consideration and support for policies like repatriation, which had hitherto been regarded as not only extreme but also illegitimate; and it consequently stimulated recruitment to organizations like the National Front, which were the most open advocates of such policies. In the general election of 1970 the National Front fielded ten candidates and gained 11,449 votes, thus achieving an average of only 3.6% of the vote in the seats it contested.

The election of the Heath government in 1970 and its commitment to a tough new immigration bill limited the scope for the far right until 1972, when the crisis and publicity surrounding the Ugandan Asian panic provided the National Front with a major campaigning issue. Naturally the Front, like Enoch Powell, was opposed to the admission of the Ugandan Asians, and felt that Heath was betraying his promises of stringent immigration controls by allowing them in. Many local Conservatives, who were angry at the 'betrayal' and furious at the support that Heath gained at the annual party conference, left the Conservatives and joined the National Front.

The Ugandan Asian crisis stimulated a period of rapid growth for the National Front, and its claimed membership soared to a peak of 14,000 in 1973. It achieved a spectacular coup in May of that year when its candidate Martin Webster gained 4,789 votes, 16.3% of the poll, in the West Bromwich by-election, saving his deposit. The public refusal of Powell to support the Conservative candidate because of his liberal views on immigration undoubted helped Webster in this seat, which was close to Powell's own constituency. But despite some respectable polls in the non-metropolitan district elections in June, the Front was unable to sustain the electoral impact made by the by-election and its candidates fared badly at the general elections of February and October 1974.

The influx of new members and the increased activity of the National Front caused problems for the party. Many of the new members were disillusioned Conservatives, strongly opposed to black immigration, but not aware of the anti-Semitism and support for violent street politics of some of the long-standing members of the extreme right. This was to cause bitter internal conflict over strategy, tactics and leadership positions. Second, the more publicity and activity the National Front achieved, the more active opposition it generated from the wide range of organizations which abhorred its policies – these included groups on the far left, the unions, the major parties, Jewish organizations, the media and immigrant groups. Marches and counter-marches became a feature of intense conflict between the National Front and its opponents, particularly those on the far left, in the mid-1970s.

The relationship between the National Front and the Conservative party was ambiguous. The parties were in direct competition for activists and voters. They claimed much of the same political ground. The Front considered itself to be a patriotic party and ostentatiously used the Union Jack as its symbol. It supported the Ulster Unionists against the IRA; it was anti-Communist; it was anti-Common Market, as this undermined British sovereignty; it favoured capital punishment and tough penalties for criminals; and it was violently opposed to black immigration and in favour of compulsory repatriation.[49] These policies would find favour with many right-wing Conservatives, especially those in organizations like the Monday Club. It was not surprising, therefore, that some disillusioned Conservatives were attracted to the Natinal Front and that there were accusations of cooperation between far-right groups in the Conservative party and the Front.[50] Many Conservatives who joined the Front quickly became disillusioned with the depth of anti-Semitism and the commitment to violent street politics rather than electoral politics. Nevertheless, something of an inverse relationship existed between the National Front and the Conservative Party: when the Conservative party was seen as failing to prevent black immigration, this provided the Front with greater opportunities for recruiting members and mobilizing support.

In May 1976 a media panic over small numbers of Asians from Malawi coming to Britain caused an upsurge of support for the National Front in local elections. There was substantial support for Front candidates in Leicester, Sandwell (West Bromwich), Bradford and Wolverhampton. In Blackburn the National Party, which had previously split off from the National Front, gained two council seats.[51] The next two years were a period of intense media interest in race relations and immigration issues. Powell was continuing his anti-immigration campaign, and there were a number of murders where racial motives were assumed. The murder of an eighteen year-old Sikh, Gurdip Singh Chaggar, for example, provoked massive demonstrations in Southall by the Asian community and fury at the reported comment by John Kingsley Read, leader of the National Party and one of its councillors in Blackburn: 'One down – a million to go.' Read was unsuccesfully prosecuted under the incitement to racial hatred provisions of the Public Order Act.

There was a fundamental contradiction at the heart of the

National Front's strategy. Those supporters, often ex-Conservatives, who favoured the electoral path to political success and wanted to present the party as respectable and mainstream, were at odds with the hard core of anti-Semites and neo-Nazis who also favoured violent street confrontations and attacks on immigrants and their allies. And many of those attracted to the National Front by its aggressive stance were not interested in, and even hostile to, the efforts to make it respectable and electorally successful. However, in the 1970s the party pursued both strategies at the same time. For example, considerable violence was associated with the National Front campaign in the Ladywood by-election in August 1977. Also, marches through immigrant areas were deliberate provocations meant to intimidate and incite retaliation. They often resulted in violence with groups like the Socialist Workers Party, which were only too eager to respond in kind – as at the Lewisham march on 15 August 1977.

Both street politics and electoral politics needed the lifeblood of publicity, as well as indications of voter appeal, to maintain the enthusiasm and unity of the fractionalist membership. In 1977 the National Front achieved both, with a series of reasonable electoral results in by-elections. At Stechford in March it achieved 8.2% of the poll and pushed the Liberals into fourth place, and in the May Greater London elections it contested 91 of the 92 seats, winning 120,000 votes: it achieved its best results of 17.8% in Tower Hamlets, 13.9% in Hackney and 12.5% in Newham.[52] In July the *Guardian* suggested that the National Front might achieve 25 seats at a general election, in a report on a survey carried out by researchers at Essex University.[53] In August tremendous publicity, some of it favourable to the Front, accompanied the Lewisham march and the Ladywood by-election, where the Front gained 5.7% of the poll and again pushed the Liberals into fourth place.

The publicity and the increasing activity of the National Front provided the seeds of its own destruction. The growing violence attending party marches made the police more willing to ban them, thereby depriving the Front of the publicity it craved. In November the Anti-Nazi League was launched with the support of prominent figures in sport, the universities, the theatre, the trade unions, the Labour party and far-left groups. In December the more moderate Joint Committee Against Racialism was launched, with support from the Conservative, Labour and Liberal parties, the British Council of Churches, the Board of Deputies of British Jews, the National Union of Students and immigrant organizations. The Labour party and the TUC also launched a joint campaign which involved the wide distribution of a leaflet entitled *The National Front is a Nazi Front*. This included the phrases 'Yesterday – the Jews; today – coloured people; to-morrow – you'.[54]

This counter-offensive against the National Front was massive, but an even more damaging blow was shortly to follow. The Malawi Asian mini-crisis in May 1976 had stimulated an astounding 140 resolutions on immigration at the annual Conservative party conference in October. Mrs Thatcher, the new leader,[55] decided that the party should harden its attitude, and Mr Whitelaw promised the conference that the party would develop a policy which was clearly designed to work towards an end to 'immigration as we have seen it in the postwar years'.[56] On 30 January 1978 Mrs Thatcher reinforced this hardening of Conservative policy in her interview with Gordon Burns on the 'World in Action' programme. 'People are really rather afraid that this country might be rather swamped by people with a different culture', she stated, and 'We do have to hold out the prospect of an end to immigration except, of course, for compassionate cases.' She went on to argue that although she would not make immigration a major issue in the general election expected shortly, she felt that for major parties to neglect people's fears about immigration would only drive them to support the National Front. When Burns asked, 'So, some of the support that the National Front has been attracting in recent by-elections you would hope to bring back behind the Tory party?' she replied, 'Oh, very much back, certainly, but I think that the National Front has, in fact, attracted more people from Labour voters than from us. But never be afraid to tackle something which people are worried about. We are not in politics to ignore people's worries; we are in politics to deal with them.'[57]

Mrs Thatcher's remarks were widely condemned as pandering to popular prejudices, and even as 'giving aid and comfort to the National Front'.[58] They had certainly once again raised the promi-nence of the 'race' issue and brought about a surge in popular support for the Conservative opposition, even though Mrs Thatcher had difficulty in indicating where further cuts of a compassionate kind could be made in Britain's already tough immigration policy. But as the National Front had been most successful in recruiting members and winning support when the prominence of the 'race' issue was combined with neglect by the major parties, particularly the Conservative party, of popular anxieties, Mrs Thatcher's statement was potentially even more damaging to the National Front than the efforts of its opponents on the left. At the Ilford North by-election the next month the Conservatives easily captured the seat from Labour, and Mrs Thatcher's initiative seems to have been an important factor. Here the National Front gained 4.7% of the vote, and in the Lambeth Central by-election held in an area of major immigrant settlement in March, Labour held the seat while the National Front took 6.2% of the vote.

Opposition to the National Front continued at a high level throughout 1978, with teachers' organizations taking a strong stand against the party's activity in the schools, a carnival against racism organized by the Anti-Nazi League in April, and action by local authorities to ban the use of facilities by the National Front. Stronger police action over marches and demonstrations deprived the party of the publicity accruing from violent confrontations with their opponents. In the local elections in May the Front performed less well than in the previous year, and in July did very badly in a by-election in Manchester, Moss Side, where it had hoped to exploit once again the existence of a substantial immigrant population.

The leaders of the National Front decided to put all their resources into a major display of strength at the long-anticipated general election, promising its members to field 300 candidates and to gain its legitimate right to the television and radio facilities that went with this. The party was also entitled to free postal delivery of literature in each constituency where it put up a candidate. When the election was announced in March 1979 the Front was able to field an unprecedented 303 candidates. The Anti-Nazi League mobilized its supporters to oppose the Front wherever it held election meetings, and major clashes took place in Leicester and Southall. In Southall on 23 April the Anti-Nazi League and the local Asian community rallied in thousands to prevent a National Front meeting. It was estimated that 10,000 people joined the anti-National Front demonstration, which was in major contrast to the mere fifty supporters that the Front was able to achieve for its meeting. Clashes took place between the police and demonstrators as the protests intensified and arrests were made. Blair Peach, a New Zealand teacher, was killed during these clashes, and the Special Patrol Group of the Metropolitan Police was blamed by the demonstrators. Peach's death became a *cause célèbre*, and the Anti-Nazi League mobilized a massive demonstration of support at his funeral on 28 April. The role of the police in Southall became a major issue of civil liberties, and subject to both official and unofficial inquiries by distinguished investigators. The results of official inquiries into the evidence at Southall and the death of Blair Peach were not published, but the Director of Public Prosecutions decided that there was insufficient evidence to charge anybody with murder. The jury at his inquest agreed a verdict of death by misadventure. The unofficial inquiry − *Southall 23 April 1979* − was published by the National Council for Civil Liberties in 1980.

The general election results were a total disaster for the National Front. It won only 0.6% of the total vote compared with 0.4% in October 1974, despite its massive increase in candidates from 90 to 303. Its share of the vote in each constituency fell from 3.1% in October 1974 to 1.4% in 1979. Even in its East End strongholds of Tower Hamlets, Newham and Hackney, the party achieved an average of only 5.2% of the vote. In the Leicester area it gained only 2.4%, and in its West Midlands bastions of Wolverhampton, West Bromwich, Walsall and Dudley, only 2.5%. These areas include almost all the 49 seats where the National Front achieved over 2% of the poll.[59]

It seems clear that the major reason for the electoral reverse was Mrs Thatcher's public identification of the Conservative party with a hard line on immigration. The massive swings to the Conservatives through the East End to Dagenham, which averaged 14.2%, took place in areas where the Front had achieved some of its highest support; now it appeared to have lost much of it to the Conservatives. The defeat was devastating to the leadership of the Front, which had placed so much of its prestige and so much of the movement's resources on fighting the election. The bill for lost deposits alone had come to £45,450 and the free publicity available on television and radio as party political broadcasts had certainly not paid off in terms of votes or recruits. Moreover, the massive mobilization of the left through the Anti-Nazi League had shown the National Front that it was unlikely ever to achieve its goal of becoming a respectable and accepted political party. Its leaders were forced to reconsider their whole strategy, as dissatisfaction mounted in the movement. John Tyndall attempted to strengthen his leadership by constitutional reforms, but this was rejected by the membership and he was unable to prevent fragmentation and disintegration. In November Andrew Fountaine and his supporters formed the National Front Constitutional Movement, and the leaders of the powerful Leicester branch also left the National Front and established the British Democratic Party. Tyndall, unable to assert his authority, resigned in January 1980 and formed the New National Front.

The collapse and disintegration of the National Front ended speculation about its possible rise as a fourth English party representing English chauvinism and nationalism. It also undermined the momentum of the Anti-Nazi League, though this was also disintegrating under internal divisions.[60] However, the fragmentation of the far right and the loss of support for it have not ended its activity, but appear to have diverted it away from electoral politics and more towards sporadic violence and racial attacks against black people.

Notes

1 E.g., Parliamentary Debates, Commons (Hansard), vol. 563, col. 392, 24 January 1957.
2 'Immigration', in Z. Layton–Henry (ed.), *Conservative Party Politics* (Macmillan, 1980).
3 Parliamentary Debates, Commons (Hansard), vol. 596, col. 1563, 5 December 1958.
4 Ibid., cols 1579–80.
5 Labour Party, *Racial Discrimination*, September 1958.
6 *Economist*, 29 November 1958.
7 The Commonwealth Immigrants Act 1968 and the Immigration Act 1971 restricted the rights of British subjects without a close connection with the UK through descent or citizenship from access to the UK.
8 Z. Layton–Henry, *The Politics of Race in Britain* (Allen & Unwin,

1984), pp. 52–5.
9   Ibid.
10 'Listeners Answer Back', BBC Radio, Light Programme, 31 August 1961.
11 *Sunday Telegraph*, 2 December 1962.
12 P. Foot, *Immigration and Race in British Politics* (Penguin Books, 1965).
13 Hugh Gaitskell died on 18 January 1963.
14 Parliamentary Debates, Commons (Hansard), vol. 685, col. 383, 27 November 1963.
15 Labour Party, *Labour Party Manifesto*, 1964.
16 Foot, *Immigration and Race*, pp. 148, 180.
17 Ibid.; M. Hartley-Brewer, 'Smethwick', in N. Deakin (ed.), *Colour and the British Electorate 1964* (Pall Mall Press, 1965).
18 R. Crossman, *Diaries of a Cabinet Minister*, vol. 1 (Hamish Hamilton and Jonathan Cape, 1975), pp. 149–50, 299.
19 *Immigration from the Commonwealth*, Cmnd 2739, HMSO, 1965.
20 Crossman, *Diaries*, vol. 1, p. 299.
21 Parliamentary Debates, Commons (Hansard), vol. 701, col. 71, 3 November 1964.
22 J. Callaghan, *Time and Chance* (Fontana, 1988), pp. 263–70; P. Cosgrave, *The Lives of Enoch Powell* (Pan Books, 1990), pp. 243–4. And for more information on the Kenyan Asian crisis, see pp. 51–3.
23 Cosgrave, *Lives of Enoch Powell*, p. 246.
24 Ibid., p. 236.
25 Text of speech delivered to the annual general meeting of the West Midlands Area Conservative Political Centre at the Midland Hotel, Birmingham, 20 April 1968, in B. Smithies and P. Fiddick (eds), *Enoch Powell on Immigration* (Sphere Books, 1969), pp. 35–43.
26 D. Spearman, 'Enoch Powell's postbag', *New Society*, 9 May 1968, 667–8.
27 D. Schoen, *Enoch Powell and the Powellites* (Macmillan, 1977).
28 Speech delivered to the annual conference of the Rotary Club of London, Eastbourne, 16 November 1968, in Smithies and Fiddick, *Powell on Immigration*, pp. 63–77.
29 Ibid.
30 P. Foot, *The Rise of Enoch Powell* (Penguin Books, 1969), p. 121; Schoen, *Powell and the Powellites*, p. 41.
31 M. Walker, *The National Front* (Fontana, 1977), p. 111.
32 Ibid.
33 Schoen, *Powell and the Powellites*, pp. 51–2.
34 J. Wood, *Powell and the 1970 Election* (Elliot Right Way Books, 1970).
35 Schoen, *Powell and the Powellites*, p. 53.
36 D. Butler and M. Pinto-Duschinsky, *The British General Election of 1970* (Macmillan, 1971), p. 163.

37 The major studies supporting this view are: D. T. Studlar, 'Policy voting in Britain: the coloured immigration issue in the 1964, 1966 and 1970 general elections', *American Political Science Review*, vol. 72 (1978), 46–72; W. L. Miller, 'What was the profit in following the crowd?: aspects of Conservative and Labour strategy since 1970', *British Journal of Political Science*, vol. 10 (1980), 15–38; Schoen, *Powell and the Powellites*. Two studies are sceptical of Powell's influence: namely, N. Deakin and J. Bourne, 'The minorities and the general election of 1970', *Race Today*, vol. 2 (July 1970), 205–10; and M. Steed, 'An analysis of the results', in Butler and Pinto-Duschinsky, *General Election of 1970*; but these are less convincing.

38 Home Office, *Immigration Act 1971*, HMSO, 1971.

39 D. Humphrey and M. Ward, *Passports and Politics* (Penguin Books, 1974), p. 31.

40 Labour Party, *Annual Conference Report*, 1970, p. 205.

41 Labour Party, *Citizenship, Immigration and Integration: A Policy for the 1970s*, 1972.

42 Ibid., pp. 31–6.

43 Labour Party, *Labour's Programme 1973*, 1973; *Labour Party Manifesto*, 1974.

44 Parliamentary Debates, Commons (Hansard), vol. 818, cols 380–5, 26 May 1971.

45 Labour Party, *Annual Conference Report*, 1972, pp. 383–4.

46 Ibid., pp. 153–8.

47 Layton–Henry, *Politics of Race*, ch. 7.

48 Foot, *Rise of Enoch Powell*, pp. 126–7.

49 M. Walker, *The National Front* (Fontana, 1977); N. Fielding, *The National Front* (Routledge & Kegan Paul, 1981).

50 At the Uxbridge by-election in December 1972 the West Middlesex branch of the Monday Club supported the NF candidate, who gained 2,960 votes, or 8.2% of the poll. The branch was dissolved. In June 1972 the Essex branch of the Monday Club was closed down because of its close links with the NF.

51 Layton–Henry, *Politics of Race*, pp. 98–9.

52 S. Taylor, *The National Front in English Politics* (Macmillan, 1982).

53 *Guardian*, 5 July 1977.

54 Taylor, *National Front*, pp. 138–9.

55 Mrs Thatcher was elected leader of the Conservative party on 11 February 1975.

56 Layton–Henry 'Immigration', p. 67.

57 Verbatim report of part of an interview with Gordon Burns, given by Mrs Thatcher on Monday 30 January 1978, 'World in Action', Granada Television.

58 *Sunday Times*, 26 February 1978.

59 Taylor, *National Front*.

60 Ibid.

5 Black electoral participation

The recruitment of migrant workers from the Commonwealth and colonial territories provided one of the major contrasts with post-war immigration to most other West European countries. Most immigrants to Britain were British subjects and therefore had full political rights. They could vote in local and national elections and stand as candidates, and they had the automatic right, until the Nationality Act of 1981, to register as British citizens. Even citizens of the Republic of Ireland, who were not British subjects after Ireland withdrew from the Commonwealth in 1948, were granted full political rights under the Ireland Act 1949, because of the historic relationship between Britain and Ireland and the large numbers of Irish people settled in the United Kingdom, many of whom were British citizens. By contrast, most migrant workers entering France, Germany and other European countries were foreigners; so they were excluded from local or national political participation, and often from public sector employment as well, unless they became naturalized citizens of their new countries of work and residence.

Concern about racism in British society and the impact of racial discrimination upon the ethnic minorities has led to anxiety that the political response of the black communities might be political apathy, alienation or even rebellion. Participation in elections, in contrast, is often seen as a hallmark of political integration and support for democratic politics. Registration, turn-out, the distribution of political opinions, the salience of issues and the levels of party support can all be used as bases for assessing the similarity or distinctiveness of groups in the electorate and their involvement in the mainstream of politics. Electoral behaviour may thus throw some light on the degree of political efficacy or feelings of power-lessness, and even on the alienation, of groups of electors.[1]

Considerable interest and research has thus been devoted to the electoral participation and voting behaviour of the black elec-torate, despite its relatively small size and the host of methodological problems involved in obtaining representative samples and accurate data.[2] This interest has arisen partly because political scientists and the media are as obsessed with elections, whether local or parliamentary, as politicians; and partly because the British electoral system in the post-war period has facilitated both close results and governmental change. The parliamentary ascendancy of the Con-servative party in the 1980s and 1990s is exceptional, even compared with the 1950s when it won three successive general elections. This ascendancy is, of course, much more marked in parliament than it is among the electorate and cannot therefore be taken too much for granted, even though the Conservatives now appear almost unbeatable in the light of their electoral victory of 1992. The entry of new, distinctive and rapidly expanding groups in the electorate is naturally of considerable interest to both politicians and political scientists in such an electoral system, and it is thus not surprising that the electoral behaviour of black voters has attracted widespread attention.

In the 1960s there was little interest in the voting behaviour of black Britons. The numbers of black voters were relatively small and, though residentially concentrated, they were scattered over many urban centres in different parts of the country. It was widely believed that many black voters were not registered and that most lived in safe Labour seats where, even if they voted, the result was a foregone conclusion. It was the impact of the immigration issue on the white electorate that was the centre of attention, especially after the Smethwick result in the general election of 1964.[3] This was also true in the 1970 general election, although a Nuffield election study noted a considerable rise in the registration and turn-out of black voters as compared with the 1966 election. This increased participation was, the authors felt, due to the impact of Enoch Powell's anti-immigrant campaign which, they argued, mobilized immigrant voters against the Conservatives.[4] Nationally, Powell's campaign is thought to have contributed significantly to the Conservatives' unexpected victory in the 1970 general election.[5]

The defeat of Mr David Pitt (now Lord Pitt) at Clapham, normally a secure Labour seat, was also thought to have been partly due to anti-immigrant voting by voters who usually supported the Labour party candidate.

It was the two general elections of 1974 that stimulated interest in the electoral importance of black voters. These hard-fought and close-run elections created a situation where the major parties were anxious to attract every vote and were willing to appeal to even small, distinctive groups in the electorate. This opportunity was brilliantly exploited by the Community Relations Commission in their publication, *The Participation of Ethnic Minorities in the General Election, October 1974.*[6] The main conclusions of the report were that:

1 the ethnic minorities played a significant part in determining the outcome of the election;
2 the minorities swung more to Labour than the electorate as a whole, partly at least in response to the Labour government's action to benefit the minorities;
3 members of minority groups were five times as likely not to be registered to vote as whites in the same area;
4 although most members of the minorities conformed with their socio-economic group in voting Labour, other parties were able to attract support among the minorities when they made the effort;
5 anti-immigrant candidates made little or no progress at the election.

The report argued that there were 76 constituencies in the February 1974 election and 85 in the October election where ethnic minority voters could have made a significant impact on the outcome, as the size of the black population was larger than the majority of the winning candidate. These seats were described as 'ethnic marginals'. It emphasized that 13 of the 17 seats won by Labour from the Conservatives in the general election of October 1974 were seats where the black population was larger than the majority of the winning candidates in both these elections.

The assumptions and conclusions of the report were controversial and were hotly disputed. It now seems clear that it exaggerated the significance of black voters in marginal constituencies and their willingness to switch votes between the major parties.[7] In particular it incorrectly equated the black population with the black electorate, when a high proportion of black people were too young to vote and many adults were not registered to vote.[8] However, the report was a political success. It alerted the parties, especially the Conservatives, to the fact that many black voters resided in marginal constituencies and that they were a rapidly expanding part of the electorate that should not be ignored.[9]

The growth in the black electorate has been dramatic in the last twenty years, and this has had an important impact on parliamentary candidates and parliamentarians sitting for urban constituencies in England. Since the late 1960s immigration has been a major source of the problems raised in MPs' surgeries in inner-city areas. Many MPs have seen their constituencies transformed and have had to adjust their priorities in order to keep in touch with their new electors.[10] Also, as the Labour party's support has declined among the white working class in the 1980s and early 1990s, so the importance of black voters for Labour party MPs has risen. This growing displacement of black voters is reflected in the campaign for black sections in the Labour party, and is one of the reasons why the parliamentary leadership wishes to reach an accommodation with black activists.

An indication of the expansion of the black electorate can be given if we compare the constituency census data for 1971 and 1981. In 1971 there were 18 constituencies where the black population (defined as those born, or with one parent born, in the New Commonwealth or Pakistan) made up 15% or more of the population. They ranged from 29.6% in Birmingham, Ladywood, to 15.3% in Newham North-West. In 1981 there were 51 such seats, ranging from 45.7% in Brent South to 15% in Westminster North. In the general election of 1987, 33 of these seats were held by the Labour party and 18 by the Conservatives. There is no doubt that when the census data for 1991 becomes available it will show a considerable increase in the number of such seats, given the youthfulness of the black population and also the fact that the ethnic question in the census will enable the black population to be more accurately determined.[11] Thus, despite the qualifications that need to be made about 'ethnic marginals' and the electoral significance of black voters, they have become a very important part of the electorate in such cities as London, Birmingham, Bradford and Leicester and in northern towns such as Blackburn and Huddersfield.

The impact of black voters in local politics

It is at the local level that the impact of black voters is potentially the most significant. The residential concentration of the black population in declining inner-city areas means that they are well represented in many safe Labour constituencies as well as in Conservative and Labour urban marginals, and are in a position to play a significant role in local ward and constituency branches in these areas. FitzGerald calculated that in 1983 the average Labour constituency in inner London had a black population of 23% compared with one of only 12% in non-Labour seats. In the seven Labour-held seats in outer London the black population was 22% while in Conservative-held seats it was only 9%.[12]

The natural tendency for black immigrants to support the Labour party – for class reasons, because of Labour's past support for colonial independence (especially for India) and its general opposition to racial discrimination – was reinforced by their settlement in Labour-dominated areas. Labour councillors and MPs were the focus of requests for help in dealing with housing, social welfare, education and immigration problems. The assistance provided reinforced black immigrants' support for the Labour party. Gradually, as the black vote grew more important in these wards and constituencies, inner-city Labour politicians worked even harder to consolidate their political support among members of minority ethnic communities. Local politics in areas like Brent, Southall, Bradford and Leicester has been transformed by the settlement of Afro-Caribbeans, Sikhs and Pakistanis. LeLohé has found in Bradford that Asians, mainly Pakistanis, have very high rates of electoral turn-out compared with their white neighbours, especially in local and European elections where white turn-out falls. This high turn-out is crucially important in several marginal wards. All local parties in Bradford have taken account of these dedicated voters and have selected Asians as local candidates. A Labour councillor, Mohammed Ajeeb, has served as Lord Mayor.[13]

In areas where the Labour party has been less welcoming it has sometimes been challenged by members of the minority ethnic communities. Eade argues that the Labour party's failure in Tower Hamlets to involve Bangladeshi community leaders in its affairs led to the emergence of Bangladeshi Independent candidates at the 1982 borough elections. One of these successfully unseated a Labour councillor and, as a result, the local Labour party made the recruitment of Bangladeshis a high priority and selected seven to stand as Labour party candidates in the local elections of 1986. Five of these were elected. The party also campaigned on issues of concern to the Bangladeshi community such as racial attacks, and mobilized their new recruits to support more general Labour party causes.[14]

In the Greater London area there are now over 130 councillors from the ethnic minority communities and they have played leading, and often controversial, roles in such boroughs as Brent, Haringey, Lambeth and Southall. While most publicity has focused on black Labour councillors, there has also been ethnic minority involvement in the other major parties. Maidenhead and Leamington Spa have both had Conservative Asian mayors, and John Taylor, the unsuccessful black Conservative parliamentary candidate in Cheltenham, in the 1992 general election, was a Conservative councillor in Solihull. As the ethnic minority population expands, their members will play a much greater role in local politics; for some, this will be a springboard to national politics. Diane Abbott, Bernie Grant and Keith Vaz all played a role in local politics before moving on to national politics at Westminster. More ethnic minority politicians are certain to follow this path.

Trends in black registration and electoral turn-out

The Community Relations Commission (CRC) and the Commission for Racial Equality (CRE) have been concerned to investigate levels of electoral registration among the adult black population, and to encourage increased registration so that members of the Afro-Caribbean and Asian communities, by taking part in electing the decision-makers in society, are in a position to exert some influence on them. The CRC report found substantial levels of non-registration among members of the ethnic minorities in

October 1974. Only 6% of whites were not registered, as compared with 24% of non-whites. If we exclude new voters and recent movers, 94% of whites, 73% of Asians and 63% of Afro-Caribbeans were registered.[15] In 1979 the CRE carried out a survey of 24 constituencies, with a sample of 1,927, to establish the proportions of people from different groups who were registered to vote. Most of the constituencies surveyed included significant proportions of ethnic minority voters and so were not representative of the population as a whole. This survey found higher levels of registration among black voters than in the earlier survey. The results revealed that 93% of whites were registered, compared with 81% of Afro-Caribbeans and 77% of Asians.[16] In 1983 the CRE found 79% of Asians and 76% of Afro-Caribbeans registered, but only 81% of whites[17] − a dramatic fall in white registration which does not accord with other studies, even of inner-city constituencies. It seems probable that this is an unrepresentative result which is exaggerated by the inner-city nature of the constituencies in the sample. The Harris poll in 1983 found 82% of Afro-Caribbeans and 94% of Asians to be registered.

A study by the Office of Population Censuses and Surveys in inner London in 1981 found 25% of ethnic minorities and 12% of whites to be unregistered. The national figures for non-registration in England and Wales were 14% for those born in the New Commonwealth, compared with 3% of those born in the UK, Ireland or the Old Commonwealth.[18]

The diversity of these results suggests that registration varies significantly in inner-city areas, where such factors as poverty, population mobility and residence in multi-occupied buildings − for example, hotels specializing in bed and breakfast accommodation for people on benefit − combine to reduce electoral registration. The ethnic minority population is more settled than the white population in inner-city areas, and electoral registration among them is rising, especially among Asians.

The turn-out of Afro-Caribbean and Asian voters is likely to vary considerably, depending on such factors as length of settlement, education, occupation, area of residence, membership of associations and feelings of political confidence and integration. Generally, surveys suggest that Asian voters participate much more than their white neighbours, and often more than the electorate as a whole. Evidence of exceptionally high electoral turn-out by Asians was found in some polling districts monitored by the CRE in 1979; for example, 95% in Nuneaton and Brent East, and 91% in Leicester South. The lowest turn-out rates were 72% in Hackney and Stoke Newington and 69% in Wandsworth and Battersea.[19] In contrast to Asians, Afro-Caribbean voters appear to participate very much less in elections, though in the by-election in Lambeth Central in April 1978 Afro-Caribbean turn-out was recorded as being very similar to that of whites.[20] In a local by-election again in Lambeth Central, monitored by the CRE, it was found that Afro-Caribbean turn-out was higher than that of their white neighbours, confirming the trend, according to Anwar, of increasing levels of turn-out of ethnic minority voters.[21]

The data from national sample surveys suggest that Asian and white voters have rather similar rates of turn-out, significantly above those of Afro-Caribbeans. The 1979 pooled Gallup surveys found that between 76 and 80% of Asians and whites claimed to be certain to vote, compared with 66% of Afro-Caribbeans.[22] In 1983 the Harris poll found the voting intentions of Afro-Caribbeans and Asians in 1983 were as shown in table 5.1.

Interestingly, the analysis of the pooled Gallup surveys taken in the run-up to the general election of 1979 found that Afro-Caribbean voters were more interested in who would win the general election, felt the result mattered more, and discussed politics more than Asian voters.[23] The paradox of a relatively apolitical

Table 5.1 Voting intentions among non-whites, 1983

	Afro-Caribbean (649) (%)	*Asian* (527) (%)
Absolutely certain to	33	61
Certain to	18	23
Probably will	21	10
Probably won't	9	1
Certainly won't	13	2
Don't know	6	3

Source: Harris Poll, 1983

but voting Asian electorate and a more politically interested but non-voting Afro-Caribbean electorate has been confirmed by the Greater London survey of the political attitudes of white, Afro-Caribbean and Asian Londoners carried out in 1984.[24] Explanations for the relatively high turn-out of Asians may relate to membership of associations and groups with positive attitudes to voting and to voting traditions in the Indian subcontinent. The Greater London survey found a strong positive response by Asians to the question, 'Does voting at general elections give people a say in how the country is run?' Seventy per cent of Asians thought that it did, compared with 65% of whites and 55% of Afro-Caribbeans. Only 17% of Asians said it did not, compared with 32% of whites and 40% of Afro-Caribbeans.[25] Surveys suggest that while Afro-Caribbeans have resided in Britain longer than Asians, they are more disenchanted with life in Britain. Thus their relative unwillingness to vote, despite their interest in politics, may include a degree of political alienation, particularly among young people who may reject voting as a pointless activity.[26]

Political attitudes and party support

Surveys of public opinion, of party support and the preferences of black voters have been plagued by problems of inadequate sampling procedure and the possibility of environmental effects due to the geographical distribution and residential concentration of the minority ethnic communities. However, these surveys suggest an overwhelming concern among black voters with economic issues – a concern that is, of course, shared equally by the white electorate. Unemployment and the cost of living have been the two most important issues for both black and white electors since 1980. In British general elections, international affairs and defence have seemed much less important issues to black voters than to whites. This does not mean, though, that particular aspects of international relations are not important for groups among the minority ethnic communities. The crisis over Khalistan, which erupted in the Anglo-Asian Conservative Society in 1984 and caused the disbandment of the national association, shows how 'homeland' politics can intrude into party politics in Britain. Some ethnic minority groups may have an intense interest in the politics of their country of origin, and also in relations between Britain and their 'homeland'. This has sometimes caused considerable embarrassment to the British government: for example, in relations with Indian when in 1984 an Indian diplomat, Mr R. H. Mhatre, the Assistant Commissioner in Birmingham, was murdered by members of the Kashmiri Liberation Front.

Immigration and nationality issues appear to be a low priority for Afro-Caribbeans and a declining issue among Asians, particularly the young, but it remains important for about a third of the Asian electorate. The actions of the Conservative government to phase out the right of Commonwealth citizens to registration rather than naturalization, and the continuing efforts to increase immigration controls by the introduction of visas, 'carrier' liability and restrictions on dependants, may increase the salience of these issues. Education and relations with the police are continuing to grow in importance for black voters, but remain far behind economic issues. There thus appears to be no distinctive set of political priorities that divide black and white electors.[27]

However, responses to general questions in surveys may fail to elicit the distinctive concerns of black people such as might become apparent if questions were asked on how best to resolve such issues as unemployment, the educational problems that face their children and relations with the police. When offered three alternative ways of reducing unemployment, significant minorities of Afro-Caribbeans and Asians felt there should be stronger action to stop employers discriminating against ethnic minorities in the allocation of jobs. The preferred solution was the creation of new jobs through increased government spending.[28] On education, a majority of Afro-Caribbeans and Asians felt more attention should be paid to the specific needs of their children and that there should be more ethnic minority teachers. As far as relations with the police were concerned, the priorities of Afro-Caribbeans and Asians diverged significantly. Afro-Caribbeans were strongly in favour of the police being more accountable to local people, and saw little need to give them more powers to catch criminals. Asians wished the police to devote greater efforts and resources to preventing racial attacks, and were more likely to endorse the proposition that they should have more powers to catch criminals.[29]

It has long been clear that support for the Labour party is very high among Afro-Caribbean and Asian voters. The level of this support may have been exaggerated in the past by quota sampling in areas of ethnic minority concentration, where class, housing and environmental factors all contribute to extensive labour party support. In some cases the timing of the polls may also have produced this result.[30] Table 5.2 shows the distribution of party support within ethnic groups given in the pooled Gallup pre-election surveys in 1979.

One of the striking features of this table is that Labour voting was higher in 1979 among professional and non-manual black voters than it was among the white working class. Overall, 28% of black voters intended to vote Conservative, 66% Labour and only 6% Liberal. Surveys carried out by the Commission for Racial Equality in inner-city areas found, not surprisingly, much higher levels of support for the Labour party.[31]

Similarly, analyses of black voting in the general election of 1983 also provide contrasting results, while confirming the high levels of support for the Labour party. A large quota sample of

Table 5.2 Voting by social class within ethnic groups, 1979

	Con. (%)	Lab. (%)	Lib. (%)	Non-voter (%)	(Nos)
White					
A, B, C1	57	20	9	15	(3,588)
C2	40	35	5	20	(3,290)
D, E	32	38	5	25	(3,145)
Afro-Caribbean					
A, B, C1	17	41	7	35	(29)
C2	11	49	8	32	(37)
D, E	15	48	3	35	(40)
Asian					
A, B, C1	25	42	6	28	(36)
C2	28	50	3	19	(32)
D, E	25	50	0	25	(40)

Source: Gallup pre-election surveys, 1979, in Z. Laylon-Henry and D. T. Strudlar, 'The electoral participation of black and Asian Britons', *Parliamentary Affairs*, vol. 38 (1985), pp. 307–18

black voters in inner-city areas carried out by the Harris Research Centre for the television programmes 'Black on Black' and 'Eastern Eye' found that 86% of Afro-Caribbeans and 80% of Asians intended to vote Labour, 8% of Afro-Caribbeans and 6% of Asians intended to vote Conservative, and 5% of Afro-Caribbeans and 12% of Asians intended to vote Alliance. In contrast, the Gallup–BBC exit poll found that 21% of black voters claimed to have supported the Conservatives, 64% Labour, and 15% the Alliance. The Harris–ITN exit poll found that 24% of black voters said they had voted Conservative, 57% Labour and 16% Alliance, while 3% refused to say how they had voted. Although the exit poll results are based on relatively small numbers of black respondents, it seems clear that inner-city polls significantly exaggerate black support for the Labour party, particularly among Asian voters.

The Harris poll in 1983 found that 76% of Labour voters among Afro-Caribbeans and 64% of Labour-voting Asians gave their reason for Labour support as being that Labour supports the working class. Only 7% of Afro-Caribbeans and 31% of Asians said it was because Labour supported Afro-Caribbeans and Asians. Interestingly, the GLC survey of 1983 found white respondents more likely to assign themselves to a class, and to the working class in particular, than either Afro-Caribbeans or Asians. The willingness to assign themselves to a class was particularly low among Asian respondents.

Black voters and the general election, 1987

The data on which this analysis is based consist of two polls carried out by the Harris Research Centre. The first is a poll of 871 black people interviewed face to face at 40 sampling points in areas of high ethnic concentration. In addition, 136 black people in areas of low ethnic concentration were interviewed by telephone. The areas of low ethnic concentration chosen included Dorking, Edinburgh and Ipswich. The interviews took place between 25 and 29 May 1987. The first poll was carried out for the *Asian Times* and was published in June just before the general election. The second poll is a national poll of 1,072 electors carried out by the Harris Research Centre for the *Observer* at the same time as the first poll. This second poll will be used for purposes of comparison.[32]

The Harris poll indicates that the Labour party remained the overwhelmingly popular choice among black voters. Taking the ethnic minorities as a whole, 72% intended to vote Labour, 18% Conservative, and 10% Alliance. Women were slightly less likely to support the Conservatives (15%) than men (20%), and were more likely to support Labour (75% to 70%). Labour support was highest among the older age groups and lowest in the 25–44 range. There were significant differences in the distribution of support between Asians and Afro-Caribbeans, as table 5.3 shows.

The comparable figures from the poll of the national electorate for May 1987 were Conservative 41.2%, Labour 36.8%, Alliance 20.5% and other party 1.5%. Support for the Labour party among black voters is thus almost double that among the national electorate.

The Harris poll for the *Asian Times* was the first that attempted to survey ethnic minority voters in areas of low ethnic concentration. As a telephone poll, it may be biased towards more prosperous ethnic minority voters in these areas, and biased also by the fact that almost all those in the sample are Asian. Nevertheless, if we compare ethnic minority support for the parties in areas of high and low ethnic concentration, then we find a considerable rise in Conservative support in areas of low ethnic concentration. It is

Table 5.3 Voting intentions of Asians and Afro-Caribbeans, May 1987

	Asians (592) *(%)*	*Afro-Caribbeans* (228) *(%)*
Conservative	23	6
Labour	67	86
Alliance	10	7
Other party	–	–

Source: Harris poll, May 1987

also significant that support for the Alliance more than doubled there (see table 5.4).

It seems clear that as members of the ethnic minority communities become more prosperous and move out into suburban areas, there will be some attrition in support for the Labour party. This may not be as dramatic as the table 5.4 suggests, where the most prosperous groups may be over-represented among the ethnic minority sample in areas of low ethnic concentration. Support for the Conservative party and the Alliance will be influenced by the prominence of 'race' and immigration issues, by the willingness of local constituency parties to mobilize ethnic minority support and welcome them as members, and by the scale of suburbanization and whether it occurs close to or far from existing areas of ethnic minority concentration. One can speculate (1) that the attrition in the Labour vote will proceed relatively slowly and (2) that it will occur much faster among Asians than among Afro-Caribbean voters. The first is suggested by the distribution of party support by class among ethnic minority voters in table 5.5, which confirms that while class differences in party support are significant among black voters, a majority of all class groups continue to support the Labour party.

In the Harris poll of May 1987, the groups of Asians and Afro-Caribbeans most likely to vote were Conservative supporters, professional and managerial groups and those over 65 years of age. Those least likely to vote were Afro-Caribbeans, skilled workers, and those between 18 and 24 years. Women were less certain

Table 5.4 Party support of ethnic minority voters in areas of high and low ethnic concentration, May 1987

	High (709) (%)	*Low* (111) (%)
Conservative	15	39
Labour	77	43
Alliance	8	17
Other party	–	1

Source: Harris poll, May 1987

Table 5.5 Party support by class among ethnic minority voters, May 1987

	A, B (48) (%)	C1 (206) (%)	C2 (241) (%)	DE (290) (%)
Conservative	33	30	14	10
Labour	54	52	78	84
Alliance	13	17	9	5

Source: Harris poll, May 1987

about going to vote than were men, and Alliance supporters were less sure than either Conservative or Labour supporters. The most significant differences were between Asians and Afro-Caribbeans, and by age, as table 5.6 shows.

However, if we compare tables 5.1 and 5.6, we find a remarkable rise in the proportions of both Asian and Afro-Caribbean voters who report that they are absolutely certain to vote in the general

Table 5.6 Intention to vote of ethnic minority voters in the general election, 1987

			Asian and Afro-Caribbean, by age			
	Asian (707) (%)	Afro-Caribbean (299) (%)	18−24 (200) (%)	25−44 (519) (%)	45−64 (257) (%)	65+ (30) (%)
Absolutely certain to	74	51	58	69	70	77
Fairly certain to	13	18	16	14	15	13
Not very certain to	7	14	14	8	6	10
Not at all certain to	2	2	2	3	1	−
Don't know	4	15	11	7	7	−

Source: Harris poll, May 1987

elections of 1983 and 1987. (The 'absolutely certain' category is the one that pollsters find is the best indicator of actual turn-out.) One can speculate that the much larger number of black candidates selected by the major parties in 1987, the fact that a number of these were in safe Labour seats and stood an excellent chance of being elected, combined with the publicity that these candidates received, may have increased black voters' commitment to voting in the 1987 election. In the national poll carried out by the Harris Research Centre 72% of all electors said they were absolutely certain to vote, a further 20% said they were fairly certain, 4% not very certain, and 2% not at all certain. Only 1% said they did not know.[33]

The most important issues

When ethnic minority electors were asked what issues would be the most important in determining how they would vote, unemployment was by far the most often mentioned. It was equally important for Asians and Afro-Caribbeans, and most important for the young and for those in the lowest occupational categories. Law and order was the issue most often mentioned second, and was most important for the professional and managerial groups, those over 65 years of age, and Conservative supporters. Housing was next in order of priority, being mentioned almost as often as law and order. In fact for Afro-Caribbeans housing was the second most important issue, significantly above law and order, but for Asians the reverse was true. Housing was a particularly important issue for semi-skilled and unskilled workers, the very young, the very old and women. Racial discrimination was the fourth most important issue for ethnic minority voters, and was particularly so for Afro-Caribbean respondents.

Conservative supporters emphasized unemployment, law and order and economic policy most often. Labour supporters emphasized unemployment, housing and law and order, and Alliance supporters emphasized unemployment, economic policy and racial discrimination. The major contrast between ethnic minority voters and the electorate as a whole was the low priority given to defence and foreign policy issues, including nuclear disarmament. Neither were the trade unions seen as an important electoral issue. Afro-Caribbeans were overwhelmingly concerned with standard of living issues, being most anxious about unemployment, housing, racial discrimination, law and order and poverty. One quarter of Afro-Caribbeans mentioned poverty as an important issue which would influence how they decided to vote. Asian voters had similar concerns, listing unemployment, law and order, housing, economic policy and racial discrimination as their five most important issues.

A majority of ethnic minority respondents were satisfied with Labour's policies on 'race' and immigration issues (54%), and dissatisfied with the government's record on these issues (55%). Most did not know whether they were satisfied or not with the Alliance's policies (59%), but more said they were dissatisfied (25%) than satisfied (16%), which confirms that the Alliance failed to make the impact they hoped on ethnic minority voters. When asked whether the parties' stand on 'race' and immigration issues would affect their vote in the general election, black voters were equally divided, with 38% responding 'Yes' and 40% saying 'No', and 23% indicating that they did not know. Alliance supporters were the most likely to reply positively, and Conservative supporters negatively.

Most respondents reported that it would make no difference to their vote whether there was an ethnic minority candidate or not (51%), but many older voters (63%) and a significant minority of Afro-Caribbeans (38%) said that they would be more likely to vote for an ethnic minority candidate. There was some support for the view that ethnic minority candidates would represent respondents' interests better than another member of parliament (37%), but again more said it would make no difference (43%).

Finally, a question was asked about whether respondents approved or disapproved of the setting-up of black sections in the Labour party. More disapproved (45%) than approved (33%), and 21% did not know. Disapproval was highest among those groups least likely to be sympathetic to the Labour party, such as professional and managerial people (63%), those in areas of low ethnic concentration (58%), Alliance supporters (58%) and Conservative supporters (57%). Older respondents (43%), Afro-Caribbeans (39%) and Labour supporters (39%) were the most approving, but only among older respondents was there a majority in favour.

Black electoral behaviour in 1987

The Harris poll data indicate that the black electorate continues to remain a bulwark of Labour party support, with 72% of black voters intending to vote Labour in the general election of 1987, compared with a national result for Labour of only 31.6%. Only 18% of black voters intended to vote Conservative, compared with 43.3% of the electorate as a whole, and only 10% intended to vote Alliance, compared with 23.1% of the electorate. Even middle-class black voters were more likely to vote Labour than Conservative, although a significant minority of Asians in areas of low ethnic concentration supported the Conservatives (39%). However, more Asians in these areas still preferred the Labour party (43%).

Support for the Labour party is high for a number of reasons. The black electorate is more working-class than the electorate as a whole. In the Harris samples 68% of the black sample were manual working-class compared to 60% of the national sample, and only 6.1 of the black sample were professional and managerial compared to 16.4% of the national sample. In addition, black voters give a higher priority to issues where the Labour party is seen as more worthy of the electorate's trust, such as unemployment, housing and racial discrimination. They give a low priority to issues where the Conservatives are more highly ranked, such as defence and foreign affairs. The exception is law and order, which is a major concern for both Asians and Afro-Caribbeans; but, although the national electorate trust the Conservatives more than Labour on law and order,[34] this may not be the case among the ethnic minorities. Afro-Caribbeans, in particular, prefer Labour's proposals to make the police accountable to local communities. On racial discrimination Labour's policies are endorsed much more strongly than those of the Conservatives. Satisfaction with Labour's policies on 'race' and immigration is particularly high among Asians (60% satisfied to 13% dissatisfied), and dissatisfaction with the government's record is very high among Afro-Caribbeans (76% dissatisfied to 8% satisfied).

It is widely believed that there is a trend towards the Conservatives among Asian voters, compared with previous elections. This may be true among particular groups such as Asians from East Africa, but this is speculation, as there is little evidence available on particular Asian communities. Among the Asian electorate as a whole no such trend can be clearly established. This is because most surveys before 1987, with the exception of the pre-election Gallup surveys in 1979, were carried out in inner-city areas and thus exaggerate Labour party support among Asian voters. The Harris poll in 1987 shows that there is significant support for the Conservatives among Asians in areas of low ethnic concentration, which is to be expected and is likely to have always been the case. Among Asians as a whole the pooled Gallup surveys in 1979 found support for the Labour party to be 57%. The Gallup and Harris exit polls in 1983 found total ethnic minority support for Labour to be 64% and 57% respectively. The 1987 Harris poll finding that 67% of Asian voters intended to support the Labour party suggests that Asian support for Labour has been consolidated rather than eroded since 1979. This appears to be confirmed by a National Opinion Poll on racial attitudes commissioned for the *Independent on Sunday* and the Runnymede Trust in June 1991. This survey found that support for the Labour party was 80% among Afro-Caribbeans, 76% among Asians and 39% for whites. Even allowing for the inner-city nature of the samples, this confirms the very high levels of black support for the Labour party.[35]

The continuing concern of the Conservative government, especially under Mrs Thatcher, to tighten immigration controls by new legislation and tough administrative action is likely to be a major factor contributing to the reluctance of middle-class Asians to support the Conservatives. Similarly, the willingness of Labour members of parliament to take up immigration problems and oppose Conservative legislation consolidates support for the Labour party. The impact of the poll tax on ethnic minority families, especially Asian families, is another factor increasing Conservative unpopularity. This could have been a major factor inhibiting any swing to the Conservatives among Asian voters. The publicity given to the increased number of Labour parliamentary candidates from the ethnic minorities and the selection of several of these for 'safe' Labour seats must also have consolidated and increased black support for Labour in the general election of 1987.

The general election of 1992

Most attention during the election campaign focused on the minority ethnic candidates selected by the major parties. The Conservatives had selected eight black candidates, including two defending Conservative-held seats. These were Nirj Deva in Brentford and Isleworth and John Taylor defending Cheltenham after his controversial selection.[36] The Labour party had nine black candidates, five of whom were sitting MPs, though one of these, Ashok Kumar, was defending a recent by-election gain at Langbaurgh. The Liberal Democrats had seven ethnic minority candidates.

Immigration and race relations issues were given little prominence in the party manifestos. The Conservatives promised to give the police stronger powers to combat racial attacks and also to reintroduce the Asylum Bill (lost because of the election), which was aimed at restraining the rise in asylum applications. The Major government thus showed its determination to continue the dual strategy of tough immigration controls combined with some measures to assist integration.[37] The Labour party promised to strengthen the 'race' discrimination laws and the CRE, to reform the citizenship laws and introduce new legislation to guarantee sanctuary for genuine refugees. It also promised to introduce legislation to allow contract compliance which would guarantee black people their fair share of jobs.[38] Liberal Democratic proposals were similar to those of the Labour party.[39]

During the election campaign in Cheltenham racist posters were handed out in local pubs, leading to accusations of racism.[40] There was also some publicity for a group of illegal immigrants who were caught being smuggled into Britain by lorry,[41] but generally the issue attracted little attention. Late in the campaign Nicholas Fairbairn, a former Scottish solicitor-general, tried to resurrect the swamping issue by stating that 'under Labour the country would be swamped by immigrants of every colour and race',[42] but he was condemned by Conservative party leaders, and Lord Whitelaw cancelled a trip to his constituency.

The results of the election seemed to indicate that black candidates were more widely accepted by the electorate than ever before. The Labour MPs Keith Vaz and Bernie Grant both showed swings of over 9% and consolidated their majorities, as did Diane Abbott and Paul Boateng, who also showed good swings. Piara Khabra easily won in Ealing Southall. Ashok Kumar, though, was one of many candidates who failed to hold their by-election gains. Nirj Deva, elected in Brentford and Isleworth, was the first Conservative Asian MP since Sir Mancherjee Bhownagree was elected for Bethnal Green North-East in the elections of 1895 and 1900.[43] John Taylor failed to hold Cheltenham for the Conservatives and missed becoming, at this election, the first ever Afro-Caribbean Conservative MP. The swing against him was 5.2% to the Liberal Democrats – only slightly higher than the 4.9% which ousted the Conservative party chairman, Chris Patten, in Bath. Generally the election suggested that parliamentary politics was slowly becoming multiracial and that prejudiced voting was much less significant than, for example, in the 1960s and 1970s.

Are black voters becoming more or less integrated into electoral politics? Detailed data are not yet available from the general election of 1992, but the evidence from the general election of 1987 suggests that they are becoming more integrated, even though the distribution of party support is very different in their case from that of the rest of the electorate, and acknowledging that significant levels of political alienation may exist, especially among young Afro-Caribbeans. One striking feature of the evidence from the Harris poll in 1987 is the considerable rise among both Asians and Afro-Caribbeans in the proportion saying that they were *absolutely certain* to vote in the general election, compared with 1983. The number of Asians saying they were absolutely certain to vote rose from 61% to 74%, a figure very close to the national turn-out of 75.5%. Afro-Caribbeans' intentions to vote rose even more strongly, albeit from a lower base: those saying they were absolutely certain to vote rose from 33% in 1983 to 51% in 1987, a rise of 18%.

The nomination of more black candidates in 1987 by the major parties (28 compared with 18 in 1983) must have raised black interest in the campaign and in the election. The success of four of these candidates in becoming the first black members of parliament since the war is of tremendous symbolic importance for the minority ethnic communities. Furthermore, they have greatly reduced the fears that black candidates will cause prejudiced voting by white electors, or abstentions. In Leicester East, Keith Vaz achieved a remarkable swing to Labour of 9.42% from the Social Democratic Party, and an above-average rise in turn-out of 5.4% to 78.6%. There was also an above-average rise in turn-out at Hackney North and Stoke Newington, where Diane Abbott was elected. The election results generally suggested that voters were more willing to support black candidates than in the past. This trend continued in the general election of 1992.

In the future, one would expect that class voting will increase among members of the black electorate, but there are a number of reasons why this is likely to be rather slow. These include the Conservative party's continuing determination to bring New Commonwealth immigration to an end, their lack of sympathy for anti-discrimination measures, and their willingness to allow the Labour party to be identified with what Conservatives regard as unpopular minorities.

Notes

1 Z. Layton–Henry and D. T. Studlar, 'The electoral participation of black and Asian Britons: integration or alienation?', *Parliamentary Affairs*, vol. 38, no. 3 (1985), 307–18.

2 D. Studlar, 'The ethnic vote, 1983: problems of analysis and interpretation', *New Community*, vol. 11 (1983), 92–100.

3 See ch. 4; and P. Foot, *Immigration and Race in British Politics* (Penguin Books, 1965); D. T. Studlar, 'Policy voting in Britain: the coloured immigration issue in the 1964, 1966 and 1970 general elections', *American Political Science Review*, vol. 72 (1978), 42–70.

4 D. Butler and M. Pinto-Duschinsky, *The British General Election of 1970* (Macmillan, 1971), pp. 406–7.

5 W. L. Miller, 'What was the profit in following the crowd?: aspects of Conservative and Labour strategy since 1970', *British Journal of Political Science*, vol. 10 (1980), 15–38; D. Schoen, *Enoch Powell and the Powellites* (Macmillan, 1977); Studlar, 'Policy voting in Britain'.

6 Community Relations Commission, *The Participation of Ethnic Minorities in the General Election, October 1974*, 1975.

7   I. Crewe, 'The black, brown and green votes', *New Society*, 12 April 1979, 76–8; Z. Layton–Henry, 'Race, electoral strategy and the major parties', *Parliamentary Affairs*, vol. 31, no. 3 (1978), 268–81.

8   The 1981 census shows that while 22% of the general population was under 16 years, the proportion of the Asian population under 16 was 40%, and of the Afro-Caribbean, 30%. As the voting age is 18 years, about two fifths of the ethnic minority population were too young to vote.

9   Layton–Henry, 'Race, electoral strategy'.

10 A good example of an MP who now devotes much more attention to the concerns of his Asian electors than in the past is Mr Roy Hattersley in Sparkbrook.

11 The 1991 census was the first to ask people to identify their ethnic origins.

12 M. FitzGerald, 'Different roads? The development of Afro-Caribbean and Asian political organisations in London', *New Community*, vol. 14, no. 3 (1988), 385–96.

13 M. J. LeLohé, 'The Asian vote in a northern city', in H. Goulbourne (ed.), *Black Politics in Britain* (Avebury, 1990).

14 J. Eade, 'The political construction of class and community: Bangladeshi political leadership in Tower Hamlets, East London, in P. Werbner and M. Anwar (eds), *Black and Ethnic Leaderships: The Cultural Dimensions of Political Action* (Routledge & Kegan Paul, 1991).

15 Community Relations Commission, *Participation of Ethnic Minorities*, pp. 13–14.

16 M. Anwar, *Votes and Policies: Ethnic Minorities and the General Election 1979*, Commission for Racial Equality, 1980.

17 Commission for Racial Equality, *Ethnic Minorities and the 1983 General Election*, 1984.

18 M. FitzGerald, *Black People and Party Politics in Britain* (Runnymede Trust, 1987), p. 8.

19 Anwar, *Votes and Policies*, p. 38.

20 I. Crewe, 'Representation and ethnic minorities in Britain', in N. Glazer and K. Young (eds), *Ethnic Pluralism and Public Policy* (Heinemann, 1983).

21 Anwar, *Votes and Policies*, p. 37.

22 Layton–Henry and Studlar, 'Electoral participation of black and Asian Britons', p. 310.

23 Ibid.

24 FitzGerald, *Black People and Party Politics*, p. 17.

25 Ibid., p. 18.

26 M. J. LeLohé, *A Study of Non-registration among Ethnic Minorities*, a report to the Commission for Racial Equality, 1987.

27 D. T. Studlar, 'Non-white policy preferences, political participation and the political agenda in Britain', in Z. Layton–Henry and P. B.

Rich (eds), *Race, Government and Politics in Britain* (Macmillan, 1986).

28 FitzGerald, *Black People and Party Politics*, p. 17.

29 Ibid.

30 The survey on attitudes to race and immigration published by National Opinion Polls in February 1978 gave the following distribution of support for the Labour party among West Indians and Asians:
Social classes A, B, C: West Indians, 90; Asians, 86%
Social class C2: West Indians, 94%; Asians, 93%
Social classes D, E: West Indians, 99%; Asians, 97%
This Poll was conducted shortly after Mrs Thatcher's 'swamping' interview on Granada Television, which greatly raised the prominence of the immigration issue.

31 M. Anwar, *Race and Politics: Ethnic Minorities and the British Political System* (Tavistock Publications, 1986), p. 80.

32 I am grateful to Mr Robert Waller of the Harris Research Centre for making these data available and for permission to re-analyse them.

33 Harris Research Centre, national poll 3, 27−8 May 1987.

34 Ibid. The Harris poll found that 42% of the electorate trusted the Conservatives most on law and order, 28% Labour, 12% Alliance, and 18% did not know.

35 National Opinion Poll on racial attitudes, 22−25 June 1991, published in the *Independent on Sunday*, 7 July 1991.

36 Z. Layton−Henry, 'A triumph for one-nation Toryism', *The Times*, 11 February 1991.

37 *The Best Future for Britain*, Conservative manifesto 1992, Conservative Central Office, 1992, pp. 25−6.

38 *It's Time to Get Britain Working Again*, Labour manifesto 1992, Labour Party, 1992, p. 24.

39 *Changing Britain for Good*, Liberal Democrat manifesto 1992, Liberal Democrat Publications, 1992 p. 41.

40 *Guardian*, 29 March 1992.

41 *The Times*, 24 March 1992.

42 *Observer*, April 1992.

43 Jonathan Sayeed, who lost his Conservative seat in Bristol East to Labour, never regarded himself as an ethnic minority candidate, although he was partly of Asian descent.

6 Law and order and violence

British policy-makers, even in the early post-war period, were concerned that non-white immigration would lead to social conflict, to discrimination against black people and to problems with the police. These concerns seem to have been related to the 'race relations' problems that were seen to exist in American cities, with their black ghettos, high levels of unemployment, violence and crime. It was assumed that black immigration would result in similar 'problems' being created in British cities, and that the solution was to prevent this happening by restricting black immigration.[1]

In their search for reasons to justify immigration controls, the Interdepartmental Working Party on Coloured Immigration to the UK, which was re-established in 1953, asked the police for information on immigrant crime. The police reports to the working party did not suggest that black immigrants were responsible for a disproportionate amount of crime, though adverse comments were made about the numbers of black men convicted for living off the immoral earnings of white women, particularly in parts of London. As far as drugs were concerned, there were 134 convictions under the Dangerous Drugs Act in the first nine months of 1953, of which 56 were of black men in possession of Indian hemp (cannabis). Not surprisingly, the police did not consider this to be a serious problem.[2]

However, despite the police evidence that immigrants were generally law-abiding and less involved in crime than the rest of the population, they continued to be blamed for a disproportionate amount of crime and for sponging off National Assistance, even though, in the latter case, their higher levels of unemployment were probably due to racial discrimination and not to the implied unwillingness to work resulting from generous unemployment benefits. These sorts of prejudice against black people were widespread among all sections of the population. MPs were lobbied by their constituents with complaints against black immigrants, and MPs in turn lobbied ministers, demanding the government take powers to deport criminals and immigrants who became dependent on public funds.[3] From a confidential meeting in the Colonial Office between members of government and opposition in April 1954, to discuss the imposition of controls, an insight into elite prejudices can be obtained. Lord Glyn, the government representative, said that many of the 'best type of colonials' disliked the lower levels of their society coming to the UK and giving their colony a bad name.[1] He believed there would be quite strong backing in the colonies for some restrictions. Lord Listowel, the Labour representative, said that, given the size of the black population, the power of deportation for certain offences would not prevent the evils arising, so he was in favour of general immigration controls.[4] These evils were overcrowding, ghettos, crime, disease, dependence on National Assistance and the creation of racial friction – all of which were blamed on the presence of black immigrants rather than on the racism which denied them decent accommodation, jobs and social acceptance.[5]

It seems clear that, in the early phase of migration, black people were more law-abiding than the general population and more likely to be the victims of crime, particularly crimes of violence, than perpetrators. There was racist violence against black people on a significant scale in Liverpool, Deptford and Birmingham in 1948. The Nottingham and Notting Hill riots in 1958 were manifestations of anti-black violence on a substantial scale, but unprovoked attacks by white youths on blacks, particularly Asians, were not uncommon, and, as mentioned earlier, in the 1960s came to be known by the populist term 'Paki-bashing'. Pearson describes one such outbreak in Accrington in the summer of 1964 and attempts to link it with other forms of violent working-class behaviour in times of economic stress, such as machine-breaking in the early nineteenth century. The immediate causes of the violence were competition for jobs and girls, while the underlying cause was the economic insecurity of the cotton towns for which the Pakistani migrant workers became a convenient scapegoat and thus the object of attack.[6] The incidence of 'Paki-bashing' reached a peak in 1969–70 in the heightened racial tension following Powell's speeches, and took place in widely dispersed locations over the whole country. *Race Today* gives numerous examples during this period of racial attacks and fights in widely dispersed locations, some resulting in death.[7]

In spite of the law-abiding nature of the immigrant population, the media tended to highlight crimes committed by immigrants, especially those involving a sexual element. This contributed to the reinforcing of stereotypes of immigrants held by both the public and the police. Cain, for example, found that many policemen considered that 'niggers were in the main . . . pimps and layabouts living off what we pay in taxes.'[8] These attitudes among ordinary policemen led to the over-policing of the black communities and accusations of harassment, racial abuse and even police brutality. As early as 1966 a report for the West Indian Standing Conference made such accusations. Its title was *Nigger-Hunting in England*, as police officers leaving their stations were sometimes heard to say that they were going 'nigger-hunting'.[9]

In 1971 a major investigation into police–immigrant relations was carried out by the House of Commons Select Committee on Race Relations and Immigration.[10] This confirmed the view that there was a low rate of crime among black immigrants: 'Of all the police forces from whom we took evidence not one had found that crime committed by black people was proportionately greater than that by the rest of the population. Indeed in many places it was somewhat less. Both the Police Federation which represents all policemen up to and including inspector, and the Metropolitan Police, confirmed this.'[11] The evidence suggested that black people were not disproportionately involved in particular types of crime such as violence, prostitution and drugs. However, the committee did find that police officers often believed that black people were more involved in crime. This was largely due to prejudice, but may also have been related to crime statistics, which show a connection between high rates of crime and the deprived areas where most black people are forced to live. According to the *British Crime Survey*, published in 1988, 39% of whites live in high crime risk areas compared with 70% of Asians and 80% of Afro-Caribbeans.[12]

The Select Committee found a substantial difference in relations between Asians and the police and between Afro-Caribbeans and the police. Asian organizations described relations as cordial and non-confrontational, with Asians avoiding situations where they might have problems with the police. On the other hand Carribbean organizations complained of discrimination, harassment, intimidation, wrongful arrests and police violence. Relations between young Afro-Caribbeans and the police were described as hostile and explosive. The West Indian Standing Conference argued that if urgent action was not taken to resolve these grave issues, violence on a large scale could not be ruled out.[13] An example of the extreme hostility between young Afro-Caribbeans and the police was found by the Committee when it met a group of young blacks in Notting Hill. The suggestion made to the group that there should be more black policemen was greeted with scornful laughter, and one of the group told the members of the Committee that being black policemen in Notting Hill would be like being Jews working in a concentration camp.[14]

A survey commissioned in 1972 by the British Caribbean Association on West Indian attitudes to the police, from a representative sample of West Indians living in London, found that 20% claimed to have been unfairly treated by the police, most believed the police discriminated against West Indians, and the opinions of young West Indians, and the unemployed were found to be particularly hostile to the police. Also, there was very little confidence in the police complaints procedure, which might explain why so few West Indians made any formal complaints. It was widely felt that the police would continue to fail to recruit from the ethnic minorities unless they adopted a more positive attitude towards them.[15]

There was strong evidence to support these suspicions of police discrimination. A detailed study of the working of the 'Sus' law[16] found that of the 2,112 people arrested under this law in 1976, 42% were black − an incredibly high proportion.[17] A Home Office research study in 1979 revealed that a black person was fifteen times more likely to be arrested for 'Sus' than a white person.[18] It was the realization of the harm that this was doing to police−black relations that caused the Home Affairs Select Committee to recommend, unanimously, the repeal of this legislation, and it was replaced by the Criminal Attempts Act 1981.[19]

However, the police did not lose their power to stop and search people or vehicles as long as they had reasonable grounds for suspicion, and research has shown that young black people are likely to be stopped repeatedly. In one study it was found that 63% of young West Indian men and 44% of young white men had been stopped in a twelve-month period; and among those who had been stopped at all the West Indians had been stopped about four times and the whites about two and a half times, on average, over the same period.[20] This procedure did not seem to be an effective method of uncovering crime, and was very annoying to a large number of innocent people.[21]

Nonetheless, some policemen did see it as a valuable method of crime prevention. An extreme example of this was provided in October 1982 when Inspector Basil Griffiths, Deputy Chairman of the Police Federation, said at a fringe meeting of the Conservative party conference organized by the Monday Club: 'There is in our inner cities a very large minority of people who are not fit for salvage ... the only way in which the police can protect society is quite simply by harassing these people and frightening them so they are afraid to commit crimes.'[22] The damage that such attitudes and actions do to police–community relations in inner-city areas is incalculable.

Tension between black people and the police continued to increase in the 1970s, with growing media and public concern over street robberies, which became labelled as 'muggings', and small-scale confrontations between young Afro-Carribbeans and the police becoming a regular occurrence. The clashes between the police and young Afro-Caribbeans at the Notting Hill carnival of 1976 and at other carnivals were the most publicized of these conflicts.[23] There was also irritation at the police protection given to National Front marches in areas of non-white settlement, and this led to conflict between the police and anti-National Front demonstrators, as occurred on the Lewisham march in August 1977. As already mentioned, during the general election of 1979 there were fierce clashes in Southall between thousands of people mobilized by the Anti-Nazi League and the local Asian community, and the police, who were deployed to allow fifty National Front supporters to hold an election meeting.[24]

Spontaneous combustion: the inner-city riots

By the end of the 1970s relations between the police and the black community were tense and hostile. A generalized belief was widespread among young blacks, especially young Afro-Caribbean men, that the police were grossly unfair and that they used their superior power to oppress and harass them. The situation exploded with riots in Bristol in 1980, in places such as Brixton and Toxteth in 1981, and in Handsworth and Tottenham in 1985. The major riots were all precipitated by police action. In Bristol on Wednesday 2 April, a police raid on the Black and White Café in the St Paul's area led to violent clashes between young people and the police. For a period of four hours, when a crowd of some 2,000 people was on the streets, the police withdrew from the area. Clashes between the police and members of the crowd resulted in 21 policemen, three firemen and nine members of the public being injured, and 21 people were arrested. During the evening some 12 police vehicles were damaged or destroyed, and several shops and businesses were broken into, robbed and set on fire.[25]

Much more serious were the 1981 riots in Brixton and Toxteth. The Brixton riots were precipitated by a major police operation, 'Swamp 81', whose purpose was to detect and arrest burglars and robbers on the streets of Lambeth. During the course of the operation, from 6 to 11 April, 112 police officers made 943 stops, 118 people were arrested, and 75 were charged. One charge was for robbery, one for attempted burglary and 20 for theft or attempted theft. Lord Scarman in his inquiry described the operation as a serious mistake.[26] The Brixton rioting lasted from 10 to 12 April: during those three days 226 people were injured, including 150 policemen, and 200 arrests were made. There was extensive damage to property, and 26 buildings and 20 vehicles were burnt by rioters.

The riots in July of the same year in Liverpool (Toxteth) were even more serious, with greater damage to property and larger numbers injured. The Toxteth riots were notable for the fact that, for the first time in Britain, CS gas was used to quell rioters.

The immediate political response to the Brixton riots was one of condemnation of the rioters and support for the police. Mr

William Whitelaw, the Home Secretary, in his statement to the House of Commons after the riots, said:

> We in Parliament, on behalf of the people of this country, have placed on the police the heavy burden of maintaining peace on the streets and of preserving order and the rule of law. Whatever questions may arise in people's minds about the reasons why this outbreak of violence occurred, there is no doubt in my mind, nor should there be in the mind of any member of this house, that Metropolitan Police officers of all ranks carried out their duty with great bravery and professionalism.

He announced the setting-up of an inquiry into the Brixton disorders, under the terms of the Police Act 1964, to establish what happened and to investigate the role of the police. The inquiry would be undertaken by Lord Scarman.[27]

Before the Scarman inquiry was complete, an influential and well publicized report on racial disadvantage was published in August by the Select Committee on Home Affairs. This report was given added importance by the Toxteth riots of the previous month. Liverpool was one of the areas to which the Select Committee had given particular attention, and the members had visited Toxteth in the course of their investigations. The report provided evidence of continuing discrimination and disadvantage among Liverpool's black population, despite the fact that most were British-born and not immigrants. The Committee reported:

> The situation of Liverpool's ethnic minority population is ... of particular interest because of the way in which patterns of disadvantage in employment, education and housing, so far from disappearing with the passage of time have, if anything, been reinforced over the years to the extent that Chinese or Asian 'newcomers' are in a better position than Liverpool's indigenous blacks. If we cannot combat racial disadvantage in our other cities now, we will soon have a dozen Liverpools but on a far greater scale.[28]

The Liverpool Black Organization had warned the Committee: 'What you see in Liverpool is a sign of things to come.'[29]

The Scarman report into the Brixton disorders of 10–12 April 1981 was published in November. The major focus of the inquiry was to establish what happened and to investigate the role of the police in Brixton. Partly in response to the threat of a boycott by black organizations, Lord Scarman agreed to investigate the underlying causes of the riots; but this formed only a relatively small part of his inquiry, which concentrated on the role of the police, policing practices and law reform. The report was well prepared, and surprisingly liberal. After a short description of the social conditions in Brixton – namely, inner-city deprivation, unemployment and discrimination, which, Scarman argues, cannot provide an excuse for disorder – the course and pattern of the disturbances are outlined in detail. They are described as communal disturbances arising from a complex political, social and economic situation which includes a strong 'racial' element. Putting it bluntly, Lord Scarman found that the riots were essentially an outburst of anger and resentment by young blacks against the police.[30]

Lord Scarman was satisfied that police forces generally recognized the significance of good relations with the community that they police, and that the Metropolitan Police at district command level and above did not lack awareness of the need for good community relations. The police in Lambeth had not, however, succeeded in achieving the degree of public approval and respect necessary for the effective fulfilment of their functions and duties. Among the reasons for this loss of confidence were the collapse of the police liaison committee in 1979; hard policing methods, which caused offence and apprehension to many; lack of consultation about police operations; distrust of the procedure for investigating complaints against the police; and unlawful and, in particular, racially prejudiced conduct by some police officers. The police had to cope with rising crime in Brixton, while retaining the confidence of all sections of the community. Lord Scarman concluded that, while nothing could excuse the unlawful behaviour of the rioters, both police and community leaders should carry some responsibility for the outbreak of disorder. Broadly, however, the police response to the disorders, once they had broken out, was commended and not criticized.[31]

In spite of the commendation of police action, the majority of the Scarman recommendations were concerned with police recruitment, training, supervision and methods of policing. The aim of these recommendations was to secure more recruits from the ethnic minorities, to establish better relations with the minority communities, and to avoid the recruitment of racially prejudiced people into the police force. The report recommended that racially discriminatory behaviour should be a specific offence in the police disciplinary code.[32] On law reform, Lord Scarman concluded that 'stop and search' powers were necessary to combat crime, but that an independent element in the police complaints procedure should be quickly introduced to improve public confidence. Finally, he recommended that the Public Order Act 1936 should be amended to include a requirement of advance notice to the police of a procession or march, and the deletion of 'serious' from the public order test for banning such marches, to make it easier to prevent them. He suggested that the Act might also be revised to enable selective bans to be placed on racist marches.

On the social questions relating to racial disadvantage, Lord Scarman endorsed the findings of the Select Committee report on racial disadvantage. He argued that there lacked a sufficiently well coordinated programme for combating the problem of racial disadvantage, and that, if racial disadvantage was to be effectively redressed, positive action, presumably by the government, was necessary.

The Scarman report is diplomatic and well balanced. All parties can find recommendations on which they agree and disagree. It puts the blame for the disorders on both the police and local community leaders. The direction and policies of the Metropolitan Police are found not to be racist, but instances of misconduct are found to occur on the streets. The contention that Britain is an 'institutionally racist' society is rejected, although nowhere in the report is a definition of institutional racism provided. Elsewhere in the report Lord Scarman admits that 'it is unlikely ... that racial prejudice can be wholly eliminated from the police so long as it is endemic in society as a whole.'[33]

In the debate on the Scarman report, Mr William Whitelaw, as Home Secretary, reported his acceptance of Lord Scarman's recommendations on police training and liaison arrangements with local committees, and the need to reform the police complaints procedures.[34] There was some reservation about including racially prejudiced behaviour as an offence in the police code, and opposition to making automatic dismissal – which Scarman had in any event rejected – the penalty for such an offence. On Lord Scarman's support for the Select Committee's report on racial disadvantage the government promised a detailed reply in a White Paper which, when it was published, was to reject most of the Select Committee's recommendations.[35] Whitelaw also announced that the government would conduct an experiment into ethnic monitoring in the civil service. In an effort to show that the government was responding positively, he also referred to the small increase in its contribution to the Urban Aid Programme, which had earlier been announced by Mr Michael Heseltine, Environment Secretary. Opposition speakers in the debate tended to focus on economic deprivation and unemployment as the fundamental causes of the disturbances, and urged the government to take action to promote economic recovery which, they argued, was the only sure remedy for the disorders. Roy Hattersley, opposition spokesman on home affairs, also called on the Home Secretary to implement all the recommendations concerning the police and to revise the Public Order Act in order to enable selective bans to be placed on racist marches.[36]

The police response was initially positive and, even before the Scarman report was published, the Police Federation announced that it would wholeheartedly support a new independent body to investigate complaints against the force.[37] However, negative reactions were soon manifest. First, it quickly became clear that the Police Federation was opposed to the introduction of a specific disciplinary offence of racially prejudiced conduct, on the grounds that it was already covered by the existing police disciplinary code – a view supported by the Police Superintendents' Association. They were not prepared in the interests of fostering good community relations to allow the offence to be specifically incorporated in the code. Second, the Association of Chief Police Officers told the Home Affairs Select Committee that they were opposed to statutory liaison committees. Third, the chairman of the Police Federation attacked Lord Scarman's criticism of saturation policing to stop street crime, and argued that operations like 'Swamp 81' were necessary. Fourth, on 10 March 1982 the Metropolitan Police issued statistics on recorded crime in London for the previous year, which included breakdowns by 'race' and which purported to show that blacks were disproportionately involved in street crime. In spite of it being well known that statistics of reported crime are very unreliable, it was clear that the police were prepared to use highly controversial and political methods as part of their response to the criticisms of their actions made by Lord Scarman in his report. They wanted better equipment to deal with rioters and wider powers, and were unwilling to accept reforms which would make them more sensitive and accountable to local communities.

The government, however, was forced to take action in view of the seriousness of the riots. A major coordinated attempt to combat racial disadvantage in the inner cities was recommended by Michael Heseltine in a confidential report, 'It took a riot', prepared for the Prime Minister. This was reinforced by Lord Scarman, who made a similar recommendation in his report. Inner-city policy was transformed by the riots from a minor item on the Cabinet agenda to a matter of urgent and substantial importance.[38] Heseltine was quickly appointed Minister with special responsibility for Merseyside, for one year, backed by a special Merseyside task force consisting of civil servants from the Departments of the Environment and Industry, the Manpower Services Commission and managers from Merseyside companies. More generally, the government expanded the number of ethnic minority projects under the Partnership Schemes and the Urban Aid Programmes. Funding for voluntary sector schemes to combat racial disadvantage was more than doubled between 1918/2 and 1984/5, rising from £7 million to £15 million. More substantially, spending under the Urban Aid Programme rose from £202 million in 1918/2 to £338 million in 1984/5. Also in 1985/6, some £127 million was spent in Partnership Scheme areas.[39] A variety of other initiatives to combat racial disadvantage were also taken under the Youth Training Scheme and the Manpower Services Commission. The scale of the problems caused by inner-city decline is so large, and the massive concentrated unemployment in these areas, especially among young blacks, so high, that even substantial spending can have only a marginal impact. The government was therefore nervous that its initiatives might not go far enough to prevent further riots. These fears were well founded.

In 1985 there were more major outbreaks of rioting in Handsworth in Birmingham and Tottenham in London, in both cases ignited by police action. In Handsworth changes in policing practices seem to have increased tension between young people and the police, and this contributed to two serious disturbances in July 1985. In the first of these, some 70 youths rioted, attacking police vehicles and looting a shop. In the second, police officers questioning a youth were attacked by a large group.

The outbreak of violence which took place in the Lozells Road area of Handsworth on 9 and 10 September seems to have occurred within the context of a deteriorating situation between young people, especially young Afro-Caribbeans, and the police, and in conditions of widespread social and economic deprivation. The attacks on firemen as well as on policemen, the widespread looting and arson, and the deaths of two shopkeepers all showed the depth of alienation and resentment against authority which exist in many inner-city areas. There is no doubt that a collective consciousness has developed among young black people – although young whites were involved in the riots too[40] – of the injustice of their situation, which they see as racial subordination caused by racial prejudice and discrimination. This collective consciousness of injustice is seen as legitimizing collective action against those in authority, who are regarded as agents of a racist state and of a racist society. Invariably, what transforms these smouldering feelings of alienation into spontaneous violent outbursts or riots are clashes with the police or resentment against what is considered unfair or illegitimate police behaviour. Such factors contributed to the London riots in September and October 1985. At 7.00 am on 28 September, armed police entered the house of Mrs Cherry Groce in Brixton. Two shots were fired by an officer and a bullet damaged Mrs Groce's spine, causing serious injury. This incident triggered considerable violence during the rest of the weekend. The local police station was attacked with petrol bombs on the Saturday evening, and the burning and looting caused damage estimated at £3 million. During the riot the police reported 724 major crimes, 53 people injured, including 10 police officers, and 230 arrests. Tragically, a freelance photographer, Mr David Lodge, sustained injuries from which he died three weeks later.

The most serious of the disorders occurred in Tottenham, North London, on Sunday 6 October at the Broadwater Farm estate. The precipitating event was a police raid on the home of a

West Indian family, during which Mrs Jarrett, the mother of the man being sought, collapsed and died. Rumours of what had happened swept around the estate and provoked a night of extraordinary violence, during which PC Keith Blakelock was stabbed to death. Two hundred police officers were injured and a substantial amount of property was damaged. The riot saw a marked escalation of violence, which for the first time included the use of guns, which injured several policemen and reporters. The police deployed CS gas and plastic bullets, but did not use them.

The political reactions to the riots in 1985 were much more critical and hostile than the reactions to the 1981 riots. Conservative politicians, in particular, described the riots as acts of wickedness and condemned the 'disgraceful criminal behaviour'.[41] The Home Secretary, after visiting Handsworth after the rioting, said, 'The sound which law abiding people in Handsworth heard on Monday night, the echoes of which I picked up on Tuesday, was not a cry for help but a cry for loot.'[42] Labour politicians responded in a similar way. Birmingham MPs like Jeff Rooker and Roy Hattersley condemned the riots as criminal. Hattersley argued that the Handsworth riot was totally different from the previous riots in Brixton and Toxteth. He said that what had happened in Brixton was a spontaneous outburst, largely generated by the conditions of the area, the behaviour of the police and the quality of the property. In contrast, what had happened in Handsworth was 'an act of pure wickedness'.[43]

The opposition demanded an independent judicial inquiry into the riots similar to the Scarman inquiry, but the government was firmly opposed to this. The Home Secretary, Douglas Hurd, argued that such an inquiry would delay the prompt action that was needed and would also prejudice the possibility of criminal proceedings against some of the 700 people arrested.[44] Mr Hurd stressed the support that the government was giving to the police, and their strong support for urban regeneration. He said that the Urban Aid Programme had more than trebled, from £93 million in 1978–9 to £335 million in 1985–6; that the Department of Employment and the Manpower Services Commission were spending more than £100 million in Partnership Scheme areas; and that the Home Office planned to spend £90 million in 1985–6 in Section 11 grants.[45] The Home Secretary's arguments failed to impress the opposition: they emphasized the huge cuts in rate support grants, which had hit urban areas particularly hard, and the appalling levels of unemployment, particularly among young blacks in inner-city areas.[46]

One unexpected response to the riots by the Labour opposition was their decision to attack the government's record on law and order. Gerald Kaufman, the opposition spokesman on home affairs, stressed that reports of serious crime had risen dramatically since 1978, from 2.5 million to 3.5 million; offences of criminal damage had risen by 63% and the clear-up rate had fallen nationally to only 35%, despite the Conservatives' emphasis on law and order.[47] The Labour party also devoted a whole party political broadcast to law and order. These were attempts to reassure the public that the Labour party was just as concerned about violence and crime as the government, and to deny the Conservatives any political gains they might have hoped for by emphasizing these issues. Both parties were well aware that the government was at least halfway through its term of office. The Conservatives responded by criticizing the Greater London Council and other Labour local authorities for their anti-police policies, and by demanding that Neil Kinnock repudiate Mr Bernie Grant, then the black Labour prospective parliamentary candidate for Tottenham, for his widely reported remark on the Broadwater Farm riot, that 'the police were given a bloody good hiding. They deserved it'.[48] Mr Kinnock, though clearly embarrassed, refused to do so.

The underlying causes of the riots are complex, but the frustration and alienation of young people, particularly young blacks, who feel constrained and subordinated by racism and forced to fail in the education, labour and housing markets, are important factors. However, it is the growth of a generalized belief among a community, which collectively defines their situation as unjust, that is the crucial factor. The consciousness of a significant proportion of the aggrieved population must be transformed into a collective feeling of injustice, in order for collective action to be realized. The failure of political institutions to articulate and remedy these grievances is also important. Sustained insurgency or the development of a revolutionary movement – rather than temporary hostile outbursts – depends in large part on the organizational resources that supporters of such a movement are able to maintain. Efforts to mobilize such a flow of resources usually lead to the establishment of formal bodies, like the Republican and Loyalist organizations in Northern Ireland, to supplement and supplant the spontaneous groups from which such movements emerge.

The relations between the police and the community are vitally important. The police are highly visible symbols of authority. They are closer to the public than other such symbols − local councillors, local government officers, magistrates, or members of parliament. If the police are believed to harass, abuse, unfairly arrest and charge a particular group, then intense collective feelings of injustice will develop and spontaneous eruptions of violence may well occur. There are continual complaints about police conduct, and a significant number of cases in which police misconduct has been proved. Substantial damages have had to be paid to black people by police forces, especially the Metropolitan Police, for gross misconduct.[49] The priority of politicians, especially Conservative politicians, has been to support the police, but a higher priority should have been to institute major reforms as Scarman recommended, to develop trust and respect between the police and the ethnic minorities, and particularly between the police and young blacks. Otherwise, future outbursts of violence could easily recur.

Racial attacks

During the early period of New Commonwealth immigration there were few public manifestations of violence towards black immigrants. As noted earlier, the anti-black riots in Nottingham and Notting Hill in 1958 shattered this tranquillity, though the severe sentences passed on the perpetrators of the attacks in Notting Hill may have prevented an early recurrence. The murder of Kelso Cockrane, a young West Indian carpenter, who was stabbed to death in Notting Hill in May 1959 by a gang of white youths, suggested that tension remained high in the area. In the 1960s there were sporadic, unprovoked attacks, particularly on Asians, usually by white youths. 'Paki-bashing' occurred widely over the country, but appeared to be unorganized and unsystematic.

However, in the 1970s and 1980s the incidence and the level of racist attacks grew significantly and appeared – at least in some areas, such as the East End of London – to become more regular, organized and systematic.[50] The continuing campaigns against immigration and the increased publicity and activity of the National Front created a climate of hostility towards black immigration and immigrants, as we observed in chapter 4. In particular, the speeches of Enoch Powell may have legitimized anti-immigrant violence by implying that black people were 'attacking' the white English by taking over their areas, frightening them out of their houses and even putting excreta through their letter-boxes.[51] Similarly, Powell's use of phrases like 'unparalleled invasion' and the 'transformation of whole areas into alien territory'[52] may have encouraged some young people to treat blacks as alien invaders and legitimate targets for attack. Young gangs of skinheads, who enjoy violence, may thus have defined black people both as vulnerable and as legitimate opponents. There is some evidence that people with a violent predisposition and authoritarian attitudes are attracted to the National Front.[53]

In 1978 the Bethnal Green and Stepney Trades Council published a report listing over a hundred separate racial attacks in Tower Hamlets between January 1976 and August 1978. These included two murders and numerous serious assaults, resulting in physical injury. The report concluded that racial abuse and attack were no longer rare and unexpected events, but a constant factor of everyday life for Bengalis living in the East End of London. This report was the first to suggest that large-scale harassment and physical assaults were being perpetrated against members of the Bengali community. 'There now exists in the East End a barrage of harassment, insult and intimidation, week in, week out, which fundamentally determines how the immigrant community lives and works, and how the Bengali people think and act.'[54]

The growing incidence of racial attacks, it was argued, had undermined Bengali confidence in the police. Many complainants felt their complaints were not followed up, and they were sometimes advised to take out private prosecutions against their assailants, which they were naturally extremely reluctant to do. Some victims reported that they were themselves treated by the police as if they were guilty of an offence by complaining, often being asked to produce passports to prove they were not illegal immigrants. The report alleged that Asian victims of attacks were more likely to be arrested by the police than their white assailants, especially if they had reacted to provocation and in defending themselves had become involved in an affray. The arrest of two Bengali youths in such an incident led to a protest demonstration and sit-down by some 3,000 people outside Bethnal Green police station on 17 July 1978. A number of strikes and demonstrations occurred in the Brick Lane area in the summer of 1978, after the murder of Altab Ali on 4 May. Disillusionment with the police, it was claimed, had caused Bengalis to give up complaining and to tolerate attacks as a fact of life which they could do little to prevent, except by retreating further into their own ghetto for the protection and security provided by living close to members of their own community.

A crucial, question which the Trades Council, and later the Commission for Racial Equality,[55] wished to examine was the role of the far right, especially the National Front, in encouraging and organizing racial attacks. The National Front at this time was very active in Tower Hamlets; but that it encouraged racial hostility and incited racial attacks was hard to prove, as most such attacks appeared to be the work of 'apolitical' white youths. The local community leaders, however, had no doubts about the role of the Front. One respondent in the CRE inquiry stated: 'The National Front organize street corner meetings. These meetings are used for hate campaigns against the Bengalis ... they use all sorts of ploys to incite the local whites against us. They tell shopkeepers that Bengalis are taking over their businesses.'[56] Another said: 'The National Front keeps on coming to Brick Lane, apparently to sell their papers which are highly offensive anyway ... but they take the opportunity to hurl abuse and insults on the Bengalis. The adult Bengalis ignore these insults but the youths react ... Brick Lane has become a flashpoint of racial violence.'[57] The CRE study found that the attitudes of young Asians towards the police were very negative, that they were resentful about being stopped and searched, and that they accused the police of giving protection to the National Front and clamping down on Asians.

The murder of Akhtar Ali Baig on 17 July 1980 focused national attention on racist attacks and led to two protest demonstrations in East Ham, over the murder and over the alleged lack of police protection for Asians in the borough. On 21 February

1981 a seventeen-year-old skinhead, Paul Mullery, was convicted of Baig's murder at the Old Bailey. The motive was said by the prosecution during the trial to be pure 'race' hatred.[58]

On 18 January 1981 a fire at a West Indian party in Deptford underlined the fears, insecurity and frustration of the black community, of which racial attacks are a significant cause. The fire resulted in the deaths of the thirteen young people and injured a further twenty-nine. Many members of the Afro-Caribbean community were convinced that the fire and deaths were caused by a racist attack, although the authorities failed to discover the cause. Even if the fire did in fact start accidentally, in an area where National Front activity was relatively high and given the regular occurrence of racist attacks it is not surprising that anguished parents and relatives should suspect arson. The fears and anger of the community were expressed on 2 March 1981, when over 6,000 people joined in a march organized by the New Cross Massacre Action Committee.

In February 1981 the all-party Joint Committee Against Racialism (JCAR) presented to the Home Secretary a dossier of over 1,000 racial attacks, and requested a meeting to discuss what they argued was an increasing degree of violence being inflicted upon the persons and property of members of the ethnic minorities in Britain. The Home Secretary, William Whitelaw, was impressed by the detailed evidence collected by the JCAR on individual cases and specific incidents. Also, he was concerned by the contention that the frequency of racial attacks was increasing, and that this was not entirely attributable to sporadic incidents of hooliganism but was the result of organized attempts at intimidation by extreme right-wing movements. The JCAR also reported that the police response to the problem was variable, but generally inadequate; they therefore suggested that specialized police units should be set up to investigate and monitor the incidence of racial harassment and violence. In response to the JCAR's approach and also to the Deptford fire, the Home Secretary agreed to set up a Home Office inquiry into racial attacks and the activities of the racist organizations alleged to be responsible, and to consider the suggestion that specialized police units be set up. During the months before the meeting with the JCAR the Home Secretary had also been lobbied on the subject of racist attacks and harassment by the CRE, the Board of Deputies of British Jews and ethnic minority organizations.[59]

During the spring and summer of 1981 continuing evidence of violence against members of the ethnic minorities was widely reported. On 10 April a black youth was murdered in what was described by the local press as a 'race riot'.[60] On the 18th a twenty-year-old student, Satnum Singh Gill, was stabbed in Coventry city centre in a fight with skinheads. A sixteen-year-old youth was later charged with murder. Further incidents followed, including another murder, the petrol-bombing of a Sikh temple and arson at the India and Commonwealth Club in London, as well as numerous attacks on individual Asians and threats to shopkeepers. A march against racial attacks organized by the Coventry Committee Against Racism prompted further violence involving skinheads, who appear to have been encouraged to attack marchers by two members of the British Movement and by Robert Relf, then a well known anti-immigrant campaigner in the Midlands.[61] On 2 July in Walthamstow an arson attack on an Asian house led to the death of Mrs Barene Khan and her three children. Questions were raised in parliament concerning the incidence of racial attacks, and in October 1981 Leon Brittan reported to parliament that in 1975 there had been 2,690 cases of assault, robbery and other violent theft on victims of Afro-Caribbean or Asian appearance. In 1977 there had been 3,492 such incidents, in 1978, 3,686, and in 1979, 3,827.[62]

As it is only the worst incidents that gain national publicity, and since these are often geographically disparate, increasing efforts to collect systematic evidence were made in 1981 by a number of groups. For example, Dr Zahi Khan, General Secretary of the Union of Pakistani Organizations, presented William Whitelaw with a report showing that racist attacks had grown from an average of 20 to 25 a week in 1980 to 60 a week in 1981.[63] Ealing Community Relations Council compiled a report, *Racialist Activity in Ealing*, and the police, partly responding to the Home Office inquiry, began compiling data on racist attacks. In a written submission to the Home Affairs Select Committee the Metropolitan Police reported an increase in racial incidents from 177 in 1980 to 727 in 1981. The most important systematic report, *Racial Attacks*, was published by the Home Office in November 1981.

The Home Office report on racial attacks

The Home Office report defined a racial attack as 'an incident or alleged offence by a person or persons of one racial group against a person or persons or property of another racial group, where there are clear indications of a racial motive'. The research team carried out a survey of inter-racial incidents in thirteen police areas over a two-month period, from mid-May to mid-July 1981. The thirteen were the major areas of immigrant settlement: Bedfordshire, Greater Manchester, Kent, Lancashire, Leicestershire, Merseyside, the Metropolitan Police District, South Wales, Sussex, Thames Valley, Warwickshire, West Midlands and West Yorkshire. Information was collected on 2,630 racial incidents, involving 2,851 victims. In 10% of the incidents reported there was strong evidence of a racial motive (both the police and the victim agreed this was the case). In a further 15% of cases there was some evidence of a racial motive, with either the police or the victim believing this to be so. In 52% of the incidents there was clear evidence of a non-racial motive, and in the remaining cases the evidence was unclear. There was a high degree of agreement on the classification of incidents by the victims and the police. The report argued that racial attacks constituted only a very small proportion of recorded crime – less than 0.25% – though if only offences of violence against the person and property were considered, this rose to 3%. Moreover, it admitted that reported incidents represented only a small proportion of all such incidents. Even so, the Home Office estimated that some 7,000 racially motivated incidents would be reported in the UK in 1982, and that this estimate was likely to be on the low side.[64]

The cases where such motivation appeared to be a factor indicated that members of the ethnic minorities were the victims far more often than white people. The rate for Asians was 50 times higher than for white people, and for Afro-Caribbeans it was 36 times higher. The report argued that there was evidence that the incidence of racial attacks was rising and that there had been a substantial increase in the past year. The JCAR's view that gangs of white youths were often involved was confirmed. Jostlings in the street, abusive remarks, broken windows and slogans daubed on walls are among the less serious kinds of racial harassment which many

Asians and Afro-Caribbeans experience. The fact that these are interwoven with far more serious, racially motivated, attacks — such as murders, physical assaults and gang attacks on homes at night — makes for considerable fear and insecurity, for example, among Bengalis in East London. The Home Office research team stated in their report:

> It was clear to us that the Asian community widely believes that it is the object of a campaign of unremitting racial harassment which it fears will grow in the future. In many places we were told that Asian families were too frightened to leave their homes at night or to visit shopping centres at weekends where gangs of skinheads congregate. Even in places where few racial incidents have occurred, the awareness of what is happening in other parts of the country induces a widespread apprehension that the climate locally is likely to deteriorate and that more serious incidents are likely in the future. In some places there was a sense of uncomplaining acceptance among some Asians of manifestations of racial violence. The problem was thought to be so widespread that they regarded it as little more than an unwelcome feature of contemporary British life.[65]

A major weakness in the Home Office report was its inadequate coverage of the role of extremist organizations in instigating and encouraging racial violence and harassment. It accepted the police view that the direct involvement of the extreme right in organizing racial violence is hard to prove, as many of the attacks are carried out by young men influenced by racist propaganda but not formally involved with any particular right-wing group. However, there is considerable evidence that the extreme right does attempt to promote anti-immigrant violence by its actions, as well as indirectly through its propaganda and language. Fielding[66] discusses the relationship between the National Front and violence, and certain other right-wing groups are known to have been involved in paramilitary activities; Column 88 and members of the British Movement have been convicted for illegal possession of firearms.[67] Violence is functional for the extreme right, as it provides it with publicity and new recruits. It is particularly valuable if it can provoke violence in its left-wing opponents, who may then be blamed by the media while the far right appear respectable by comparison. The violence surrounding the National Front's

Lewisham march in August 1977 was blamed on the Socialist Workers Party, and some of the publicity praised the National Front.[68] Many young men have been attracted to the National Front by the excitement of violence at such events as provocative marches in areas of immigrant settlement, at demonstrations and at the breaking-up of opponents' meetings. Some senior members of the far right have been guilty of more serious offences. In January 1981 Roderick Roberts, said to have been the quartermaster of the British Movement in the West Midlands, was jailed by Birmingham Crown Court for seven years on conviction of arson, ten charges of possession of firearms and ammunition, and conspiracy to incite racial hatred. He was said by the judge to have wanted to provoke racial violence and then use his cache of weapons to escalate such violence.[69]. It seems clear that violence and paramilitary activities are an integral part of the activities of extreme right-wing parties.

The fear and insecurity generated by racist attacks have caused some members of the Asian community to take the law into their own hands. In June 1982 twelve young Asians in Bradford were found not guilty of charges of conspiracy and making petrol bombs with intent to endanger life and property, after 38 petrol bombs had been discovered on waste ground in the city. The defendants did not deny making the bombs, but argued that they did so in self-defence against expected racial attacks, and also that the Asian community could not rely on police protection against such attacks. The jury believed them.[70]

Concern about racial attacks led to increased monitoring of such incidents in the 1980s and to two Select Committee reports. In 1986 the Home Affairs Committee described racial attacks and harassment as the most shameful and dispiriting aspect of race relations in the United Kingdom.[71] Its report also led to a wider definition of racial attacks being adopted by the Association of Chief Police Officers, to emphasize the victim's perception of the incident: 'any incident in which it appears to the reporting or investigating officer that the complaint involves an element of racial motivation; or any incident which includes an allegation of racial motivation by any person'.[72] The Committee was not sure that the police response to the issue of racial attacks and harassment was adequate, given the continuing vulnerability of the Asian community, especially in East London, to such attacks.[73] Tompson describes the relentless violence directed at the Bangladeshi community in the 1980s and the inadequate official response − for example, by the police, and also by local authorities in dealing with racial harassment on local authority estates.[74]

The criminalization of Afro-Caribbeans?

During the 1980s there was growing concern with the operation of the criminal justice system as a whole, regarding its ability to adapt to Britain as a multiracial society. The reasons for concern relate in particular to the growing black prison population. A wholly disproportionate number of black people are being incarcerated, and this appears to relate not to the level of crime among the black population but to the criminalization of black people by society and the agencies of law and order. Moreover, it is the Afro-Caribbean population which seems most affected; Asians do not appear to be over-represented in the prison population. Table 6.1 shows that in 1989 Afro-Caribbeans comprise 11% of the prison population, an extraordinarily high figure, bearing in mind that they form only 1% of the total population. The even higher figures for female Afro-Caribbean prisoners is due, in part, to the high proportion of African prisoners in the female population, most of whom are imprisoned for drugs-related offences such as acting as couriers. If the proportion of Afro-Caribbean prisoners who are resident were compared, then the discrepancy for men and women would be greatly reduced.[75] But Afro-Caribbean women, like Afro-Caribbean men, appear to be over-represented in the prison population.

A considerable research effort is needed to explain why Afro-Caribbeans are so over-represented in the prison population. Is it due to their relative youthfulness, their concentration in inner-city areas known for their high rates of certain types of crime, to their high levels of unemployment, to homelessness, poverty or involvement in leisure activities which bring them into contact with the police? Is it due to their greater involvement in the types of crime which lead to prison sentences? Or is it due to the cumulative effects of discriminatory decision-making at each stage of the

Table 6.1 Non-white prison population, as % of total prison population, 1985 and 1989

	Afro-Caribbean 1985	%	1989	%	Asian[a] 1985	%	1989	%	All non-white 1985	%	1989	%
Men	3,662	(8)	4,988	(11)	1,052	(2)	1,324	(3)	5,453	(12)	6,804	(16)
Women	192	(12)	353	(20)	28	(2)	27	(2)	270	(17)	425	(24)
Total	3,854	(8)[b]	5,341	(11)	1,080	(2)	1,351	(3)	5,723	(12)	7,229	(16)

[a] Asian = Indians, Pakistanis and Bangladeshis
[b] Because the female prison population is so small, the total percentages are almost identical to those for the male prison population.
Source: Black People's Experience of Criminal Justice, National Association for the Care and Resettlement of Offenders, 1991.

criminal justice system – for example, stricter surveillance by the police resulting in the discovery of a higher proportion of black crime than white or Asian, a greater readiness to prosecute black people, and harsher sentencing once they are brought before the courts?

It seems likely that it is a combination of factors that has brought about the criminalization of the black population, but socio-demographic factors can explain only a small part of the over-representation of black people in prison. Moreover, the Asian population also has many of the same characteristics – youthfulness, residence in high-crime inner-city areas (it is worth mentioning that both Afro-Caribbeans and Asians are more likely to be victims of household and personal crime than the white population)[76] and high levels of unemployment – as the Afro-Caribbeans,[77] and yet they are not over-represented in prison. Cultural differences in behaviour and attitude, which may be thought partly to explain differences in treatment by the criminal justice system, are just as likely to be a result of experiences in British society (such as unemployment, racial discrimination and harsh treatment by police and officials) as of 'cultural' attributes learnt from their immigrant parents or grandparents. They are emphatically not a matter of inherent characteristics based on false notions of 'racial' differences.[78]

As noted earlier, research findings suggest that Afro-Caribbeans are far more likely to be stopped by the police than Asians or whites. They are more likely to be arrested, and once arrested they are more likely to be prosecuted than cautioned, warned or released. There is no clear evidence that in court Afro-Caribbeans are more likely to be found guilty and to be treated more harshly than whites or Asians with similar previous convictions, nor that they are more likely to receive a custodial sentence.[79]

However, there is a widespread perception by Afro-Caribbean people that they are treated harshly by the police and the criminal justice system in general. Some black parents feel there is some sort of collusion by the police and the courts to criminalize their children in order to ensure that they cannot succeed in British society. The different experiences of Afro-Caribbeans and Asians have led to a different set of attitudes towards the police and the courts. FitzGerald found that a high priority for Afro-Caribbeans was to make the police more responsive and accountable to the local communities they police, while for Asians the highest law and order priority was for the police to put more resources into combating racial attacks. Afro-Caribbeans were against the police having more powers to catch criminals, reflecting the widespread feeling in the Afro-Caribbean community that they are over-policed. Asians are less opposed to the police having more powers to catch criminals, reflecting their lower levels of conflict with the police.[80]

There is certainly a crisis of legitimacy in the relations between Afro-Caribbeans and the police, as well as alienation from the criminal justice system as a whole. Some action has been taken to counter this, by encouraging ethnic minority recruitment into the police, the probation service, the prison service, the magistracy and other branches of the law. Ethnic monitoring and research is being introduced, but progress is very slow or is only just beginning. In August 1990 there were only 1,352 ethnic minority police officers — just 1% of all police officers in England and Wales. In Greater London, where 14% of the population is non-white, only 1.6% of Metropolitan police officers were from the ethnic minorities. In the West Midlands, where 13% of the population is non-white, 2.3% of the police were from ethnic minorities. Such disparities show the huge gap between the police and an important part of the community that they are meant to serve. Similarly, only 2% of probation officers and 1% of solicitors in 1988 were non-white. In 1987, 2% of all magistrates were from the ethnic minorities, though annual recruitment had risen to 5%. Among stipendiary magistrates and judges, the number from the ethnic minorities is infinitesimal.

It is impossible to exaggerate the importance of the police and the criminal justice system in contributing to the legitimacy and authority of the state and to the stability of society. Every citizen expects the protection of the law and equal treatment under the law. If racial attacks are allowed to continue and are even encouraged by the speeches and actions of those in authority, then not only will the lives of members of minority communities be made miserable and intolerable, but alienation will grow. Similarly, if police actions discriminate against sections of society, then the legitimacy of public authorities will be undermined and the danger of violent confrontations and hostile outbursts will grow. Alienation and resentment will be compounded if black people are faced with cumulative discrimination in education, housing and employment, as well as in the criminal justice system.

Notes

1 See pp. 30–36.
2 Z. Layton–Henry, 'The state and New Commonwealth immigration: 1951–56', *New Community*, vol. 14, nos 1/2 (1987), 64–75.
3 Ibid., p. 68.
4 Ibid., pp. 68–9.
5 P. Foot, *Immigration and Race in British Politics* (Penguin Books, 1965).
6 G. Pearson, '"Paki-bashing" in a north-east Lancashire cotton town: a case study and its history' in G. Mungham and G. Pearson (eds), *Working-Class Youth Culture* (Routledge & Kegan Paul, 1976), pp. 48–81.
7 Institute of Race Relations, *Race Today*, 1969–71.
8 M. Cain, *Society and the Policeman's Role* (Routledge & Kegan Paul, 1973), p. 117.
9 J. Benyon, 'Spiral of decline: race and policing', in Z. Layton–Henry and P. B. Rich, *Race, Government and Politics in Britain* (Macmillan, 1986), p. 239.
10 House of Commons, *Police – Immigrant Relations*, report by the Select Committee on Race Relations and Immigration, Session 1971–2, HMSO, 1972.
11 Ibid., vol. 1, p. 70.
12 J. Lambert, *Crime, Police and Race Relations* (Oxford University Press, 1970), pp. 281, 291; *British Crime Survey*, HMSO, 1988.
13 *Police – Immigrant Relations*, 1972, vol. 1, p. 4.
14 Ibid., p. 55.
15 Ibid., pp. 889–93.
16 The 'Sus' law referred to the suspected persons provision of Section 4 of the Vagrancy Act 1824. A person could be convicted of being in a public place, of having the intention of performing a criminal act, without even having to have acted in a suspicious way. The Select Committee argued that this was fundamentally unsatisfactory.
17 J. Benyon, 'Spiral of decline', p. 230.
18 P. Stevens and C. Willis, *Race, Crime and Arrests*, Home Office Research Study no. 58, HMSO, 1979, pp. 31–3.
19 House of Commons, *Race Relations and the 'Sus' law*, second report from the Home Affairs Committee, Session 1979–80, HMSO,

1980.
20 D. J. Smith and J. Gray, *Police and People in London: The PSI Report* (Gower, 1985), p. 90.
21 Ibid., pp. 106–7.
22 *The Times*, 7 October 1982.
23 J. Solomos, *Race and Racism in Contemporary Britain* (Macmillan, 1989).
24 For details on the Southall incident, see p. 000.
25 *Runnymede Trust Bulletin* no. 120 (May 1980), pp. 1–2.
26 Lord Scarman, *The Brixton Disorders, 10–12 April 1981*, report of an inquiry, Cmnd 8427, HMSO, 1981, pp. 56–9.
27 Parliamentary Debates, Commons (Hansard), vol. 3, col. 21, 13 April, 1981.
28 House of Commons, *Racial Disadvantage*, fifth report from the Home Affairs Committee, Session 1980–1, HMSO, 1981, vol. 1.
29 Ibid.
30 Scarman, *Brixton Disorders*, p. 45.
31 Ibid., pp. 126–8.
32 Ibid., p. 130.
33 Ibid., pp. 11, 79.
34 Parliamentary Debates, Commons (Hansard), vol. 15, cols 1001–8, 20 December 1981.
35 Home Office, government reply to the fifth report from the Home Affairs Committee, 1981–2, *Racial Disadvantage*, HMSO, 1982.
36 Parliamentary Debates, Commons (Hansard), vol. 14, cols 1008–16, 10 December 1981.
37 *Runnymede Trust Bulletin*, December 1981, p. 2.
38 P. Lindley, 'The Merseyside task force', paper presented at the annual conference of the Political Studies Association, Oxford, August 1983.
39 D. Webber, 'Defusing the time bombs in Britain's inner cities', *The Times*, 14 May 1985.
40 362 people were arrested in the disturbances at Handsworth: 105 were white, 182 were Afro-Caribbean and 72 were Asian.
41 Parliamentary Debates, Commons (Hansard), vol. 84, col. 30, 21 October 1985.
42 *Financial Times*, 13 September 1985.
43 Roy Hattersley, speaking on the Radio 4 programme, 'File on 4', two weeks after the riots. See J. Clare, 'The Handsworth reports', *Listener*, 6 March 1986, 2–4.
44 Parliamentary Debates, Commons (Hansard), vol. 84, col. 357, 23 October 1985.
45 Parliamentary Debates, Commons (Hansard), vol. 84, col. 81, 21 October 1985. For an explanation of Section 11, see p. 161.
46 Parliamentary Debates, Commons (Hansard), vol. 84, cols 350–6, 23 October 1985.

47 Ibid.
48 *The Times*, 9 October 1985; Parliamentary Debates, Commons (Hansard), vol. 84, col. 366, 23 October 1985.
49 J. Benyon, 'Spiral of decline', pp. 243–9.
50 For details of involvement of the far right in racial violence, see the magazine *Searchlight* with monitors such activities. See also N. Fielding, *The National Front* (Routledge & Kegan Paul, 1981).
51 Speech by the Rt Hon. Enoch Powell, MP, to the annual general meeting of the West Midlands Area Conservative Political Centre, 20 April 1968, in B. Smithies and P. Fiddick (eds), *Enoch Powell on Immigration* (Sphere Books, 1969), pp. 35–43.
52 Ibid., p. 74.
53 M. Billig, *Fascists: A Social Psychological View of the National Front* (Academic Press, 1978); Fielding, *National Front*.
54 Bethnal Green and Stepney Trades Council, *Blood on the Streets: A Report on Racial Attacks in East London*, 1978.
55 Commission for Racial Equality, *Brick Lane and Beyond: An Inquiry into Racial Strife and Violence in Tower Hamlets*, 1979.
56 Ibid.
57 Ibid.
58 *Guardian*, 13 February 1981.
59 Home Office, *Racial Attacks*, report of a Home Office study, HMSO, 1981.
60 Swindon *Evening Advertiser*, 13 April 1981.
61 S. Taylor, *The National Front in English Politics* (Macmillan, 1982), p. 200.
62 Parliamentary Debates, Commons (Hansard), vol. 85, cols 380–1, 31 October 1981.
63 *Observer* 14 June 1981.
64 Home Office, *Racial Attacks*, pp. 7–14.
65 Ibid., p. 16.
66 Fielding, *National Front*, ch. 8.
67 *Runnymede Trust Bulletin*, March 1981, pp. 4–5.
68 *Daily Express*, 15 August 1977; *Sunday Times*, 21 August 1977.
69 *Runnymede Trust Bulletin*, March 1981, p. 5.
70 *Runnymede Trust Bulletin*, August 1982, pp. 1–2; *Guardian*, 21 June 1982.
71 House of Commons, *Racial Attacks and Harassment*, third report from the Home Affairs Committee, Session 1985–6, HMSO, 1986.
72 House of Commons, *Racial Attacks and Harassment*, first report of the Home Affairs Committee, Session 1989–90, HMSO, 1990.
73 Ibid.
74 K. Tompson, *Under Siege: Racial Violence in Britain Today* (Penguin Books, 1988).
75 M. FitzGerald, 'Ethnic minorities and the criminal justice system in

the UK: research issues', paper presented at the British Criminology Conference, July 1991.

76 *British Crime Survey*, HMSO, 1988.
77 For example, while 28% of West Indian males between 16 and 24 were unemployed in 1988, the figure for Pakistanis and Bangladeshis was 32% (*Employment Gazette*, HMSO, March 1990).
78 FitzGerald, 'Ethnic minorities and the criminal justice system'.
79 Ibid.
80 M. FitzGerald, *Black People and Party Politics in Britain* (Runnymede Trust, 1987), p. 16.

7 Labour dilemmas

The contrast between the actions of the Labour party in government and in opposition has been the subject of considerable critical comment. Foot draws attention to the curious political phenomenon of the Labour Home Secretary, who behaves in office in direct contrast to his principles and promises in opposition, and, strives mightily to be less humane than the Tories.[1] This is an exaggeration and there have been notable exceptions, such as Roy Jenkins, but it does contain a large element of truth. Labour Home Secretaries have often been forced on to the defensive, in a way that Conservatives have never been, by accusations of being soft on criminals or foreigners. It is ironic, for example, that Marx, Engels and Lenin were all able to enjoy refuge in Britain under Conservative and Liberal administrations, while Trotsky was refused asylum by a Labour Home Secretary.[2]

The most dramatic shift occurred between 1962 and 1965, when Labour's official immigration policy changed from one of total opposition to controlling Commonwealth immigration on grounds of high moral principle, to criticizing the Conservatives for passing inadequate legislation and tightening the controls, in order to maintain Labour's electoral credibility. The Commonwealth Immigrants Act '1968', imposing controls on British passport-holders without close connections with the UK but granting favourable treatment to those of British descent, was the culmination of the Wilson government's retreat from principle and its determination to outdo the Conservatives in its commitment to control New Commonwealth immigration. Some attempts were made to balance these tough policies with legislation against racial discrimination and against incitement to racial hatred in public places, but this legislation was largely symbolic.

The determination of the Labour government after 1964 to eliminate immigration as an electoral issue dividing the parties to the advantage of the Conservatives was successful for a time in the 1960s, when a bipartisan consensus was achieved with the acquiescence of Heath and the Tory leadership. The policy collapsed in 1968 as a result of the success of Enoch Powell's anti-immigration campaign, which associated more stringent policies on immigration, once again, with the Conservative party.

In the early 1970s a number of factors caused the Labour party to change its strategy and adopt a more positive approach to the interests of Afro-Caribbean and Asian voters and a more vigorous opposition to racism. Firstly, the party was back in opposition and free from the responsibility of managing and justifying immigration controls. Second, the early 1970s saw a marked shift to the left in the Labour party, both on the National Executive Committee and more widely in the constituency parties and the trade union movement.[3] This provided a stronger basis for a more principled stand to be taken on issues like immigration control and racism. Third, the growing activity of the National Front in the 1970s and its exploitation of issues such as the entry of the Ugandan Asians in 1972 and the media panic over the Malawi Asians in 1976 demanded a response from the major party on the left, especially as the Front was making great efforts to encourage white working-class voters to oppose immigration and vote for its candidates.[4] Fourth, the growing electoral registration and turn-out of Afro-Caribbean and Asian voters, which at this time was exaggerated by the Community Relations Commission's report, appeared to make it more worthwhile for the party to take their interests into account, especially as most of them supported the Labour party.[5]

An additional reason for the Labour party reconsidering its race relations and immigration policies was that many members were convinced that the unexpected defeat in the general election of 1970 was largely due to the party's failure to counter Powell's anti-immigration campaign. There was thus considerable pressure to abandon the policy of appeasement and to try and develop coherent and consistent non-racist policies. The NEC's study group on immigration tried to do this in the opposition's Green Paper, *Citizenship, Immigration and Integration*.[6] One of the major strategies advocated by this Green Paper was a non-discriminatory immigration policy based on a redefinition of British citizenship. Ironically, this was a strategy already proposed by Enoch Powell in his Eastbourne speech,[7] and was to become the basis for the Nationality Act of 1981. The study group also proposed a wide range of measures to assist integration. As already described, the more positive stance of Labour in opposition between 1970 and 1974 was undermined by the legacy of its inconsistent immigration and race relations policies while in government between 1964 and 1970.

Labour in government, 1974–9

The Labour government that came into office in February 1974 was not committed to specific policies on 'race' relations and immigration matters, but Roy Jenkins embarked on a cautious programme of positive reforms. In April he announced an amnesty for illegal immigrants who were Commonwealth citizens, or citizens of Pakistan who were adversely affected by the retrospective operation of the 1971 Immigration Act. In June the restriction imposed by the Labour government in 1969 on the admission of husbands and fiancés of women settled in the UK was lifted. In February 1975 the quota for UK passport-holders was raised from 3,600 to 5,000. In September the White Paper, *Racial Discrimination*,[8] was published. This proposed the extension of the Race Relations Act, and the following year the new, greatly strengthened, Race Relations Act was passed and the Commission for Racial Equality established. These substantial achievements did not go unchallenged by Enoch Powell and the Conservative right, though the official opposition cooperated with the government, especially with regard to the new 'race' relations legislation.

By the beginning of 1976 it had become clear that New Commonwealth immigration was rising again – to the fury of Powell and his supporters. The government decided it had to adopt a more restrictive approach, partly to counter growing opposition criticism and to preserve Conservative support for the Race Relations Bill. On the second reading of that Bill, Jenkins conceded that 'there is a clear limit to the amount of immigration which this country can absorb and ... it is in the interests of the racial

minorities themselves to maintain a strict control over immigration.'[9]
In April Alex Lyon, the Home Office minister responsible for
immigration, was dropped from the government, allegedly for
being too liberal in his administration of immigration controls.

In May, during a debate on immigration, Enoch Powell leaked
details of a confidential report on immigration from the Indian
subcontinent prepared by a Foreign Office official. The Hawley
report suggested that the Home Office estimates for dependants
entitled to come to Britain were far too low, that there was a
substantial illegal immigrants industry in India helping migrants to
come to Britain, and that arrangements in India were too generous
for intending migrants.[10] Under mounting pressure, Jenkins announced the establishment of a small parliamentary group under
Lord Franks, 'to look into the feasibility and usefulness of a
register [of dependants] with all the problems and evidence available to them from official sources'.[11] The report was published in
February 1977, and the government concluded that such a register
would not be practicable or desirable, or a basis for certainty.
However, in March the government moved towards a more restrictive policy by amending the immigration rules to prevent men
being accepted for settlement through marriages of convenience.

The government's suggestions for the reform of the nationality
and citizenship laws were published in April 1977 in a Green Paper
entitled *British Nationality Law: Discussion of Possible Changes*.[12]
This contained the proposal that there should be two forms of
British citizenship: the first, UK citizenship for those with close
connections with the UK, and the second, British overseas citizenship for those who were citizens of UK colonies. These proposals
were adopted in a modified form by the subsequent Conservative
government, and were incorporated in the Nationality Act 1981.

In March 1978 the Select Committee on Race and Immigration
published a controversial but unanimous report, recommending
tighter immigration controls, an end to amnesties for illegal immigrants, a system of internal controls of immigration and a
register of dependants. There were some liberal recommendations,
such as the need to speed up immigration procedures for dependants so that families could be reunited more quickly, but on
balance it was a restrictive report.[13] The government rejected it,
but the fact that the Labour members of the Committee supported

the recommendations showed how Conservative pressure, and in particular Mrs Thatcher's initiatives on immigration, had influenced the political climate and forced the Labour party on to the defensive.

Outside parliament in the constituency parties, the unions and on the NEC, pressure was growing for a stronger response to the National Front and for an all-out campaign against racism. The Labour Party Race Action Group and Afro-Caribbean and Asian members within the party were pressing hard for such a campaign. In particular, the success of the National Front in exploiting the 'media scare' over the Malawi Asians and in increasing its vote in the local elections of May 1976 greatly concerned the NEC. In Blackburn the far-right National Party, which had split from the National Front, gained two seats on the district council. This shocked Barbara Castle, the local MP, and she urged the NEC to take vigorous action.

In September 1976 the NEC launched an anti-racialist campaign, together with the TUC. The intention was mainly to educate party members and trade unionists in the evils of racialism, and to expose the neo-fascist policies of the National Front and their dangerous implications. An additional incentive for positive action was the launching, also in 1976, of the Conservative party's Anglo-Asian Society, which alerted the NEC to the danger of taking Asian and Afro-Caribbean votes for granted. In particular, some members of the NEC were concerned that a sustained Conservative initiative might attract substantial numbers of Asian voters. Furthermore, there was an added danger that if the Labour party continued to emphasize firm support for immigration control and failed to combat publicly the activities of the National Front, Afro-Caribbean and Asian voters might become sufficiently disillusioned with both the major parties to nominate candidates from their own communities in areas where they were electorally strong.

There was a major debate on racialism at the annual party conference in September 1976 and calls from all sides for a major offensive against the far right, especially the National Front. The conference also passed a resolution demanding the repeal of the Immigration Acts 1968 and 1971.[14] The annual conference debated racialism again in 1978, but the combination of the Conservative offensive and the impending election caused the NEC to oppose a strongly framed composite resolution condemning the Select Committee report, opposing all Immigration Acts and supporting the right of blacks to organize self-defence groups. This resolution was lost, and a more moderately phrased resolution was remitted to the NEC for further consideration.[15] The Labour party downplayed immigration and 'race' relations in its 1979 election manifesto. Its modest proposals emphasized the need to strengthen the legislation protecting the ethnic minorities against discrimination and racialism. It promised that the next Labour government would:

1 give a strong lead, by promoting equality of opportunity at work throughout the public sector;
2 help those whose first language is not English;
3 monitor all government and local authority services to ensure that minorities are receiving fair treatment;
4 consider what measures may be necessary to clarify the role of the Public Order Act and to strengthen and widen the scope of the Race Relations Act;
5 review the 1824 Vagrancy Act with a view to repealing Section 4.[16]

There was no mention of repealing the immigration control legislation or even of reviewing its more racist and discriminatory parts.

Labour in opposition, 1979–83

Labour's defeat in 1979 substantially increased the importance of Afro-Caribbean and Asian voters for the party's remaining MPs. The erosion of Labour's support among the white working class meant that the most loyal supporters of inner-city Labour MPs were electors from the Afro-Caribbean and Asian communities. The Labour Party Race Action Group capitalized on this by circulating a leaflet to all constituency Labour parties entitled *Don't Take Black Votes for Granted*.[17] The NEC was also keen to adopt a positive stance, and included in its Human Rights Committee a number of people critical of the party's record. In February 1980 the NEC circulated an advice note to all constituency parties, called *Labour and the Black Electorate*.[18] This document urged local parties to encourage greater black involvement in the party, and was highly critical of the record of the recent Labour government in spite of Jenkins' reforms and the 1976 Race Relations Act. It argued that the government

> [had] failed to deliver the promised changes to working conditions of Britain's ethnic minorities. We failed to replace the racist immigration laws: or to make immigration laws more flexible in operation; or to end the harassment of blacks by the police — by, for example, repealing 'Sus' and disbanding the Special Patrol Group; or to take adequate steps to tackle racial disadvantage and give a clear lead in the promotion of equal opportunity policies, especially in employment.[19]

In the autumn of 1980 a new front-bench team on home affairs, consisting of Roy Hattersley and John Tilley, replaced Merlyn Rees and Shirley Summerskill, to lead Labour's attack on the Nationality Bill. Both were from constituencies with large numbers of Afro-Caribbean and Asian voters. Hattersley mounted a vigorous campaign against the Bill but, although the minority ethnic communities were deeply concerned by the Bill, the general public was largely indifferent and uninterested. Labour's fierce opposition was less credible on account of their own commitment to reform the nationality laws.

The opposition also responded vigorously to the issues raised by the inner-city riots of 1980 and 1981, arguing that they were not 'racial' but caused by the conditions of deprivation and despair in the inner cities, particularly unemployment, poor housing and education, and a general lack of amenities.[20] There was wide Labour support for Lord Scarman's recommendations, especially the introduction of lay visitors to police stations, the reform of the police complaints procedure, the revision of Section 3 of the Public Order Act to enable selective bans to be placed on marches, and the inclusion in the police disciplinary code of an offence of 'racially prejudiced behaviour'.[21] However, while the parliamentary Labour party welcomed the Scarman report enthusiastically and unequivocally, it confusingly decided to vote against the government motion accepting it, 'to show our concern lest the government should not implement it with the determination and enthusiasm that we believe it deserves'.[22]

The greater importance of Afro-Caribbean and Asian electors for Labour MPs in this period could be seen in the wide range of 'race'-related issues raised in the House by back-bench MPs. These included the effects of immigration controls, the need for 'racially' mixed juries, the 'Sus' law, the treatment of Rastafarians in prison and the use made of Section 11 funds. (Section 11 of the Local Government Act 1966 provides supplementary finance to meet the special needs of Commonwealth immigrants. Most of the money (75%) is provided by the Home Office and the rest by local authorities. All the money is spent on staff in education and social services, with three quarters of it being spent on teachers.) Newly elected MPs from areas with significant numbers of minority ethnic electors were naturally active in taking up such issues, both to represent their constituents and to build up electoral support. Alf Dubbs, the new member for Battersea South, for example, raised the issue of 'fishing raids' for illegal immigrants by the police and immigration officers, and campaigned on behalf of Filipino women threatened by deportation. He was a founder member of the Labour Party Race Action Group.[23]

Lack of coherence and consistency was a feature of Labour's policy in this period. Labour MPs were divided over whether National Front marches should be banned, whether they should support or oppose the inclusion of an ethnic question in the census, and over legally obliging employers to ensure that Afro-Caribbean and Asian people were represented in their workforces. There were also disagreements over Labour's policy towards British 'protected persons' and British subjects with citizenship who were non-patrial and living overseas.[24]

In 1982 the NEC working group on 'race' relations produced proposals to form the basis for new legislation to replace the Immigration Act 1971. These affirmed the right of free entry to all British citizens, but made it clear that Britain would not unilaterally abandon immigration control. The main innovation in nationality policy was that citizens of the British Dependent Territories would become citizens of their colonies of residence; they would not have the right of abode in Britain, but only in their territory of residence and citizenship. The principles under which non-citizens would qualify for admission to the UK would include the rights to family reunification, to study and travel, and to seek asylum. Other recommendations included the liberalization of rules for the admission of dependants, the elimination of 'race' and sex discrimination over the admission of husbands and fiancés, the right of appeal prior to deportation or removal, the improvement of the appeals procedure, the publication of instructions to immigration officers on how to interpret the immigration rules, and the discontinuation of medical examinations for administrative purposes.[25] These recommendations had the full support of the NEC and of Roy Hattersley, the shadow Home Secretary, and were unanimously passed by the conference. While party policy was still to repeal the Immigration Act 1971 and the Nationality Act 1981, it was clear that broadly similar legislation would be enacted to replace both. Thus the election manifesto for the 1983 general election stated: 'We accept the need for immigration controls. But we will repeal the 1971 Immigration Act and the 1981 Nationality Act and replace them with a citizenship law that does not discriminate against either women or black and Asian Britons.[26]

The manifesto promised that the new immigration and nationality legislation proposed by Labour would be more liberal and humanely administered, with greater facilities for appeals against the decisions of immigration officials or of the Home Secretary. The manifesto indicated that within days of taking office a new Labour government would introduce an emergency programme of action, which would include not only new immigration and citizenship laws but also a positive action programme for the ethnic minorities. There would be a political offensive against racial disadvantage, discrimination and harassment. A senior minister would be appointed to lead the offensive against racial inequality. Positive action programmes would be stimulated, to ensure that the ethnic minorities received a fair deal in employment, education, housing and social services. The keeping of ethnic records would be encouraged in order to assess the needs of the ethnic minorities and take steps to meet them. The Race Relations Act 1976 would be strengthened, and a major public education initiative aimed at eliminating racial prejudice would be launched.[27]

The campaign for black sections

The dilemmas confronting the Labour leadership in managing 'race' issues were dramatically exposed in the early 1980s by the development of the campaign for black sections in the party. The impetus for the campaign came from a number of sources. First, the campaigns by Enoch Powell and the National Front had mobilized Afro-Caribbean and Asian people, and throughout the 1970s political participation among members of the minority ethnic communities was growing. This was reflected in rising levels of electoral registration, turn-out and active membership of political parties. As black people were predominantly working-class and geographically concentrated in inner-city areas, and as they identified the Conservative party with tough immigration controls and an anti-immigrant bias, most of this political participation found expression in the Labour party. By the early 1980s small numbers of Afro-Caribbeans and Asians were being elected as councillors in Greater London and other major cities. In 1986, for example, some 130 black councillors were elected in Greater London, and an additional 70 in places like Birmingham, Bradford and Leicester.[28]

Second, the Labour party itself was encouraging greater black political participation. Already, many local parties were recruiting black members and putting up black candidates, sometimes on the assumption that they could deliver the votes of their local communities.[29] The NEC, prompted by the Labour Party Race Action Group, was concerned that local parties should be aware of the growing importance of the black electorate, and should recruit black people and encourage them to stand for positions within the party and for public office.[30] The campaign for greater democracy in the Labour party and the more militant stand against racism and the National Front in the late 1970s also made the Labour party appear more attractive to black activists.

However, black activists' expectations that they would advance rapidly to high positions in the party were disappointed. In 1979 Labour party constituencies had nominated only one black person as a parliamentary candidate for the general election. In 1983, despite much NEC encouragement, only six black candidates were selected, and none of these were in winnable seats. Black activists were well aware that black voters were the most loyal part of the Labour electorate and that they were concentrated in the safest Labour seats. There was considerable frustration that selection committees in safe Labour seats were unwilling to nominate black candidates.[31]

The first black sections were founded in 1980–1, and three composite resolutions were debated at the annual conference, supporting the establishment of black sections. They were all lost. However, the NEC promised that it would establish a working party to examine constitutional reforms to provide more equal representation for disadvantaged groups at all levels of the party.[32] In the meantime the movement gathered momentum, especially in London, and by October 1984 some 25 constituency parties had allowed the formation of black sections, with representation on general and executive committees – even though, strictly speaking, this was unconstitutional. The agenda for the 1983 conference had contained four resolutions in favour of black sections. The 1984 agenda contained 18 resolutions and seven amendments favouring black sections, and one resolution opposed. In all, 25 constituency parties and one trade union (the EETPU) submitted resolutions or amendments in favour. Some of these resolutions went further than merely proposing the establishment of black sections at constituency level, and supported representation at regional level and on the NEC. Two resolutions called for the mandatory inclusion of at least one black person on candidate short-lists for local and parliamentary elections.

The Campaign for Black Sections held its first national conference in Birmingham in June 1984. It endorsed the demand for the creation of a constituional black section within the party, and elected a steering committee. Later in the year a Black Labour Activists' Campaign was formed, to promote left politics in black sections.[33]

However, even before the conference, substantial blows had been struck against the Campaign by the Labour leadership. Roy Hattersley declined an invitation to attend the Birmingham conference, saying that the Campaign's aims did not conform to party policy and that he would regard the establishment of a black section in his constituency as a retrograde step.[34] Neil Kinnock, interviewed on the BBC 2 television programme 'Ebony', warned of the danger of cutting blacks off from the mainstream of the party, of the problems of defining who should count as black, and of imposing quotas for parliamentary seats. People should rise to high positions in the party through individual merit, he argued. He emphasized that there was no place for racism in the party, maintaining that the Labour leadership was in touch with black people' and was well aware of their aspirations, which were for jobs, housing and education.[35] Gerald Kaufman warned of the dangers of pushing black people into some sort of ghetto, and claimed that the real cause of the problem was that blacks were not politically active enough and that more should join the party. He would look into the possibility of introducing affirmative action policies in the area of employment, he said, but he was opposed to quotas. Better education and training facilities were also urgently needed for young blacks.[36]

There were additional reasons why the party leadership faced a dilemma, with the creation of black sections, and it decided to oppose their recognition. The proliferation of sections within the party has not been an entirely happy experience. The youth sections have always demanded a great deal of autonomy, have usually been hostile to the party leadership, and have been dominated by far-left groups.[37] Other sections have often been used as a means by which cliques, factions or individuals have gained places on general committees which might have been denied them by the more intense competition at ward level. In the 1980s the position of the women's sections has provoked much heart-searching in the party. There is little evidence to suggest that they have diverted the energies of female activists away from the mainstream of the party or to specific areas, but nor have they acted as an agency for recruiting substantial numbers of women members. However, if the women's sections were abolished, female representation would be reduced at all levels of the party.

There was a danger that black sections, like the youth sections, would develop a very different style of politics from the rest of the party, and that they would increase intra-party conflict. While they would be concerned with a wide range of issues, they would focus on them not in terms of different political perspectives, but from a community perspective. They would also be concerned with racism and racial discrimination, within the party as well as without.

Inevitably, the black sections would be involved in criticizing the policies of their own party, demanding a degree of positive action and pressing for the adoption of more black candidates and party officers. There were already signs of this at the Birmingham conference. As one delegate said, 'Black sections are absolutely necessary to challenge racism in the Labour party, to change the party so that it becomes one that campaigns against racism, and to draw more black people into it to campaign for socialism and against racism.'[38]

Substantial representation for black sections at constituency, regional and national level would increase the enthusiasm of black party members and supporters, but could change the balance of power within party committees. Second, it would publicize in a dramatic way the identification of black people with the Labour party, and its espousal of ethnic minority causes. This could be exploited by the tabloid press, and be electorally damaging to the party.

The annual party conference in October 1984 proved to be a major setback for the Campaign for Black Sections. The NEC working party failed to produce the promised report on constitutional reforms. Instead, a consultative document, *'Black people and the Labour Party'*, [39] was produced which outlined the arguments for and against black sections. The NEC wished, once again, to persuade the supporters of black sections to remit their motions for further consideration by the working party. The members of the Black Sections' National Committee were determined to force a showdown and refused to agree to remit their resolutions, which were then heavily defeated. The first resolution advocating the establishment of black sections was defeated by 5,427,000 to 500,000.[40] The second motion, which was more ambitious, stated:

> Conference instructs the working party to put forward proposals for constitutional amendments for submission by the NEC to the 1985 conference: a) to increase the composition of the NEC by five members to be elected by an annual conference of black sections; b) mandatory inclusion of at least one black person, if any apply, on all parliamentary and local government shortlists; c) the promotion of a substantial extension of affiliation to the party by suitable ethnic minority organisations at local, regional and national level. Conference believes that such action is essential for the party

to be able to speak with credibility on behalf of underprivileged members of the electorate.[41]

This motion was defeated by 5,645,000 votes to 418,000, and conference finally carried a motion by 4,018,000 to 2,019,000 disapproving the setting-up of black or ethnic minority sections.[42]

In 1985 the left-wing Black Labour Activists' Campaign became the leading group in the black sections movement, and aligned the campaign firmly on the left of the party. They continued to agitate for recognition, but without success. In July the NEC rejected a working party's majority recommendation in favour of recognising black sections, and the rejection was overwhelmingly endorsed by the annual conference. The establishment of an ethnic minority officer in Labour party headquarters and a Black and Asian Advisory Committee did not satisfy black sections activists, who decided to boycott both. However, by 1987 a combination of factors had dissipated some of the steam behind the black sections campaign.

First, there was a substantial increase in black Labour parliamentary nominations for the 1987 general election. These involved some of the leading black activists associated with the campaign, such as Diane Abbott, Sharon Atkin, Bernie Grant and Keith Vaz. There is no doubt that the highly publicized campaign organized by black sections activists contributed greatly to the increase in black nominations by constituency labour parties, especially in the safe and winnable seats. Only one black person was nominated as a Labour parliamentary candidate in 1979, and six in 1983. But none was chosen for safe Labour inner-city constituencies where Afro-Caribbean and Asian voters were concentrated. In 1987 there were 14 black parliamentary candidates in a much better spread of safe, marginal and hopeless seats.

The success of the campaign for improved black representation among Labour candidates led to a crisis of identity and loyalty. Sharon Atkin, the prospective parliamentary candidate for Nottingham East, said at a black sections rally in Birmingham in April that it was more important to represent black people than to win a seat for the Labour party.[43] She was quoted as saying, 'I don't give a damn about Neil Kinnock and the racist Labour party.' She was immediately threatened with expulsion by the

NEC, which had already warned black sections activists not to organize outside the party's constitution. Four prominent black prospective candidates, Diane Abbott, Paul Boateng, Bernie Grant and Russell Profitt, immediately issued a joint statement saying that a Labour victory at the next election was a more urgent priority than achieving representation for black sections within the party: 'We are accountable to our constituency Labour parties and we will be fighting the general election on manifestos drawn up . . . on the basis of Labour policy.'[44] Sharon Atkin was subsequently deselected, and Muhammed Aslam selected in her place. This was a strong warning that the Labour leadership was not prepared to allow an autonomous, militantly anti-leadership organization which would divide the party and harm its electoral prospects.

Moreover, the black communities were also divided over the value of black sections. A Harris poll in 1985, conducted for Channel 4's 'Black on Black' programme, found 63% of its black respondents against black sections and only 18% in favour. The hostile response to black sections from the Labour party leadership may have had some impact on this result, but many black people undoubtedly felt that black sections would be sectarian and marginalizing and would cut black people off from the mainstream of the party. This was confirmed by Labour party soundings among black party members, many of whom were opposed to black sections. In 1987 another Harris survey found black support for black sections had risen to 33%, but 45% remained against. There was thus little pressure from the black community on the Labour leadership to make concessions.

The continuing conflict, however, was damaging to the Labour party and, after the 1987 general election, moves were made by Bill Morris of the Transport and General Workers' Union and Bernie Grant, who was active in the Campaign for Black Sections, to negotiate a compromise. An affiliated socialist society emerged as the main alternative to black sections, and Bill Morris wrote an influential article in *Tribune* pressing the black socialist society option.[45] Inside the Campaign for Black Sections Bernie Grant was working hard for a compromise solution, and at the same time he was trying to persuade the NEC to offer something to black activists in the party.

At the annual party conference in October 1988 a formula for the affiliated black socialist society was agreed, and an NEC working party was set up to work out the details of the new organization. Its proposals to the 1989 conference for an ethnic-minority-led socialist society, open to white voting members and with a future seat on the NEC, were rejected, after opposition from both supporters and opponents of black sections. Finally, agreement was reached at the 1990 annual Labour party conference. The approved motion recognized black members' right to organize together for effective participation and representation; agreed to allow for representation of black mambers at all levels of the party; and agreed to the setting-up of a single affiliated organization for members of African, Caribbean and Asian descent, with local and regional groups and with direct representation on the NEC. A motion calling for fully recognized, constitutional black sections was once again heavily defeated.[46]

The Labour party had finally conceded the right of its black members to organize themselves, but the success of the Campaign for Black Sections was limited. It had failed to obtain recognition for black sections, as originally conceived; its more ambitious demands for representation had been turned down, and it had failed to ensure that black candidates be shortlisted for local government and parliamentary seats. It had not made much impact on Labour party policy. Most important of all, it had failed to become a mass black political movement. However, its successes were considerable. It had forced the Labour party to make greater efforts to encourage black representation and participation; it had helped to secure the selection of more black people for local government and parliamentary seats, assisting in the election of the four black Labour MPs; and it had forced the party to concede a measure of black self-organization and representation on the NEC. This was a remarkable achievement, especially given the initial opposition of the Labour party leadership and their concern with the electoral impact of their decisions.[47]

Labour in opposition after 1987

The Labour manifesto in 1987 was cautious in its commitments on race relations and immigration issues. It stated that the party's policies on employment, education, housing, health care and local government would be of equal benefit to the 'whole community', including black people. More specifically, a Labour government would take firm action to promote racial equality and attack racial discrimination—for example, by insisting that all organizations with government contracts should have effective equal opportunity policies. The manifesto highlighted the problems of racist attacks, and promised that the Labour party would strengthen the law on public order to combat racial hatred and racial attacks. Prosecutions in such cases would be made easier. On immigration, the manifesto—rather ominously—adopted Conservative phraseology, stating that Labour would be 'firm but fair' and would ensure that the law did not discriminate on the basis of 'race', colour or sex.[48]

The modest proposals in Labour's manifesto led to accusations by some of the Conservative press that Labour had omitted its electorally unpopular commitment to repeal Tory immigration and nationality laws.[49] Conservative electoral advertising targeted two of Labour's black parliamentary candidates, Diane Abbott and Bernie Grant, as extremists.

A more detailed outline of Labour's policies could be found in *Opportunity Britain: Labour's Better Way for the 1990s*, which outlined the commitment to a new, strengthened, racial equality Act, which would extend the law to government institutions such as the police, prison and immigration services. Ethnic monitoring would be encouraged to eliminate discrimination and promote equality, and strong action would be taken to combat racial attacks.[50] On citizenship, a Labour government would restore the principle of *jus soli*, whereby every child born in Britain would be entitled to British citizenship and all citizens would have equal rights.[51]

In 1991 the Home Policy Committee of the NEC decided to draw up a comprehensive campaign document on Labour's policies and their impact on Afro-Caribbean, Asian and other ethnic minorities. Much of the draft was concerned with stressing how Labour's general policies of reducing poverty, increasing opportunities for employment, improving the quality of life in the inner cities, and investing in health and education would be of benefit to all working-class people, including the minority ethnic communities. Specific policies to assist Afro-Caribbeans and Asians focused on the proposed Race Equality Bill, the introduction of contract compliance, and the replacing of existing immigration and nationality legislation with non-discriminatory legislation[52] The proposals relating to contract compliance could result in opposition from the trade unions, who have opposed such proposals in the past.

Two major crises erupted in the late 1980s which illustrated the dilemmas facing the Labour leadership in deciding party policy in the area of 'race' relations and immigration. These were the Salman Rushdie affair and the crisis over Hong Kong.

The Salman Rushdie affair

Towards the end of 1988 Muslim communities in Britain became actively involved in a campaign to ban *The Satanic Verses* by Salman Rushdie, which they regarded as an offensive and blasphemous attack on the Islamic faith.[53] When the book was published in September, it quickly brought protests from Muslim groups. On 2 December they turned to direct action, and some 7,000 people staged a demonstration in Bolton and a copy of the book was burned, in an unsuccessful effort to gain publicity. On 14 January 1989 a protest meeting was held outside Bradford Town Hall, and once again a copy of the book was burned. This time the protest was widely reported and condemned. On 14 February the campaign against *The Satanic Verses* took a dramatic turn, when Ayatollah Khomeini urged Muslims throughout the world to execute Rushdie: 'I inform the proud Muslim people of the world that the author of *The Satanic Verses* book, which is against Islam, the prophet and the Koran, and all those involved in its publication, who were aware of its content, are sentenced to death.'[54]

There was widespread shock that a head of state could urge the death of a famous writer who was the citizen of another state. The Ayatollah's *fatwa* (legal ruling) was immediately condemned in Western countries, as Salman Rushdie went into hiding. Some Muslim leaders, for example in Bradford, supported the *fatwa*, but the Council of Mosques in Britain condemned the violence and urged Muslims to obey British law. On 18 February Rushdie apologized for the distress he had caused to Muslims, but this was not accepted by Ayatollah Khomeini. On the 21st the British government withdrew its diplomats from Tehran and sent Iran's diplomats home. This action was supported by the opposition. 'In this free democracy,' said Gerald Kaufman, 'authors must have the right, within the law, to write and publish freely. In this free democracy, Moslems offended and affronted by what has been published have the right, within the law, to give full expression to their concern, their distress and their sense of serious affront to their religious convictions.' The withdrawal of diplomats from Tehran was supported by the European Community. Many writers also took the lead in supporting Rushdie and defending his right to publish.

On 24 February the Home Secretary, Douglas Hurd, addressed Muslims in the Central Mosque in Birmingham. He accepted that Muslims had been deeply hurt by the book, but warned that violence or the threat of violence was wholly unacceptable, and that nothing would do more damage to racial harmony than the idea that British Muslims were indifferent to the rule of law in this country. Respect for the rule of law was a fundamental principle for which Britain stood, as were freedom of speech and the toleration of different opinions.

The campaign against *The Satanic Verses* raised concern about the influence of Islamic fundamentalism in Britain and about efforts by Muslim groups to set up their own educational institutions, especially single-sex schools for girls. In July John Patten, Minister of State at the Home Office responsible for 'race' relations, spoke of the need for the Muslim community to integrate into British society. In a letter to the Advisory Council on Race Relations he wrote, 'One cannot be British on one's own exclusive terms or on a selective basis.'[56]

A number of factors influenced Labour's response. First, there was condemnation of the *fatwa* and support for the principle of free speech. There was also concern that racists would exploit the issue to stir up anti-Muslim and anti-Asian prejudice, and there were reports of attacks on Mosques and Muslim homes.[57] A number of Labour MPs, such as Max Madden and Keith Vaz, were supportive of the Muslim protests and called for the blasphemy laws to be changed to protect religions other than Christianity. Many Muslims, however, felt that the Labour party was generally hostile to their cause. Mr Sher Azam, president of the Bradford Council of Mosques, said, 'In the past large numbers of Moslems have traditionally voted Labour. If they will not help, we will switch our vote.'[58] Roy Hattersley, who also had many Muslim electors in his constituency, argued forcefully that the proposition that Muslims are welcome in Britain if, and only if, they stop behaving like Muslims, is incompatible with the principles of a free society, but that in a free society the Muslim community can be allowed to do whatever it likes only as long as the choice it makes is not damaging to society as a whole.[59] He hoped no paperback of the book would be published, since this would increase the hurt and anguish caused to Muslims.

The Labour party as a secular, socialist party had difficulty in supporting some of the demands of the deeply religious Muslim community, but could express solidarity with a group that felt discriminated against in a society that had little regard for Muslim customs and traditions. It could unite with Muslims in criticizing the unfair blasphemy laws, and attack the efforts of right-wing Conservatives and the far right to exploit the issue. The most extraordinary attack on Muslims was made by Mr John Townsend, Conservative MP for Bridlington, who called for Muslims to be deported if they would not accept the publication of *The Satanic Verses*. 'England must be reconquered for the English,' he said.[60]

In early 1990 there was a sharp rise in anti-Muslim feeling as a result of the outbreak of the Gulf War. This was inflamed by the tabloid press, which adopted a super-patriotic stand. The Muslim communities in Britain were divided over the war, but some supported Iraq and were attacked for doing so. The editor of the *Daily Star* for example wrote: 'It is time to deport fanatical Moslems baying for the death of our boys in the Gulf.'[61] The actions of the Home Secretary in interning Iraqis and Palestinians without good cause must also have aroused public suspicions of Muslims. The CRE reported a sharp rise in incidents of anti-Muslim violence after the outbreak of the war.[62] The Labour party supported the United Nations and the government in their prosecution of the war, though Bernie Grant described it as a racist war prosecuted by America and its allies for control of Middle-East oil.[63].

The Rushdie affair has brought the Muslim communities in Britain into much greater political prominence. The communities have become more organized, new leaders have emerged, and issues of concern to Muslims are receiving much greater attention. The campaign against *The Satanic Verses* is continuing, but few concessions are being made to Muslim demands.

The Hong Kong crisis

The agreement between the British and Chinese governments over the terms of the return of Hong Kong to China in 1997 provoked a crisis over the future of the three and a half million British passport-holders who live there. These people are citizens of the British Dependent Territories under the Nationality Act 1981, but this citizenship does not entitle them to immigrate and settle in the UK. A great number of Hong Kong people wish to emigrate because of the uncertain future of Hong Kong after 1997. The massacre in Tiananmen Square in Beijing on 3 and 4 June 1989 greatly increased insecurity in Hong Kong, and re-doubled the efforts of its people to emigrate to the most favoured destinations of Canada, the USA and Australia.

Considering that the government and opposition are so often at odds over immigration issues, it was a remarkable consensus that quickly emerged over Hong Kong. Government, opposition and Foreign affairs Select Committee all agreed that British passport-holders from Hong Kong should not be allowed the right of access to the UK. The foreign secretary said:

> The practical difficulties of absorbing hundreds of thousands – possibly millions – of people make the granting of an open-ended right of abode to all British Dependent Territory citizens impossible to contemplate. It would be wrong to raise expectations we could not possibly meet. I do not believe the House would support such a departure from the immigration policies pursued by successive British governments since the early 1960s.[64]

Mr Kaufman for the opposition agreed with the government.[65] Only Mr Paddy Ashdown for the Liberal Democrats argued that citizens of the British Dependent Territories in Hong Kong should be offered the right of abode in the UK.[66]

The mass media and public opinion have been much more

sympathetic to the plight of the Hong Kong Chinese and sensitive to Britain's moral obligations than have the politicians. The quality press has strongly argued in favour of granting the right of abode to British passport-holders, and a Gallup poll carried out soon after the slaughter in Tiananmen Square found as many as 42% of the population believed that Hong Kong citizens should be given the legal right to settle in Britain. But the government was not prepared to relax its controls, and Sir Geoffrey Howe warned of the dangers of ethnic conflict in Britain if the right of abode was conceded, given the possible scale of immigration.[67]

On 20 December the new Foreign Secretary, Douglas Hurd, announced a government proposal to increase the confidence of key people in Hong Kong while at the same time reducing the numbers who might emigrate. The government would grant full British citizenship to 50,000 people and their dependants, to a maximum of 225,000. These would be professional, business and technical experts, including Crown servants, needed to run the colony. Gerald Kaufman reiterated the opposition's belief that if would not be right to offer any commitment to the British Dependent Territories passport-holders in Hong Kong, and stated that the opposition was against the creation of specially favoured categories based on status or affluence.

The Bill giving effect to the government's proposals was the British Nationality (Hong Kong) Bill, which had its second reading on 19 April 1990. The Labour opposition decided to oppose the Bill on the grounds that Kaufman had already argued — namely, that select and affluent groups were being favoured. To Labour's embarrassment the fiercest opposition to the Bill came from Norman Tebbit and the right wing of the Conservative party who hoped, with Labour help, to defeat the Bill. Labour's parliamentary ranks were thrown into confusion by this unnatural alliance, and 54 Labour MPs refused to vote the opposition line and go into the lobbies with Mr Tebbit and the Conservative right. One, Mr Andrew Faulds, voted with the government. The crisis exposed the difficulties the Labour leadership had in managing 'race' relations and immigration issues, and the eventual decision to oppose the Bill, but on narrow and specific terms rather than in general like Tebbit and the Tory right, made the opposition appear both confused and unconvincing.

Labour's policy impasse

The Labour party has been unable to develop a coherent and consistent policy in the areas of immigration control and 'race' relations. Its original decision to oppose control of Commonwealth immigration after the 1958 anti-black riots in Notting Hill and Nottingham proved untenable in the face of strong electoral support for controls and the willingness of Conservative politicians to exploit the issue. Efforts by Labour Home Secretaries, like Roy Jenkins, to administer the controls in a fair, humane and non-discriminatory way have been short-lived and have quickly collapsed in the face of Conservative pressure. The immigration policy of the Labour party has thus fluctuated considerably, depending as much on Conservative initiatives and pressure as on whether Labour has been in government or opposition, though generally the party has been more idealistic in opposition. The Conservatives, however, have dictated immigration policy since 1962, with the support of public opinion and the media – in particular, sections of the tabloid press which have been only too willing to manufacture immigration panics and identify black immigrants and Third World asylum-seekers as unwanted scroungers, immigration cheats and potential trouble-makers.

Thus the Labour party has since 1962 been consistently on the defensive, afraid of the adverse electoral consequences of the immigration question. Its efforts to defuse the issue and remove it as a bone of contention between the parties was successful for a time in the mid-1960s and mid-1970s. But these periods of bipartisan consensus were broken in the late 1960s by Enoch Powell, and in the late 1970s by Margaret Thatcher. On both occasions the Conservative party appeared to gain electoral dividends from exploiting the issue.

The future strategy of the Labour party must be to focus on combating racial discrimination and disadvantages within the UK and at European Community level. This has considering public support,[68] and significant support within the Conservative party. It would also have the advantage of helping to maintain the substantial support that the Labour party secures from the expanding numbers of black voters in its urban heartlands. The pressure from black Labour party activist for a greater share of public nominations for local councils and for parliament creates some conflict within the party because of the intense competition for safe Labour seats especially parliamentary seats, in inner-city areas. Also, the militancy of some of its black members sometimes results in the targeting of black inidividuals by the Conservative tabloid press, ever anxious to discredit 'looney left' Labour politicians or local authorities.

On immigration there seems no political alternative for the party other than to continue its support for stringent immigration controls, even though these are inevitably open to attack as in some respects racist. This is an invidious position for a party which claims to be anti-racist; it keeps it on the defensive, and the clear electoral support for tough immigration controls leaves the initiative with its opponents. There is no easy way to escape this dilemma except perhaps to try to displace the responsibility for immigration policy from the United Kingdom government to the European Commission.

Notes

1   P. Foot, *Immigration and Race in British Politics* (Penguin Books, 1965). p. 114.
2   Ibid., p. 113.
3   M. Hatfield, *The House the Left Built: Inside Labour Policy-Making, 1970–75* (Gollancz, 1978).
4   C. T. Husbands, *Racial Exclusionism and the City: The Urban Support of the National Front* (Allen & Unwin, 1983).
5   Community Relations Commission, *The Participation of Ethnic Minorities in the General Election, October 1974*, 1975.
6   Labour Party, Citizenship, Immigration and Intergration: A Policy for the Seventies, 1972.
7   Address by the Rt Hon. Enoch Powell to the annual conference of the Rotary Club of London, Eastbourne, 16 November 1968, in B. Smithies and P. Fiddick (eds), *Enoch Powell on Immigration* (Sphere Books, 1969).
8   Home Office, *Racial Discrimination*, Cmnd 6234, HMSO, 1975.
9   Parliamentary Debates, Commons (Hansard), vol. 906, col. 1548, 4 March 1976.
10 Parliamentary Debates, Commons (Hansard), vol. 912, cols. 49–51, 24 May 1976.
11 Parliamentary Debates, Commons (Hansard), vol. 914, cols 972–87, 5 July 1976.

12　Home Office, *British Nationality Law: Discussion of Possible Changes*, Cmnd 6795, HMSO, 1977.

13　Z. Layton-Henry, 'The report on immigration', *Political Quarterly*, vol. 50, no. 2 (1979), 241–8.

14　Labour Party, *Annual Conference Report*, 1976, pp. 213–14.

15　Labour Party, *Annual Conference Report*, 1978, pp. 312–23.

16　Labour Party Manifesto, 1979, p. 29.

17　Labour Party Race Action Group, *Don't Take Black Votes for Granted*, 1979.

18　Labour Party, *Labour and the Black Electorate*, 1980.

19　Ibid.

20　Parliamentary Debates, Commons (Hansard), vol. 8, col. 1408, 16 July 1981.

21　M. FitzGerald and Z. Layton-Henry, 'Opposition parties and race policies 1979–83', in Z. Layton-Henry and P. B. Rich (eds), *Race, Government and Politics in Britain* (Macmillan, 1986).

22　Parliamentary Debates, Commons (Hansard), vol. 14, col. 1009, 10 December 1981.

23　FitzGerald and Layton-Henry, 'Opposition parties and race policies', 108–10.

24　Ibid.

25　Labour Party, 'Immigration: Labour's approach', statement to conference by the NEC, *Annual Conference Report*, 1982, pp. 144–50.

26　*The New Hope for Britain: Labour Party Manifesto*, 1983, pp. 28–9.

27　Ibid.

28　M. Anwar, 'Ethnic minorities and the electoral process: some recent developments', in H. Goulbourne (ed.), *Black Politics in Britain* (Avebury, 1990).

29　M. FitzGerald, 'Different roads? The development of Afro-Caribbean and Asian political organisations in London', *New Community*, vol. 14, (1988), 385–96.

30　For example, the advice note, *Labour and the Black Electorate: Black People and the Labour Party*, Labour Party, 1984.

31　J. Bochel and D. Denver, 'Candidate selection in the Labour party: what the selectors seek', *British Journal of Political Science*, vol. 13 (1983), 45–60.

32　Labour Party, *Annual Conference Report*, 1983, pp. 30–9.

33　K. Shukra, 'Black sections in the Labour party', in H. Goulbourne (ed.), *Black Politics in Britain* (Avebury, 1990).

34　A. Osman, 'Blacks give ultimatum to Labour', *Observer*, 10 June 1984.

35　'Ebony', BBC 2, 6 June 1984.

36　'Black on Black', Channel 4, 5 June 1984.

37　Z. Layton-Henry, 'Labour's lost youth', *Journal of Contemporary History*, vol. 11 (July 1976), 275–308.

38　Mr M. Wong Sam (Manchester, Gorton) speaking at the Birmingham conference, 10 June 1984.

39 Labour Party, *Positive Discrimination: Black People and the Labour Party*, 1984.

40 Labour Party, *Annual Conference Report*, 1984, p. 174.

41 Labour Party, *Annual Conference Composite Resolutions*, 1984, pp. 54–6.

42 Labour Party, *Annual Conference Report*, 1984, p. 174.

43 *Runnymede Trust Bulletin*, no. 203. (May 1987), p. 9.

44 Ibid.

45 B. Morris, 'Time for new thinking in the black sections debate', *Tribune*, 8 January 1988, pp. 1, 11.

46 Labour party, *Annual Conference Report*, 1990, pp. 45–50.

47 For a good discussion of the Campaign for Black Sections, see T. Sewell, *Black Tribunes: Race and Representation in British Politics*, (Lawrence & Wishart, 1992).

48 *Britain Will Win: Labour Party Manifesto*, June 1987, pp. 13–14.

49 E.g. *Daily Mail*, 20 May 1987; *Today*, 20 May 1987; *Daily Mail*, 29 May 1987.

50 Labour Party, *Opportunity Britain: Labour's Better Way for the 1990s*, 1991, pp. 48–9.

51 Ibid.

52 Labour Party, *Opportunities for All: Labour's Campaign Statement for Ethnic Minorities*, 1991.

53 For a detailed account of the Rushdie affair, see Z. Sardar and M. W. Davies, *Distorted Imagination: Lessons from the Rushdie Affair* (Grey Seal Books, 1990).

54 London, *Evening Standard*, 14 February 1989.

55 Parliamentary Debates, Commons (Hansard), vol. 147, cols 840–1, 21 February 1989.

56 *Independent*, 21 July 1989.

57 *Runnymede Trust Bulletin*, no. 225 (May 1989), pp. 7–8.

58 *Daily Mail*, 27 March 1989.

59 *Sunday Times*, 20 May 1989.

60 *Runnymede Trust Bulletin*, no. 229 (October 1989), p. 11.

61 *Daily Star*, 6 March 1991.

62 *Runnymede Trust Bulletin*, no. 243 (March 1991), pp. 1–2.

63 Parliamentary Debates, Commons (Hansard), vol. 183, cols 806–7, 15 January 1991.

64 Parliamentary Debates, Commons (Hansard), vol. 156, cols 1170–1, 13 July 1989.

65 Ibid., col. 1176.

66 Ibid., col. 1188.

67 Sir Geoffrey Howe interviewed on a BBC1 programme, 'Hong Kong – a Matter of Honour', 12 June 1989.

68 I. Crewe, and B. Särlvik, 'Popular attitudes and electoral strategy', in Z. Layton-Henry (ed.), *Conservative Party Politics* (Macmillan, 1980).

8 Mrs Thatcher's 'racecraft'

It is surprising to recall that Margaret Thatcher was elected leader of the Conservative party in February 1975 during a period of relative liberalism in Conservative 'race' relations policy. This liberalism owed much to her predecessor, Edward Heath, to those like Whitelaw and Hailsham who were in charge of Home Affairs for the party, and to considerations of electoral strategy which at this time were favourable to an appeal to black voters.[1] Heath, as party leader, had in many respects an honourable record on 'race' issues. True, he had acceded to pressure from Powell and his supporters to introduce the tough Immigration Act (1971) with its controversial partriality provisions, which favoured people of British descent, almost all of whom could be presumed to be white. However, by this time the need for firm immigration controls to restrict New Commonwealth immigration, particularly from the Indian subcontinent, had been accepted by all sections of the party. On the positive side, Heath had strenuously forbidden Conservative parliamentary candidates from exploiting the immigration issue in elections; he had sacked Powell from the shadow cabinet after his inflammatory 'river of blood' speech in April 1968; and he had honoured, albeit reluctantly, Britain's obligations to the Ugandan Asians. Unlike Powell and some of the intellectuals of the new right,[2] Heath was on record as stating that 'there is no reason why cultural diversity should not be combined with loyalty to this country.'[3]

Mrs Thatcher's views on 'race' relations and immigration issues were less sensitive and sympathetic than those of her predecessor. As a successful, self-made individualist, she had little sympathy with those who felt they suffered group disadvantages, whether they were women, working-class, or ethnic minorities. She disapproved of campaigns in favour of legislative action to remove such disabilities, and felt that people should fend for themselves. On immigration she instinctively sympathized with Enoch Powell and those on the hard right of the party. She favoured the most stringent controls of New Commonwealth immigration.

In the two years following her leadership victory, Mrs Thatcher acted cautiously while she established her new position. The opposition's policy on 'race' issues continued to be liberal, but with little support from the leader. In January 1976 Mr Andrew Rowe was appointed director of a new Department of Community Affairs, which was specifically charged with promoting the party among target groups in the electorate. These were defined as including young voters, women, small businessmen, skilled workers and ethnic minority voters. Rowe established an Ethnic Minorities Unit, whose job was to educate party members about the growing electoral importance of black voters and to promote the party more positively to the ethnic minority communities. A young graduate was put in charge of the unit, and one of his first initiatives was the establishment of the Anglo-Asian and Anglo-West Indian Conservative Societies.

These societies were formed with the help of two Conservative councillors who belonged to the ethnic minorities. Mr Basil Lewis, a West Indian, had been elected as a Conservative councillor for Haringey Borough Council in 1968, and had some support from the West Indian community in Hornsey. He became Secretary of the Anglo-West Indian Society. Major Narindar Saroop, a Conservative councillor for Kensington and Chelsea, became Chairman of the Anglo-Asian Society. Conservative Central Office decided to give high priority to the Anglo-Asian Society, as they believed Asian businessmen and professionals such as doctors and accountants could be successfully recruited into the party and would be willing to contribute to party funds. Mrs Thatcher agreed to become Honorary President of the society, and, in order to impress Asian leaders with the wholehearted support that Conservatives were giving to the new initiative, the honorary vice-presidents included some reassuringly right-wing MPs such as John Biggs-Davison, Winston Churchill and Julian Amery. The Anglo-Asian Society had some modest success, until it was riven apart in 1985 by internal conflict over an independent Sikh state of Khalistan. It was then closed down and replaced by a new organization, the One Nation Forum. The Anglo-West Indian Society failed to generate much support outside its Hornsey branch in London.

In retrospect, the decision by the shadow cabinet not to oppose the Race Relations Act 1976 was remarkable, and showed that liberal Tories still had considerable influence. Many parts of the Act were anathema to right-wing Conservatives, who opposed the intrusion of the law into areas they felt were private and personal. The Act broadened the definition of racial discrimination to include indirect, as well as direct, forms, and it merged the Community Relations Commission and the Race Relations Board to create a more powerful Commission for Racial Equality. The new Commission was granted broad powers to conduct strategic investigations. Mrs Thatcher was hostile to the legislation: Russel[4] reports that she was on the verge of ordering complete Conservative opposition to the Bill, and was prevented from doing so only by a threatened revolt of liberal Tories who felt that tough immigration controls had to be balanced by positive 'race' relations policies, in order to assist integration and equality. The shadow cabinet's decision not to oppose the Race Relations Act was criticized and resented by many right-wing Conservative MPs, 43 of whom rebelled against the decision to abstain and voted against the Bill on its third reading.

The issue had become more controversial because of the arrival in May of small numbers of Asians from Malawi. These Asians, as mentioned earlier, were UK passport-holders, entitled to come to Britain under the quotas established for non-patrials in 1968. Some of the migrants had to be temporarily housed by West Sussex County Council in a four-star hotel, and this provoked an eruption of hostile headlines and adverse comment in the tabloid press.[5] In the local elections which coincided with this anti-immigrant publicity, the immigration scare was immediately exploited by the extreme right. There was a dramatic upsurge in electoral support for the National Front, though they failed to win any council seats. The National Party, without Conservative opponents, did gain two seats in Blackburn.[6] The media panic stimulated widespread concern among Conservative constituency associations, and a massive 140 resolutions on immigration were sent for debate at the annual party conference. Margaret Thatcher, with shadow cabinet support, decided that the Immigration Act 1971 was not effective enough, and that new proposals must be found to convince party members and the electorate that the party would bring New Commonwealth immigration to an end. William Whitelaw, deputy leader and shadow Home Secretary, was charged with the production of new proposals for reducing immigration.

In October an outline of the way Conservative policy was developing appeared in *The Right Approach*, the party's proto-manifesto.[7] This stressed that the maintenance of racial harmony required an immediate reduction in immigration and a clearly defined limit to the numbers to be allowed to enter the UK. The Conservative opposition had already successfully urged the government to set up a committee, to be chaired by Lord Franks, and charged with investigating the feasibility of a register of dependants.[8] There was also a commitment to introduce a new Nationality Act to allay fears of unending immigration and to establish a rational basis for British citizenship. These themes were taken up at the annual party conference by Whitelaw who, while reaffirming that every immigrant now here should be treated as an equal and welcome member of our society, stressed the need to recognize the genuine fears of our fellow-citizens and work towards the end of immigration 'as we have seen it in these post-war years'.[9] He promised a drastic review of all the immigration laws, consideration of a register of dependants, and the creation of a new concept of nationality based on a close and real relationship with Britain and its people.[10] The following year Whitelaw asked Keith Speed, a new junior spokesman for home affairs, to investigate immigration controls with a view to drawing up new proposals.

The heightened activity of the National Front during 1976 and 1977 provoked a number of responses from its opponents. These included the launching of the Anti-Nazi League and a broader, all-party Joint Committee Against Racialism (JCAR), and an anti-racialist campaign by the Federation of Conservative Students which was launched and supported by Whitelaw in November 1977. The leaders of the National Union[11] agreed to participate with the other major parties in the JCAR. Mrs Thatcher became aware of Conservative involvement at a late stage, and was appalled to discover that the party might be engaged in an anti-racist campaign jointly with the Labour party and other left-wing groups. She indicated that she was opposed to such involvement, and vetoed the appointment of John Moore, one of the party's vice-chairmen, as joint chairperson of the JCAR with Joan Lestor, the Labour party's nominee. In an unprecedented move, the executive committee of the National Union insisted on going ahead with its involvement in the JCAR, and nominated Shelagh Roberts, who had been a member of the Race Relations Board, as its joint chairperson. Lord Thorneycroft, Chairman of the party, attempted to defuse the conflict by explaining that Conservatives could participate in the JCAR on an individual basis, but that corporate membership by the party or its constituency associations would not be encouraged.[12]

On 30 January 1978 Mrs Thatcher was able to seize the initiative and to define Conservative policy on immigration. Her opportunity came in an interview with Gordon Burns on Granada's 'World in Action' programme. When asked about immigration, she identified herself with those who felt it was too high and sympathized with those who felt 'really rather afraid that this country might be rather swamped by people with a different culture'. 'If you want good race relations', she said, 'you have got to allay peoples' fears on numbers.'[13] The Conservative party should hold out the prospect of an end to immigration except in compassionate cases, and neglect of the immigration issue by the major parties, she suggested, was driving some people to support the National Front. When asked if she wished to bring back to the Tory party some of the support the National Front had been attracting in by-elections, she replied, 'Oh, very much back, certainly, but I think that the National Front has, in fact, attracted more people from Labour voters than us, but never be afraid to tackle something which people are worried about. We are not in politics to ignore peoples' worries: we are in politics to deal with them.'[14]

Mrs Thatcher's initiative, taken without advance consultation with colleagues, re-established the Conservatives as the anti-immigration party. Mrs Thatcher was sure that this was what the electorate wanted. It accorded with her own views and those of her supporters on the back benches, many of whom felt that immigration was an issue that could, and should, be exploited to the electoral advantage of the party. She, and they, appeared to be correct. Her statement on television received considerable publicity, and the party's positive showing in the opinion polls demonstrated dramatically that the immigration issue could still provoke a popular response, in spite of the tough control legislation that had existed since the Immigration Act 1971. Not long before her television interview, the support for the Conservative and Labour parties had been equal in the polls, at 43.5%, and only 9% mentioned immigration as one of the two most urgent problems facing the country. In February the Conservatives shot into a 9% lead over Labour (48% to 39%), and 21% of those questioned in the NOP survey mentioned immigration as one of the two most urgent national problems.[15]

In this dramatic interview, Mrs Thatcher had seized the initiative on a number of fronts. First, the Labour government, which had been gaining support, was forced on to the defensive – and this was confirmed not only in the polls but also at the by-election at Ilford North in February, which the Conservatives easily gained from Labour. Mrs Thatcher had also undermined the efforts of Conservative Central Office to appeal to black voters: she had reminded the leaders of the National Union that it was she who determined party policy, and that winning public support – not participating in anti-racialist campaigns of dubious popularity – was the major priority. Her judgement was that the Conservative party had most to gain by responding to the concerns of white voters anxious about immigration. Her intervention also put pressure on Keith Speed and his committee investigating ways of tightening immigration controls to come up with specific recommendations quickly.

The calculated exploitation of the 'race' issue by Mrs Thatcher was condemned by the opposition and by immigrant organizations. In her own party, only a few criticized her. Peter Walker attacked her emotive language, and argued that the principles of a multiracial society were more important than winning votes. 'If you exploit people's worries in a way which shows hostility to minorities, you will do immense damage to racial harmony,' he said.[16] Edward Heath, her predecessor as leader, interpreted her remarks as a criticism of his administration. He attacked her in the House of Commons, arguing that the immigration issue had not been ignored, that the Immigration Act 1971 gave the government all the powers it needed to control immigration, and that she was deliberately misleading people by suggesting that significant reductions could be made in the numbers entering the country. He castigated her for the way she had callously exploited such a sensitive issue for electoral purposes.[17]

Most Conservative politicians supported Margaret Thatcher, though there was private criticism over the way she had taken a major initiative without consulting her colleagues. The ethnic minority communities were outraged, particularly by the 'swamping' remark and by her apparent eagerness to win the votes of National Front supporters for the Conservative party. Not surprisingly, the opinion polls recorded overwhelming black support for the Labour party after the interview.[18] One of the most critical responses to her television performance came from Bernard Levin in *The Times*, who exposed the fallacy in the oft-repeated argument that firm controls were a necessary condition for racial harmony: 'You cannot by promising to remove the cause of fear and resentment fail to increase both. If you talk and behave as though black men were some kind of virus that must be kept out of the body politic, then it is the shabbiest hypocrisy to preach racial harmony at the same time.'[19]

Despite the criticism, it was clear that Mrs Thatcher's statements had wide support among the electorate, as well as in the Conservative party. It was not surprising, therefore, that at the meeting of the Central Council of the party held on 7 April Mr Whitelaw outlined specific proposals that the Conservatives would make on their return to government. These included introducing a new British Nationality Act; ending the practice of allowing permanent settlement for those who came here for a temporary stay; restricting the entry of parents, grandparents and children over 18 to those who could prove urgent compassionate grounds; withdrawing the concession introduced in 1974 to husbands and male fiancés; instituting a register for eligible wives and children from the Indian subcontinent, followed by an across-the-board quota to control entry. Whitelaw also promised tougher restrictions on the issue of work permits, and intensified action against illegal immigrants. He described the proposals as a tough but fair package.[20]

The eight proposals to increase immigration control were all specifically incorporated in the Conservative party's election manifesto, and were defended on the usual grounds, that 'firm immigration control for the future is essential if we are to achieve good community relations.'[21]

The party did not emphasize its policies on immigration control during the 1979 general election campaign, though Mrs Thatcher confirmed in a radio phone-in programme that she stood absolutely by her earlier statement that people felt 'rather swamped' by immigrants, and reiterated the proposals the Conservatives intended to introduce. However, while immigration was not an issue in the campaign, Mrs Thatcher had made it very clear where the Conservative party stood. This proved popular with sections of the electorate, and there were substantial swings to the Conservatives in areas like North and East London where the National Front had been doing well in the mid-1970s. In fact, there was a complete collapse in the Front vote, which suggests that Mrs Thatcher was successful in winning many of these voters for the Conservatives.[22]

In constituencies where there were substantial numbers of ethnic minority voters the Conservatives made modest efforts to appeal to them. The Anglo-West Indian Conservative Society was formally launched in February 1979, to help attract West Indian support for the Conservative candidates in the marginal seats of Hornsey and Croydon Central. The Anglo-Asian Conservative Society attempted to assist in marginals with large numbers of Asian voters. Two Asians were selected as Conservative parliamentary candidates: Narindar Saroop in Greenwich and Farriq Saleem in Glasgow Central. Both of these seats remained safely Labour. Conservative efforts to attract support from the ethnic minorities made little impact, and Afro-Caribbean and Asian voters remained overwhelmingly Labour party supporters.[23]

The first Thatcher government, 1979–83

The election of the Conservatives in May 1979 brought an immediate clash between the populist authoritarian promises of the new regime and Whitehall pragmatism. William Whitelaw, the new Home Secretary, was charged with implementing the manifesto proposals, but senior Home Office advisers warned in particular that a register of dependants was impracticable, would greatly inflate the numbers likely to come, and would outrage Commonwealth governments, particularly India. The Franks Committee had made similar recommendations. It was also argued that it would be extremely foolish, and would raise a host of practical problems, to establish a finite quota covering everyone outside the EEC who wished to settle in Britain. Moreover, the government found that apparently simple and effective methods of reducing immigration could cause unexpected political trouble. Thus the commitment 'to end the concession to allow husbands and male fiancés the right to enter the UK for settlement'[24] affected native-born white British women who were engaged or married to foreign nationals and who might wish to return to the UK to settle with their husbands. Some Conservative MPs argued that it was normal for a wife to settle in her husband's place of residence and assume his nationality, so there should be no right of entry for husbands or fiancés. In a number of countries, including Egypt and the USA, British wives organized themselves into groups to lobby the government. Women's groups within Britain protested at the unequal treatment of the sexes that rescinding the right would involve. Conservative MPs were lobbied also by large numbers of constituents with children and grandchildren settled overseas and who did not wish them to be adversely affected. And the Home Secretary was lobbied by a number of these MPs. This unexpected resistance to the changes in the immigration rules delayed publication of the government's proposals until November, when a White Paper was laid before parliament.[25]

The new rules proposed that husbands of women settled in Britain would need an entry certificate to be admitted to the United Kingdom, and that this would be refused if the entry clearance officer had reason to believe that (1) the marriage was arranged solely to gain admission to the UK; or (2) the husband and wife did not intend living together; or (3) the couple had not met. An entry certificate could be issued if the wife had been born in the UK. Similar conditions would apply to applications from fiancés. Elderly dependants would only be admitted if wholly or mainly dependent on sons and daughters in Britain – that is, receiving money from them – and 'they must also be without relatives in their own country and have a standard of living substantially below that of their own country.' These conditions were designed to disqualify elderly dependants from Third World countries, as remittances from their children in Britain would have raised their standard of living at home. The regulations governing change of category for people entering the UK as visitors or students were tightened, in order to prevent such a change resulting in a right to settlement; and their ability to seek employment was restricted. The new provisions relating to au pair girls were restricted to those from Western European countries.

The new immigration rules were debated on 4 December 1979. They were opposed by the opposition on the grounds that they violated the principle that the rights of all British citizens legally settled here should be equal before the law, no matter their 'race', colour or creed.[26] The opposition's case was undermined by the fact that the Labour government had restricted the right of entry of husbands and male fiancés in 1969; Merlyn Rees apologized to the House for his involvement in introducing these earlier restrictions, admitting that he had been wrong.[27] The government was also criticized by some of its own back-benchers, who argued that the provision for elderly dependent relatives was very mean, and that the rules discriminated against British women not born in the United Kingdom. Although the government had a majority of 42 and thus easily won the debate, 19 Conservative MPs abstained.

The government felt the need to amend its new rules to mollify its critics. The final statement of changes in the immigration rules was published and laid before parliament on 20 February 1980. The right of entry was extended to husbands and fiancés whose wives or fiancées had been born or who had one parent born in the UK, providing the *primary purpose* of the marriage was not settlement. Also, elderly dependants would be allowed to enter the UK providing they were wholly maintained by their children or grandchildren. These final provisions were debated and approved on 10 March, when the government had a majority of 52. This time there were only five Conservative abstentions.

The new government thus experienced unexpected difficulties in fulfilling its manifesto promises. Practical problems forced it to drop two of its most widely publicized commitments – the register of dependants and the world-wide quota systems for non-EC nationals. The government was embarrassed by charges from its opponents that it was racist, and from its own right-wing back-benchers that it was failing to keep its manifesto promises. There was, it appeared, no easy way of bringing New Commonwealth immigration to an end, nor of avoiding accusations of introducing racist rules. One solution that had been suggested by Powell and taken up by the Conservative government in 1972, though for differ-ent reasons,[28] was to link the right of entry and permanent abode in the UK to citizenship. With the development and expansion of the Empire and Commonwealth, the old feudal notion of British subject had been transformed over the centuries into an imperial ideal. But Britain's decline as a great imperial power and the failure of the Commonwealth to develop into a cohesive political and economic bloc meant that British subject status was increasingly irrelevant. Britain's entry into the European Community recognized its new status as a middle-ranking European power, and provided an additional justification for changing the citizenship laws – that of bringing them into line with Britain's Community partners. A citizenship restricted to those with close ties to the UK was a recognition of these new political realities.

The status of British subject had, of course, already been undermined. The introduction of more and more restrictive immi-gration controls meant that most British subjects no longer enjoyed the full rights of British citizenship as they had before 1962. Although they still had some important rights such as the right to vote, to serve in the armed forces and to work in the public services, since they no longer had the right of free access to, or settlement in, the UK, they no longer had the means to exercise these rights easily. The way of resolving these contradictions seemed to be to create a new, narrower British citizenship for those with close ties to the UK and with the right of free entry and permanent abode. Also, as discrimination by sovereign states in favour of their own citizens over and above non-citizens was an accepted principle of international law, a new citizenship law would make it more difficult for critics to accuse the government of operating racist immigration laws. A new British Nationality Act thus had many attractions for the government, not the least of which was that it would fulfil a manifesto pledge. The immediate pressure for a new Nationality Act arose from the need to rationalize and legitimize the immigration laws. This was confirmed by a

Conservative party policy document published in March 1980: 'Future immigration policies, if they are to be sensible, realistic and fair, must be founded on a separate citizenship of the UK and it is therefore essential that a reformed law of nationality should, for the first time, make clear who are the citizens of the UK.[29] In the longer term, the government was concerned about the prospect of increasing pressure to immigrate coming from Hong Kong, given that the British lease on most of the territory would run out in 1997.

The British Nationality Act

The commitment to introduce a new Nationality Act was the most wide-reaching and important proposal in the Conservatives' election manifesto. It was not only a break with an ancient tradition, but it affected the status of millions of people from Malaysia to the Falkland Islands, from Hong Kong to Bermuda, as well as in Britain itself. It would define British citizenship for the first time and effectively make redundant the earlier status of British subject. As mentioned earlier, the Labour government of 1974–9 had also decided that the nationality law had to be revised, and had published a Green Paper in 1977 which discussed a variety of possible changes. It argued that a new scheme of citizenship should reflect the strength of the connection that various groups of people had with the UK. It proposed two categories of citizen: namely, British citizens and British overseas citizens. This latter group was to consist mainly of people connected with existing dependencies and those who had retained their British citizenship when the colonies or dependencies in which they lived became independent.[30]

The government published a White Paper on its proposed nationality legislation in July 1980.[31] There was tremendous concern and anxiety about the implications of the proposed Bill, and representations were made to the government and opposition parties by ethnic minority organizations, the Churches, the CRE and civil liberties groups. The government published its Bill in January 1981.[32]

The Bill set out three major categories of citizenship: British citizenship, citizenship of the British Dependent Territories and

British overseas citizenship. British citizens would be those citizens of the UK and colonies who had a close personal connection with the UK, either because their parents or grandparents had been born, adopted, naturalized, or registered as citizens of the UK, or through permanent settlement in the UK. One controversial proposal was that, as a general rule, British citizenship should descend only to the first generation of children born abroad to British citizens born in the UK. This caused consternation to expatriate Britons all over the world, and also to Britons working or serving abroad, many of whom had not themselves been born in Britain as their parents had been involved in imperial service or overseas trade. The Bill also proposed that children born in Britain of certain categories of foreign parents, or whose parents were of uncertain status — because of illegal immigration or through overstaying their period of residence, for example — would not automatically be entitled to citizenship. Mr Whitelaw was to tell the House of Commons: 'The Government sees no reason why a child should ever have citizenship simply because his parents happen to be in the United Kingdom when he is born.'[33] This was the first time that the Anglo-Saxon tradition of *jus soli*, conferring citizenship by virtue of birth in the territory, had been questioned. It marked a moved, albeit a modest one, towards the continental tradition of *jus sanguinis*, conferring citizenship by virtue of descent from a citizen. Persons marrying a British citizen would no longer have an automatic right to citizenship, but would be able to apply for citizenship after three years' residence.

Citizenship of the British Dependent Territories would be acquired by those citizens of the UK and colonies who had that citizenship by reason of their own or their parents' or grandparents' birth, naturalization or registration in an existing dependency or associated state. The third category, British overseas citizenship, was essentially a residual one with virtually no rights. It was intended for those citizens of the UK and colonies who did not qualify for either of the first two categories, and related mainly to holders of dual citizenship who lived in Malaysia, but also to East African Asians entitled to come to Britain under the quotas established in the Commonwealth Immigrants Act 1968. British overseas citizens would not be able to pass on this citizenship, nor would they have the right of abode in any British territory. It was hardly a citizenship at all — rather, the phasing-out of British subject status. In reality, it was a strong invitation to those British subjects permanently settled abroad and with no close connection with the UK to acquire full local citizenship as quickly as possible and end the pretence of a continuing British connection. It was a further indication that the British government wished to divest itself of overseas obligations that were a legacy of its imperial past. There was a risk that if the children of British overseas citizens were refused citizenship by their country of birth they would be born stateless, but, as most of their parents had dual citizenship, the government considered the risk to be slight.[34]

The Home Secretary introduced the Bill for its second reading on 28 January 1981. He declared that under the immigration laws it would not adversely affect the position of anyone lawfully settled in the UK. It did not discriminate on racial or sexual grounds, he claimed, and it provided the comprehensive and logical overhaul of citizenship legislation that had so long been required and which it had long been the duty of the UK government to introduce.[35]

The opposition attack on the Bill was even more ritualistic than usual, as they themselves were committed to a revision of the citizenship laws, and the government's proposals owed much to the previous Labour government's Green Paper. Conservative back-benchers spent much of the debate making representations on behalf of dependencies such as Gibraltar, the Falkland Islands and Hong Kong. Some of them also argued that it was unjust to distinguish between children born abroad to people who were British citizens by birth and those whose parents were British by naturalization or registration. There was considerable support for the sensible proposal, put forward by Roy Hattersley for the opposition, that each colony should have its own citizenship rather than the cumbersome common citizenship proposed in the Bill for British Dependent Territories. The government had a comfortable majority of 50 on the second reading.

Shortly after the debate, the Home Secretary announced two major amendments to the Bill: first, that any child born in the UK who did not acquire British citizenship at birth might acquire it after ten years' continuous residence, irrespective of the status of the parents; and second, that citizens by naturalization or registration would be allowed to transmit citizenship to children born overseas in the same way as British-born citizens. These amendments were reassuring to members of the ethnic minority communities, and were welcomed in the Rajya Sabha by the Indian Foreign Minister, Shri Navalsimha Rao. The first amendment was a move back towards the *jus soli* principle. Some right-wing Conservative back-benchers were angry at the concessions made by the government. Ivor Stanbrook, a member of the standing committee examining the Bill, said they showed a contempt for back-bench opinion and were a betrayal of government pledges on immigration.[36]

After considerable discussion in committee and on the floor of the House, the Bill received its third reading on 4 June. It then went to the Lords and returned to the Commons with 90 amendments, all except one of which were accepted by the government, including the controversial Gibraltar amendment. This gave Gibraltarians special access to British citizenship, a concession which was later extended to the Falkland Islanders after the war with Argentina. The Nationality Bill was enacted and came into force on 1 January 1983.

The consequences of the Nationality Act

The decision by the government to introduce a more restrictive British citizenship and to phase out the entitlement of Commonwealth citizens to automatic registration for UK citizenship[37] caused considerable anxiety among the permanently settled immigrant community — an anxiety that was increased by the fact that the Nationality Bill was introduced in a context which emphasized more rigorous immigration controls. The result was a huge rise in applications for registration and naturalization as British citizens: from 38,000 in 1978 to 70,000 in 1981 and 96,000 in 1982, despite a large increase in fees, which the government introduced to make the service self-financing. Naturalization fees rose from £90 in 1979 to £200 in April 1982. The fee for those entitled to registration rose from £37.50 in 1979 to £70 in 1982. According to the Select Committee, this produced a notional profit to the Home Office of £6 million in 1982–3.[38] The Committee criticized the level of the fees, which it felt was unfairly high and deterred some people from applying for citizenship. The government agreed to reduce them, which it did in 1984.[39] The Home Office was also censured for not anticipating the surge in applications, which resulted in long delays. This was criticized by the Home Affairs Committee in its 1983 report, but even more strongly in its 1990 report, which condemned the incompetence and inexcusable delays of the Immigration and Nationality Department in dealing with registrations and naturalization applications. This was particularly disgraceful, it felt, in a fee-paying service.[40]

The Home Secretary published a White Paper on 25 October 1982, setting out proposals for changes in the immigration rules made necessary by the Nationality Act. Mr Whitelaw argued that the Act now defined those belonging to the UK, and that all women who were British citizens should have the right to be joined by their husbands or fiancés; in future, all British citizens would be able to bring their husbands or wives or fiancé(e)s into Britain.[41] This was not entirely true, as the spouses or fiancé(e)s would have to satisfy immigration officers that the primary purpose of joining their partner was not immigration to the UK. The opposition criticized and opposed the changes in the rules, arguing that some were too restrictive, while fifty Conservative MPs supported a reasoned amendment tabled by Ivor Stanbrook that they would encourage abuse of the immigration laws through the arranged marriage system.[42] The new rules were finally approved by parliament on 15 February 1983.

'Racecraft' and riots

It has been persuasively argued by Bulpitt that the statecraft pursued by successive British governments regarding the 'race' issue – that is, the broad strategy behind its policies and actions – has been aimed at preserving the autonomy of the political centre and protecting it from the demands of the electorate, both black and white. This strategy leaves the government free to pursue policies it regards as much more important, such as foreign affairs, defence and managing the economy. Prime responsibility for the difficult and controversial issue of 'race' politics has been delegated as far as possible to a variety of agencies, such as the Commission for Racial Equality, the UK Immigrants Advisory Service, the Joint Council for the Welfare of Immigrants and, above all, to local authorities.[43]

This was undoubtedly the strategy of successive British governments up to 1979, but Margaret Thatcher broke with this tradition. Immigration control was a major priority for her, and she made it a major priority for her first administration. She was convinced that she was responding to the electorate's wishes, and she wanted to satisfy the demands of white voters that she had aroused in January 1978. She therefore made immigration control a central part of her general electoral strategy and programme. Other pressures also contributed to making 'race' issues a high priority for the whole of her first administration. The Nationality Act, as we have seen, was an important part of Mrs Thatcher's 'racecraft',[44] and she regarded this as a major achievement and the partial fulfilment of her promise to bring New Commonwealth immigration to an end. The tightening of the immigration rules and greater pressure on illegal immigrants were other aspects of this policy.

The riots in Bristol in 1980 and in Brixton, Toxteth and elsewhere in 1981 were the major external factors forcing 'race' issues to the top of the political agenda between 1980 and 1983. The government was seriously concerned that further riots might take place − a fear that was reinforced by the continuing clashes between young blacks and the police in 1982 and 1983, which were not widely publicized.[45] The Cabinet, urged on by Michael Heseltine, was forced to act.[46] Extra resources were deployed in inner-city areas under Partnership Schemes and the Urban Aid Programme.[47] Efforts were made to reduce black youth unemployment by expanding the Youth Training Scheme, and Mr Heseltine himself was made Minister for Merseyside, but only for one year. These efforts had only a marginal effect on the huge problems caused by inner-city decline, and did little to offset the reductions in rate support grant which hit inner-city local authorities particularly hard.

The government also took action to overhaul and improve police training, to increase black recruitment into the police, and to introduce an independent element into the police complaints procedure; it also encouraged the setting-up of local consultative arrangements between the police and local communities, especially in London. Other recommendations by Lord Scarman in his report, such as the introduction into the police code of a specific offence of racially discriminatory behaviour, were resisted by the police; a long battle was to ensue before that particular recommendation was implemented, at the insistence of the House of Lords.[48]

The Home Affairs Select Committee was also active in keeping 'race' issues high on the government's agenda. It issued a series of important reports between 1980 and 1983, to which the government had to respond.[49] An interesting clash between the government and the Select Committee occurred over its report on 'race' relations and the 'Sus' law.[50] There had been mounting criticism of the way the 'Sus' law was being used disproportionately against young black people in London and other metropolitan areas.[51] They were being arrested and proceeded against for being suspected of frequenting a public place with intent to commit an arrestable offence under Section 4 of the Vagrancy Act 1824. The law had become increasingly discredited, and the Select Committee recommended its immediate repeal, partly because they regarded it as an unsatisfactory offence in English law and partly because of the harm it was doing to police–black relations. The Committee was so angry at the initial refusal of the government to act on its recommendation that it threatened to place a Bill for repeal before the House of Commons itself.[52] The police and the Home Office were against repeal, but acquiesced when the government agreed to replace 'Sus' by new legislation on 'criminal attempts', which, for example, made it an offence to interfere with a motor vehicle without the owner's consent. The 'Sus' law was repealed, and a constitutional clash between the Select Committee and the government was avoided.

Partly by chance and partly through pressure of events in the inner cities, the first Thatcher government had to give immigration and 'race' relations issues high and continuing priority. Its major 'achievement' was the new Nationality Act, which, the government felt, had 'created a secure system of rights and a sound basis for control in the future'.[53] But the inner-city riots had shown that unrelenting pressure on young black people could reach intolerable levels, and that positive measures had to be taken to counter black youth unemployment and educational failure,[54] to improve police–

black relations, and to counter racial attacks on black people.[55] Otherwise, the government risked widespread civil disorder on a massive scale.

The second Thatcher government, 1983–7

In contrast to its 1979 campaign, immigration controls were not an important part of the Conservative electoral programme in 1983. They made no new specific commitments for tightening controls, and satisfied themselves with defending their record and claiming that immigration for settlement had fallen sharply since 1979 – to its lowest level since controls were first introduced in 1962 (see table 8.1).

Table 8.1 Total acceptances for settlement, 1973–83

	1973 (000s)	1976 (000s)	1979 (000s)	1980 (000s)	1981 (000s)	1982 (000s)	1983 (000s)
New Commonwealth and Pakistan	30.3	55.1	37.2	33.7	31.4	30.4	27.5
Total	55.2	80.7	70.7	69.7	58.1	53.8	53.5

Source: Home Office, *Control of Immigration Statistics, UK*, HMSO, 1983, 1984

The Labour administration had been criticized for relaxing the rules of entry for foreign husbands in 1974, for increasing the number of vouchers of UK passport holders from East Africa, and for granting an amnesty for illegal immigrants in 1977.[56] In contrast, the Conservative government had not only increased immigration controls, but had been more active in pursuing illegal immigrants and overstayers. The Conservative message continued to be the incantation that, to have good community relations, effective immigration controls had to be maintained. The 'firm but fair' formula was constantly reiterated by government spokesmen. It could more accurately be described as firm on immigration controls, and fair to those who opposed immigration from the New Commonwealth.

It was often unfair to genuine dependants, spouses and refugees legally entitled to enter the UK, but who were refused admission or kept waiting for years so that the government could claim a reduction in the immigration statistics.[57]

The far right

The collapse of the National Front in 1979 and Mrs Thatcher's wish to win back to the Conservative party people who had been attracted to the Front bore unexpected fruit in 1983. Tom Finnegan, the Conservative candidate for Stockton South, was exposed as a past National Front candidate. Conservative ministers, notably Nigel Lawson and Sir Keith Joseph, refused to support his campaign, and all his public meetings had to be cancelled. The adverse reaction and publicity generated by the unmasking of these political antecedents caused the Conservatives to fail to win the seat. Ian Wrigglesworth held the seat for the Social Democrats by a mere 102 votes.

The concern caused by the Finnegan candidature might have died away, had it not been for the leaking of a Young Conservative draft report into right-wing infiltration into the party.[58] This argued that the electoral collapse of the far right in 1979 and the subsequent fragmentation and disillusion had had two consequences. First, individual members had left the far right and some, like Finnegan, had joined the Conservative party. Second, some right-wing groups, it was suggested, had adopted a policy of infiltrating the Conservative party. The strongest evidence of this was provided by a letter from Richard Franklin, a past member of the National Socialist Movement, of the directorate of the National Front, of the League of St George and of the National Front Constitutional Movement. Franklin had stood as a Conservative candidate in Norwich in the council elections of May 1983, but was expelled from the party when his past affiliations became known. The letter written by Franklin to another nationalist stated:

> Those of us who have chosen to work quietly through the Conservative party are not altering one iota of our basic ideology. Far from it, the new strategy merely represents a change of style. When

some of us established the National Front Constitutional Movement, it was never seriously believed by its more intelligent members that it could ever form the nucleus of an independent political party of the right. The more far-thinking nationalists saw it as a sort of 'halfway house' between the Conservative party Right and the Outside Right. Reciprocal developments within the Tory party include the formation of Tory Action, a beefed-up Monday Club, and the *Salisbury Review* 'tendency', to borrow a phrase from the Left. WISE (Welsh, Irish, Scots and English — an association of people of British stock) also provides a useful meeting point.[59]

The Young Conservative report also investigated the bridging groups, singling out Wise, Tory Action, the London Swinton Circle and the Focus Policy Study Group run by David Irving. All these groups appeared to bring together members and supporters of both the Conservative party and far-right groups. The report named a small number of Conservative MPs who, it claimed, were associated with the groups at least to the extent of attending and speaking at functions organized by them. The Monday Club, whose membership is confined to Conservative party supporters, was also examined, and the report's conclusion was that, whilst the Club was not as extreme as it had been in the early seventies, it remained an important channel for racist sentiments. The draft report recommended that the Conservative party should establish a permanent unit to monitor the whole question of infiltration and collaboration; that it should review its procedures for the approval of candidates for British and European elections; that those who had been active members of ultra-nationalist parties should not be eligible for inclusion in any list of approved candidates; that the party should disassociate itself from the building and coordinating organizations on the far right; that it should strengthen the work of the Ethnic Minorities Unit at Conservative Central Office; and that the Prime Minister should give a lead in ensuring that the climate of opinion in the party was totally hostile to racism.[60]

Conservative party leaders were furious that a section of the party had caused such public embarrassment, and they took action to limit the damage. John Selwyn Gummer, the new Chairman of the party, announced the tightening of the rules for the selection of parliamentary candidates. Action was also taken to ensure that the motion on immigration submitted by the Billericay constituency association and voted on to the conference agenda should be strenuously opposed. The motion, proposed by Harvey Proctor, MP for Billericay, was: 'This conference urges Her Majesty's Government to end all further permanent immigration from the New Commonwealth and Pakistan, to increase the financial and material provision for voluntary repatriation and resettlement, and to repeal all 'race' relations legislation so that all UK citizens are equal before the law.'[61]

The debate was marked by booing, hissing and the ejection of a man who repeatedly heckled an Asian speaker who had stood as a Conservative parliamentary candidate at the general election. Proctor said he was honoured to propose the motion, but party leaders were embarrassed by his hard line on immigration and his alleged association with far-right groups. They were concerned that if the motion was passed it would give additional credence to the Young Conservative allegations. David Waddington, the Home Secretary, argued that the policies advocated in the motion were incapable of execution and that everyone knew it full well. It would be a tragedy if they appeared to be turning their backs on the fair and just society that Conservatives stood for, and had fought for. He also reminded delegates that great numbers of immigrants had put their faith in the Conservative party at the last general election. He urged the rejection of the motion; to the relief of party managers, it was overwhelmingly rejected by delegates.[62]

The controversy over right-wing infiltration into the Conservative party was given added impetus when, on 30 January 1984, the sixth anniversary of Mrs Thatcher's 'swamping' interview, the BBC programme 'Panorama' followed up the Young Conservative allegations. Much of the programme focused the group on Tory Action, whose chairman, George Kennedy Young, was described as a racist and anti-Semite. Young had been a Conservative parliamentary candidate, but had been removed from the candidates list. Tory Action was described as a hard-line anti-immigrant organization which was said to claim the support of 24 MPs and many local activists,[63] but the evidence provided to back these claims was very scanty. A handful of MPs, including Harvey Proctor, were named, but those interviewed refused to admit

membership or categorically denied it. Some later successfully
sued the BBC for libel. The programme included an interview
with David Irving about the activities of his Focus Policy Study
Group and some shots of a meeting of WISE, including a man
selling the National Front paper.[64] In conclusion, Gummer, the
party Chairman, was interviewed. He attacked the programme for
presenting vague and ill-substantiated claims about infiltration of
which, he maintained, there was no evidence. He emphasized that
George Kennedy Young had been thrown off the candidates list
and added; 'We are a totally non-racist party and will throw
racists out of our party.'[65] As an immediate result of the programme,
Clare Short, the Labour MP for Ladywood, asked Margaret
Thatcher: 'Will the Prime Minister find time to consider the
problem she has of Fascist and racist groups operating at all levels
of her party? Will she tell the House and the black community in
Britain what action she proposes to take?' Mrs Thatcher replied:
'There is no racism in the Conservative party. We believe in equal
opportunities for all our citizens, whatever their background.'[66]

Conservative back-benchers were angry that the Young Conservatives had contributed to media attempts to discredit the
party, and furious with the BBC for broadcasting the programme.
The anger of the 1922 Committee of back-bench MPs was conveyed
to Mr Gummer, who met Mr Alistair Milne, Director-General of
the BBC, to complain about the programme. The BBC rejected
the complaints, after an internal inquiry.[67] Gummer made a strong
speech attacking the programme at the national Young Conservative
conference in February, accusing the BBC of using techniques
utterly beyond the pale of democratic politics, including smear,
innuendo and guilt by association.[68] A further inconclusive meeting
was arranged between the Director-General and three senior
Conservatives – Mr Gummer, the Government Chief Whip,
Mr John Wakeham, and Mr Edward Du Cann, the Chairman of
the 1922 Committee.

Further embarrassment was caused to the party in March when
John Pinniger, political adviser to the Monday Club, resigned,
alleging that the Club harboured racists and extremists. Mr Pinniger
was a member of the Monday Club's immigration committee, and
worked for Harvey Proctor with whom he had written a number
of pamphlets advocating a vigorous programme of resettlement

overseas of New Commonwealth immigrants, and the abolition of the CRE.[69] Mr Pinniger's resignation was followed by nine others, in what appeared to be the fall-out after a power struggle within the Monday Club.

Problems of 'racecraft'

The Young Conservative report, the 'Panorama' programme and the crisis in the Monday Club highlighted the dilemmas facing the party leadership in managing immigration and 'race' relations issues. A tough public stand on immigration controls is electorally popular, but may encourage unrealistic expectations and foster the growth of far-right groups and individuals both inside and outside the party. At the same time, the electorate favours racial equality and fair treatment for ethnic minorities.[70] There is also electoral and media opposition to candidates with far-right connections. The Conservative party thus needs to maintain both a commitment to firm immigration controls and a credible 'race' relations policy. It also needs to create electoral support among the growing number of ethnic minority voters, to reduce the political alienation of young black people in order to avoid the spontaneous unrest of the early 1980s, and to distance itself from the more bizarre and obnoxious policies of the extreme right. The anger of back-bench Conservatives over the 'Panorama' programme underlines the difficulties inherent in Mrs Thatcher's 'racecraft'.

The second wave of inner-city riots in 1985, in Handsworth, Brixton and on the Broadwater Farm estate in Tottenham, posed further 'racecraft' problems for Margaret Thatcher and her government. Should they respond to the riots as 'race' relations issues, as had been the reaction of the opposition parties, Lord Scarman and to some extent the government in the aftermath of the 1981 riots, or should the riots be defined as an issue of law and order? A 'race' relations response would require long-term investment in the inner cities, reforms in police training and recruitment, and positive initiatives to reduce unemployment. A law and order response demanded support for tough policing practices, more resources for the police in terms of new legal powers and equipment, and harsh penalties for law-breakers. Mrs Thatcher and her government felt that a liberal response had been made to the riots in 1981, additional resources had been made available to inner-city areas, and reforms in police training and policies had been made. But the liberal response had not worked and the riots had been repeated in 1985. This suggested that the riots had more to do with human wickedness than with social deprivation. Moreover, the riots had resulted in deaths as well as damage to property, and so a tough law and order response was appropriate. The government was confident in its ability to contain the riots, given its 1981 experience and its success in defeating the miners' strike. The deaths of the two Asian shopkeepers in Handsworth and the horrific murder of PC Blakelock made them confident that the media and public opinion would endorse a tough response.

The Home Secretary's initial response to the Handsworth riot set the tone: 'It was not a cry for help, but a cry for loot,' he said.[71] He turned down opposition requests for an independent judicial inquiry, arguing that this would delay prompt action and prejudice the possibility of criminal proceedings against some of the 700 people arrested.[72] The Prime Minister strongly endorsed this approach. Her immediate response was to announce that there was 'no excuse, no justification whatsoever for the riots'. In her speech to the annual party conference in October, she said:

> We utterly condemn anyone who takes part in riots in Britain. Whoever these people are who riot, burn and murder − whoever they are organized by − there is no excuse, no justification whatsoever for such crime and vandalism. Those who take to the streets on the first available pretext, to fire, loot and plunder, will be subject to the full rigours of the criminal law.[73]

Those critical of the government's response did not feel that it had effectively invested in the inner cities after 1981. Nor had it acted vigorously to combat unemployment, racial discrimination and oppressive policing. After Handsworth and Broadwater Farm, however, the government was not prepared to make even cosmetic concessions to liberal opinion. It accepted the police version of events, that the riots were caused by Afro-Caribbean youths involved in robbery, drug abuse and other crimes.[74] The government made it a priority to invest in new police equipment and riot training.

Two other issues were of growing concern, but were managed quite differently by the government. The first was a rise in the number of applications for political asylum, especially from Sri Lanka. In May 1985 there were 1,260 Tamils applying for asylum, compared with only 350 in the whole of the previous year. The Home Secretary, Leon Brittan, responded by imposing a visa requirement on visitors from Sri Lanka, to come into force with immediate effect. This was the first time a visa requirement had been imposed on a Commonwealth country. The use of visas was a well tried strategy for regulating the flow of refugees into the United Kingdom; for example, it had been used to control the number of Jewish refugees entering Britain in 1938.[75] Then, in September 1986, the government responded to a threat of industrial action by immigration staff at Heathrow Airport, who claimed they could not cope with the volume of passengers, by imposing visa requirements on the major countries from which immigrants were arriving. These were India, Pakistan, Nigeria, Ghana and Bangladesh. A statement issued by the Home Office said that visas would be required, to 'relieve the pressures on the immigration control which have caused unacceptable delays to passengers'. The change had become necessary, 'to maintain the effectiveness of immigration control in the face of pressures upon it.'[76] The introduction of visas for the Indian subcontinent was accompanied by chaos at Heathrow on 15 October, as there was a sudden increase in visitors wanting to enter before the new requirements came into force. The opposition claimed that the influx was due to government incompetence, while the Home Secretary claimed it justified the imposition of the visa requirement. He argued that the number of people in the Third World who were seeking better prospects was large and growing.[77] The tabloid press publicized the chaos, blaming it on the flood of immigrants and supporting the government's decision. There was considerable emphasis on the problem of illegal immigration and the drain on public expenditure in having to accommodate the new arrivals. The tabloid press have consistently been willing participants in stereotyping immigrants and in pandering to the assumed prejudices of their readers.

The government kept up the pressure to control Third World immigration and reduce asylum applications. In 1987 the Immigration (Carrier's Liability) Act was passed, making it an offence for airlines or shipping companies to bring people to the UK without proper documents, and requiring these companies to enforce the immigration laws and visa regulations or face a fine of £1,000 per passenger. This was to prove an increasingly onerous burden, particularly on airlines.

The second issue of growing concern both to the ethnic minority community and to the government was the increasing and extensive problem of racial violence. The alarming number of racist murders during the 1980s were just the most appalling outrages among a huge number of acts of racial violence and harassment. This anti-immigrant behaviour was encouraged by the anti-immigration pronouncements of some politicians as well as by headlines and stereotypes that regularly appeared in the tabloid press, but it was also due to the switch in tactics of far-right groups. After the electoral setbacks of the far right in 1979 and subsequent elections, many of these groups turned to direct violence against blacks instead of trying to pursue an electoral strategy. The government's policy in dealing with racial violence was to delegate it to the Home Office, the police and local authorities to deal with. It was defined as part and parcel of the general area of law and order. Home Office research and pressure from the Select Committee was successful in making the Home Secretary demand that the police give higher priority to combating racial violence.

The third Thatcher government, 1987–90

In May 1987 the Conservative party published, together with their manifesto, a booklet entitled *Our First Eight Years: The Achievements of the Conservative Government since May 1979*. By far the shortest entry was headed 'Better race relations'; it stated: 'Firm but fair immigration controls have been applied in the interests of harmonious race relations. Last year fewer people were accepted for settlement in the United Kingdom than at any time since the control of Commonwealth immigration began in 1962.'[78] The Conservative manifesto made it clear that immigration control and tackling the problem of 'fraudulent' refugees were the government's chief priorities. It promised that the existing law would be tightened to ensure that control over settlement became even more effective. The manifesto condemned racial discrimination and racial attacks as injustices, and emphasized the wish of the party to see ethnic minorities participating fully in British culture. Reverse discrimination, however, was condemned as an injustice undermining the achievements of those who had succeeded on their own merits.[79]

One of the first acts of the new government was to introduce yet another immigration Bill. This was described by Douglas Hurd, the Home Secretary, as 'keeping immigration control in good repair',[80] but it appeared to be yet another attempt to reduce New Commonwealth immigration and to fulfil Mrs Thatcher's promise to bring immigration to an end. However, legislation had already been so extensive and draconian that only by withdrawing rights of dependants to enter the UK could a significant impact be made on the immigration statistics. The Bill repealed the absolute right of men settled in Britain before 1 January 1973 to be joined by their families. The European Court of Human Rights had ruled that this discriminated against women, and the government had chosen to comply with the ruling by abolishing the right for men rather than extending it to women. The right now became conditional on showing that dependants seeking entry to the UK would be provided with adequate accommodation and financial support, and thus would not seek resort to public funds. The Bill restricted rights of appeal against refusal of entry, and also against deportation where the appeal was based on compassionate grounds. It made overstaying a continuing criminal offence, and prohibited the entry of second or subsequent wives in a polygamous marriage. This latter measure appears to have been more an attempt to preserve the 'British character' than to close an immigration loophole, as only 25 people were admitted under this provision in 1985. Mr Hurd apparently confirmed this in debate, when he stated: 'Polygamy is not an acceptable social custom in this country.'[81] The opposition view was that this was a harsh, mean-minded Bill, even contrary to the European Convention on Human Rights, as it undermined the right to family life. It was perfectly consistent, however, with Mrs Thatcher's stated aims and those of her government to limit New Commonwealth immigration as much as possible.

The Hong Kong crisis

The government's and opposition's policies on immigration were put to the test by the agreement in September 1984 on the transfer of Hong Kong back to the People's Republic of China when the leases to most of the territory expire in 1997.[82] As mentioned earlier, under the British Nationality Act 1981 about half of Hong Kong's population are citizens of the British Dependent Territories and the remainder are Chinese citizens. Those with BDT citizenship who are of Chinese ethnic origin are regarded by China as Chinese citizens; BDT citizenship does not entitle the holder to immigrate to and settle in the UK. In addition to the resident population, Hong Kong also contains thousands of Vietnamese refugees held in camps. Some 10,000 of these were allowed to settle in Britain in 1981, but since then the government has been trying to persuade them to return to Vietnam.

The prospect of Hong Kong's incorporation into the People's Republic has created considerable nervousness in the colony and substantial emigration of professional people. By 1987 a campaign had been launched to grant BDT citizens full citizen rights, including right of abode in Britain, in case relations with China should deteriorate. The suppression of the pro-democracy reform movement in China has greatly increased insecurity in Hong Kong, and added to the pressures to emigrate before the Chinese take-over. However, neither the government, the opposition nor the Foreign Affairs Select Committee were prepared to recommend that BDT passport-holders should be allowed the right of abode in the UK. The Foreign Secretary, Sir Geoffrey Howe, argued that the assessment made by the Select Committee and many other members of the House of Commons rested on the sheer scale of the numbers involved, which could be between 3 and 5 million people.[83] In marked contrast to the British position, the Portuguese government granted full citizenship, with the right of abode in Portugal and therefore anywhere in the European Community, to the people in its colony of Macao.

The Foreign Secretary's announcement on 20 December, that the government would grant full British citizenship to 50,000 people and their dependants, to a maximum of 225,000, provoked a storm of protest within the Conservative party, led by Norman Tebbit. He argued that the concession to Hong Kong broke the manifesto pledges made by the Conservatives in the 1980s not to allow any further large-scale immigration. He was supported by a significant body of Conservative back-benchers. Mr Tebbit ran a vigorous populist campaign in the press and on television, reminiscent of Enoch Powell's anti-immigration campaign in the late 1960s. He warned of ethnic tensions and civil strife if the legislation was passed, argued that it would be electorally damaging for the Conservatives, and called for a referendum. Tebbit and eighty other Conservative MPs signed a letter stating that they would not support the legislation. Mrs Thatcher defended it, maintaining that it was not a large-scale immigration but a strictly limited concession, needed to preserve stability and prosperity in Britain's last colony.

The day before the debate on the second reading of the British Nationality (Hong Kong) Bill, Mr Tebbit provoked a furious debate among politicians and in the media when he proposed a 'cricket test' of loyalty for ethnic minorities in Britain: namely, 'Which side do they cheer for?' This would show, he argued, whether immigrants were committed to their country of origin or to the country where they live and are making their name. Most press comment, as well as responses from Conservative MP colleagues, were highly critical of his statement. It was widely felt that he had reduced his standing in the party.

Despite the threats of rebellion from the back benches, the government stood firm, and were assisted in this by the divisions within the opposition. The Labour opposition's official position was to oppose the Bill, but many labour MPs could not face the prospect of voting with Mr Tebbit and the right-wing Conservative against the Bill. The government had a majority of 97 on the second reading on 19 April: the vote was 313 to 216. The revolt threatened by Conservative MPs was less than expected, with 44 voting against the government and a further two dozen abstaining. Fifty-four labour MPs abstained and one, Mr Andrew Faulds, supported the government as did the Liberal Democrats and the Nationalists.

Mrs Thatcher's legacy

The major priorities of Mrs Thatcher's 'racecraft' were concerned with alleviating what she saw as popular anxieties about immigration, and increasing electoral support for the Conservatives by pursuing populist policies and protecting British culture and traditions. All of these were predicated on a reduction in New Commonwealth immigration. The considerable time, energy and resources spent on devising and implementing new immigration controls only brought about a modest fall in New Commonwealth immigration, but the political gains may have been greater. Certainly the tabloid press were, on the whole, only too eager to exploit racist themes and avidly supported every tough measure the government proposed.

There were elements of liberal pragmatism in government policies, as well. The decisions to admit the Vietnamese refugees from Hong Kong in 1981, to inject resources into the inner cities after the riots and to allow the Commission for Racial Equality to continue its modest efforts against racial discrimination are evidence of this. Mrs Thatcher was also more willing to compromise over extending full British citizenship to key personnel in Hong Kong than the Labour opposition front bench. She was, however, firmly opposed to positive action to aid integration or encourage multicultural diversity. The introduction, for example, of the Education Reform Act with its provisions for a national curriculum indicated that the government wished to integrate the minority ethnic communities into the majority culture.[84]

One major legacy of Mrs Thatcher's tough anti-immigration stance was the political annihilation of the National Front in 1979. The continuing efforts of her administration to maintain stringent immigration controls and reassure public opinion that the government was successfully managing the issue may well have prevented the rise of the kind of anti-immigrant parties that have been so prominent in other West European countries in the 1980s and early 1990s.

Notes

1   Z. Layton–Henry, 'Race, electoral strategy and the major parties', *Parliamentary Affairs*, vol. 31, no. 3 (1978), 268–81.

2 J. Casey, 'One nation: the politics of race', *Salisbury Review*, no. 1 (Autumn 1982), 23−8.
3 E. Heath, letter to the Bexley Community Relations Council, June 1970.
4 T. Russel, *The Tory Party: Its Policies, Divisions and Future* (Penguin Books, 1978), p. 119.
5 Z. Layton−Henry, *The Politics of Race in Britain* (Allen & Unwin, 1984), p. 98.
6 Ibid., p. 99
7 *The Right Approach: A Statement of Conservative Aims*, Conservative Central Office, October 1976, pp. 47−8.
8 Parliamentary Debates, Commons (Hansard), vol. 914, cols 985−6, 5 July 1976.
9 Speech made by Rt Hon. William Whitelaw, Conservative party conference, Brighton, 5 October 1976.
10 Ibid.
11 The National Union of Conservative and Unionist Associations is the part of the Conservative party which organizes the voluntary party membership.
12 Statement by the RT Hon. Lord Thorneycroft, 19 January 1978.
13 Verbatim report of part of an interview with Gordon Burns, given by Mrs Thatcher on Monday 30 January 1978. Extract by courtesy of 'World in Action', Granada Television.
14 Ibid.
15 National Opinion Polls, February 1978.
16 Russel, *Tory Party*, p. 117.
17 Ibid., pp. 117−18.
18 National Opinion Polls, *Race and Immigration*, February 1978.
19 *The Times*, 14 February 1978.
20 Extract of a speech by Rt Hon. William Whitelaw, replying to the debate on immigration and race relations at the Central Council annual meeting, Leicester, 7 April 1978.
21 Conservative Central Office, *Conservative Party Manifesto*, April 1979.
22 Z. Layton−Henry, *Politics of Race*, pp. 105−6.
23 See pp. 147−53.
24 On 27 June 1974 Mr Roy Jenkins, Home Secretary, relaxed the rules of entry to allow foreign husbands automatic entry to the UK. In 1973 the number of foreign husbands entering the UK was 2,400, and in 1976 it was 11,061. The proportion of new Commonwealth husbands rose from 5% in 1973 to 57% in 1976. The number of fiancés accepted for settlement was 1,010 in 1975 and 2,190 in 1976, almost all from India and Pakistan. On 22 March 1977 immediate settlement ceased to be granted automatically.
25 *Home Office, Proposals for Revision of the Immigration Rules*, Cmnd 7750, HMSO, 1979.
26 Parliamentary Debates, Commons (Hansard), vol. 974, cols 265−6,

4 December 1979.

27   Ibid.

28   Home Office, *British Nationality Law: Discussion of Possible Changes*, Cmnd 6795, HMSO, April 1977.

29   Conservative Political Centre, *Who Do We Think We Are?* March 1980.

30   Home Office, *British Nationality Law: Discussion of Possible Changes.*

31   Home Office, *British Nationality Law: Outline of Proposed Legislation*, Cmnd 7987, HMSO, July 1980.

32   Home Office, *British Nationality Bill*, Session 1980–1, HMSO, 13 January 1981.

33   Parliamentary Debates, Commons (Hansard), vol. 31, col. 697, 11 November 1982.

34   Home Office, *British Nationality Law: Outline of Proposed Legislation.*

35   Parliamentary Debates, Commons (Hansard), vol. 997, cols 931–41, 28 January 1981.

36   *Guardian*, 5 February 1981.

37   Commonwealth citizens entitled to automatic registration as British citizens had to exercise this right by 31 December 1987; otherwise, they would have to apply for naturalization on the same basis as aliens.

38   House of Commons, *British Nationality Fees*, third report from the Home Affairs Committee, Session 1982–3, HMSO, 1984.

39   Home Office, government reply to the third report from the Home Affairs Committee, Session 1982–3, *British Nationality Fees*, HMSO, 1984.

40   House of Commons, *Administrative Delays in the Immigration and Nationality Department*, fifth report of the Home Affairs Committee, Session 1989–90, HMSO, June 1990.

41   Parliamentary Debates (Hansard), vol. 31, cols 692–9, 11 November 1982.

42   *Guardian*, 11 November 1982.

43   J. Bulpitt, 'Continuity, autonomy and peripheralization: the anatomy of the centre's race statecraft in England', in Z. Layton–Henry and P. B. Rich (eds), *Race, Government and Politics in Britain* (Macmillan, 1986).

44   The term 'racecraft' is used to describe the strategy and policies of Mrs Thatcher and her administrations in the areas of immigration and race relations.

45   J. Solomos, *Race and Racism in Contemporary Britain* (Macmillan, 1989).

46   P. Lindley, 'The Merseyside task force', paper presented at the annual conference of the Political Studies Association, Oxford, August 1983.

47   D. Wallser, 'Defusing the time bombs in Britain's inner cities', *The Times*, 14 May 1985.

48 See pp. 174–8.
49 The race and immigration subcommittee of the Home Affairs Select Committee, House of Commons, published a series of reports between 1980 and 1983. They included the second report from the Home Affairs Committee, *Race Relations and the 'Sus' Law*, Session 1979–80, HMSO, April 1980 and August 1980; the fifth report from the Home Affairs Committee, *Racial Disadvantage*, Session 1980–81, HMSO, August 1981 (Commission for Racial Equality, 1981).
50 House of Commons, *Race Relations and the 'Sus' Law*, 2nd report, April 1980.
51 J. Benyon, 'Spiral of decline: race and policing', in Z. Layton–Henry and P. B. Rich, *Race, Government and Politics in Britain* (Macmillan, 1986).
52 House of Commons, *Race Relations and the 'Sus' Law*, fourth report from the Home Affairs Committee, Session 1979–80, 5 August 1980.
53 *Conservative Party Manifesto*, 1983, p. 35.
54 The educational performance of ethnic minority children was being examined by a committee under Anthony Rampton. He was replaced by Lord Swann in 1981. Its interim report, *West Indian Children in Our Schools*, was published in June 1981. The full report, *Education for All*, was published in 1985.
55 Home Office, *Racial Attacks*, report of a Home Office study, HMSO, November 1981.
56 An amnesty was announced by Roy Jenkins, the Home Secretary, on 29 November 1977 for Commonwealth and Pakistani citizens who had entered illegally before 1 January 1973. By 1980 some 2,390 people had had their position regularized.
57 A Home Office document leaked in March 1985 revealed that queues were used as a means of controlling immigration from the Indian subcontinent: *Guardian* 21 March 1985.
58 The leaked report was widely circulated but not published. It was called 'Draft report of the committee of inquiry on infiltration by the extreme right into the Conservative party and the level of collaboration with the right wing of the Conservative party', Young Conservative Organization, September 1983. Detailed accounts appeared in *The Times*, 10 October 1983 and *Searchlight*, no. 101 (November 1983), p. 11. An abridged version was circulated by Conservative Central Office in February 1984.
59 *Searchlight*, no. 101 (November 1983), p. 11.
60 Young Conservative Organization, 'Draft report', ch. 7, paras 62–74.
61 Conservative Central Office, agenda of the 100th Conservative conference, 1983, p. 80.
62 *The Times*, 14 October 1983.

63   BBC 'Panorama', 30 January 1984.
64   Ibid.
65   Ibid.
66   Parliamentary Debates, Commons (Hansard), vol. 53, col. 401, 2 February 1984.
67   *Guardian*, 17 February 1984.
68   Ibid., 13 February 1984.
69   H. Proctor and J. Pinniger, *Immigration, Repatriation and the Commission for Racial Equality*, Monday Club, April 1981.
70   For an interesting discussion of electoral attitudes, see I. Crewe and B. Särlvik, 'Popular attitudes and electoral strategy', in Z. Layton—Henry (ed.), *Conservative Party Politics* (Macmillan, 1980).
71   *Guardian*, 13 September 1985.
72   Parliamentary Debates, Commons (Hansard), vol. 84, col. 357, 23 October 1985.
73   *Financial Times*, 12 October 1985.
74   Report of the Chief Constable, West Midlands Police, *Handsworth/Lozells: September 1985*, November 1985.
75   A. J. Sherman, *Island Refuge: Britain and Refugees from the Third Reich 1933—39* (Paul Elek, 1973).
76   *Runnymede Trust Bulletin*, no. 196 (October 1986), p. 2.
77   Home Office, *Immigration and Nationality Department Report*, 1986, HMSO, 1986.
78   Conservative Central Office, *Our First Eight Years: The Achievements of the Conservative Government since May 1979*, May 1987.
79   Conservative Central Office, *The Next Moves Forward: Conservative Party Manifesto*, May 1987.
80   Parliamentary Debates, Commons (Hansard), vol. 122, col. 779, 16 November 1987.
81   Ibid., col. 785, 16 November 1987.
82   The Hong Kong crisis from the Labour party's perspective is discussed in ch. 7.
83   Sir Geoffrey Howe, statement on visit to Hong Kong, Hansard, col. 320, 5 July 1989.
84   *Education Reform Act 1988*, HMSO, ch. 40, 1988.

9 The European context

The experience of Britain in recruiting migrant workers from neighbouring countries such as Ireland and from colonial and post-colonial countries in the Caribbean, Africa and the Indian subcontinent has been by no means unique. All the advanced industrial countries of Western Europe have experienced similar processes of labour recruitment and immigration. This has held true despite their different migration histories. Traditional countries of emigration such as Belgium, Britain and Germany have been as much affected as countries like France with a long tradition of encouraging immigration in order to augment its labour force and population.

In most European countries, however, immigration from the Third World started later than in the British case, occurring mainly in the 1960s and 1970s. This was partly because it took longer for the shattered economies of mainland Europe to recover from the war, and partly because there was a considerable amount of intra-European migration. The Federal Republic of Germany, for example, had to absorb some nine million ethnic Germans seeking refuge or expelled from East European countries as a consequence of the post-war settlement, then a further three million Germans who left the German Democratic Republic between 1948 and 1961, when the building of the Berlin Wall prevented further emigration. As the post-war German economic 'miracle' proceeded in the 1960s, these people were all integrated into the economy, and additional workers were recruited from neighbouring countries such as Italy, Spain, Yugoslavia, Greece and Turkey.

In France, neighbouring countries such as Italy, Spain and

Portugal were the first to be targeted for labour recruitment, and then Algeria, Tunisia, Morocco and the countries of former French West Africa. The Netherlands initially accepted people who left or fled from the former Dutch East Indies when Indonesia became independent in December 1949; later, migrant workers came from Surinam, the Dutch Antilles, North Africa and Turkey. Large numbers of Finnish workers migrated to Sweden, to be followed by Yugoslavs, Greeks, Moroccans and Turks. In contrast to the many labour sources of most European countries, Switzerland relied almost wholly on Italian workers, though in recent years it has accepted refugees from a large number of countries. France, Germany and Britain attracted three quarters of all the migrant workers who came to Europe in the post-war period. After the economic recession in the mid-1970s most European countries halted labour recruitment, but migration continued at a high level as the wives and children of many former migrants joined their husbands and fathers in Western Europe. In the 1990s labour recruitment has resumed on a smaller scale − with one significant change: some of the countries on the European periphery which were labour exporters have now become importers, as North Africans in particular are migrating to Italy, Spain, Portugal and Greece.

By 1989 it was estimated that the seven major labour-recruiting countries of mainland Europe − namely, Belgium, France, Germany, the Netherlands, Sweden, Switzerland and the United Kingdom − had over 6.2 million foreign workers and over 14 million foreign residents, as table 9.1 shows. The figures in table 9.1 underestimate the numbers of immigrants to the European industrial countries, as many migrants to Britain, France and the Netherlands came from colonies and so had British, French or Dutch citizenship and were not counted as foreigners. Many others, in the post-war period, have become naturalized citizens of their countries of work and residence. The table also excludes the smaller but significant numbers of foreign workers in such countries as Austria, Italy, Luxembourg and Denmark.

One interesting contrast between Britain and the other major recruiting countries like France and Germany has been the lack of government planning and involvement in the recruitment process. The French had a long tradition of concern about their population

Table 9.1 Foreign workers and foreign populations of selected European countries, 1989

	Foreign workers (000s)	% labour force	Foreign population (000s)	% total population
Belgium	412[a]	9.8	881	8.9
France	1,594	6.6	3,752[b]	6.7
Germany	1,941	6.5	4,846	7.9
Netherlands	192	2.9	642	4.4
Sweden	237	5.2	456	5.4
Switzerland	632	17.9	1,040	16.0
UK[c]	1,263	4.5	2,409	4.2

[a] 1987
[b] 1985
[c] 1986–8
Source: OECD, *Continuous Reporting System on Migration (Sopemi)*, Paris, 1991; *British Labour Force Surveys*, 1986–8, HMSO

size and about the need for immigrants to compensate for France's low birth-rate and the enormous losses of the First World War. These concerns led to policies to increase the birth-rate, which were generally unsuccessful, and policies to encourage immigration, which were more successful. In the 1920s, for example, there were labour contracts with Italy and Poland. Labour recruitment ceased in the 1930s because of the recession, and then resumed again after the Second World War. In France and Germany, government and employers cooperated in the recruitment of young, healthy and relatively skilled workers. Both governments signed bilateral labour recruitment treaties with a large number of countries, and established recruitment agencies abroad. The French government signed 13 such agreements between 1946 and 1965.[1] In addition, the French government tolerated a huge amount of illegal immigration, partly because official recruitment agencies could not cope with the demand for labour and partly because illegal workers provided a cheap, insecure and cooperative labour force, from whom greater surplus value could be extracted for the French economy. There also existed in France the tradition of relying on internal rather than border controls as the means to regulate the foreign population.

The more urgent need for immigrants gave French politicians and employers, and even the general public, a greater appreciation than their British counterparts of the economic value and positive effects of immigrant labour. In the 1960s and 1970s French politicians stressed the contribution of immigrants to the French economy, to the standard of living, and to economic growth. For example, President Giscard d'Estaing said: 'Immigrant workers, being part of our national productive community, should have a place in French society which is dignified, humane and equitable.'[2] The rapid economic growth of the French economy in the 1960s and the leadership of politicians reduced anti-immigrant resentment, until the economic recession of the mid-1970s caused anti-immigrant prejudice to rise sharply. This prejudice was fostered and exploited by the French National Front which emerged as a significant force in French politics in the 1980s.

In many European countries it was assumed that post-war migration was a temporary form of labour migration, albeit on a substantial scale. The decision to migrate was viewed as a kind of economic agreement between the migrants and the receiving society. Migrant workers were seen as freely choosing to move from their own countries to Britain, Germany, France and other West European countries, where, in return for employment and wages, they worked in jobs rejected by native workers and so contributed to the receiving country's economy and economic growth, while at the same time raising their own standard of living and opportunities above those that would have been available in their country of origin. Thus, both sides were assumed to gain from this exchange, though it was clearly an unequal one and, in the case of illegal workers, extremely exploitative. However, it was widely assumed (though not by British policy-makers) that if the economic gains to the migrants were reduced or ceased altogether − for example, through unemployment − they would return to their home countries. The logic of this argument was that the receiving countries saw themselves as owing little, if anything, to the migrants. They chose to come freely, and if their expectations of work, income and savings failed to materialize, it was taken for granted that they would, and should, return home. In times of recession, therefore, policies to encourage repatriation would be both justified and successful.

These assumptions have proved to be false, although some governments have attempted to act as though they were tenable. In spite of the economic recession after 1973, which caused high unemployment among migrant workers, and despite the efforts of West European governments to halt labour recruitment and encourage repatriation, migrant workers have not only remained but have sent for their wives and children, have bought houses, and are showing every sign of settling as permanent members of their new countries. As, despite the end of the post-war European economic boom and the ending of labour recruitment, the numbers of foreign residents continue to rise, many European countries have attempted to impose strict immigration controls. The move towards a free internal market for labour and goods in the European Community and the wish of most European countries to join the Community has encouraged moves towards stricter immigration controls throughout Europe, among both Community and non-Community members. The dramatic rise in applications for political asylum since the mid-1980s, which has affected all West European countries, has had a similar effect as have the upheavals in Eastern Europe, which have caused all West European countries to fear large-scale Russian, Rumanian, Polish and Yugoslav immigration.

The move towards stricter immigration controls has made it more difficult for foreign migrant workers to risk returning to their home countries, as the opportunity to re-migrate to Europe might be lost. In any event, for most Third World migrants the attraction of returning to their home countries is very low, as these countries face a combination of economic stagnation and rapid population increase. Migrant workers can often earn more in manual jobs in Europe than they could earn in professional employment in the Third World. And their chances of finding secure employment if they return, even with new skills, are poor. Also, some Third World countries are ruled by repressive regimes and are subject to internal wars, which act as major deterrants to returning. The large majority of migrant workers in Europe thus have little choice but to remain. Furthermore, the moves towards European union, including common immigration policies, make it advantageous to remain in the Community until it is clear what the rights of immigrant workers are, including rights of entry and settlement.

Migrant workers have made a major contribution to the economies of West European countries, especially to the manufacturing and construction industries, public transport, the health services and agriculture. They have offset to some extent the adverse demographic trends that are affecting all of Europe, such as ageing populations which are failing to replace themselves and are thus incurring the damaging economic prospect of contracting labour forces. Immigrants are thus an increasingly valuable resource for West European countries, and are contributing more in work, taxes and other contributions than they receive in benefits. Large-scale immigration has also transformed the societies of West European states, with the creation of more heterogeneous populations. Associated with this has been a rise in racism and racial violence, as extremist groups have campaigned against immigrants and attempted to mobilize xenophobic and racist sentiments against them. There has also been a challenge to notions of citizenship and democracy, as long-term resident migrant workers and even their children have often been reluctant to naturalize, or have found it difficult to do so, and so are denied many political rights, particularly the right to vote in local or national elections.[3]

Multiracial Europe

One of the most striking features of post-war migration has been the diversity of the areas from which the migrants have come. West Indians, Indians, Pakistanis and Bangladeshis have been the major groups from outside the British Isles migrating to Britain, but there have been many West Africans and Latin Americans too. France and Germany have recruited people predominantly from the Mediterranean countries, but migrants have also come from Afghanistan, Vietnam, Eritrea, West Africa, the Philippines and other countries of Latin America, Africa and Asia, often as refugees and in sizeable numbers. An extensive network of immigrant associations, churches, mosques, temples, schools, cinemas, restaurants, cafés and clubs has been established, that fosters national consciousness, family ties and cultural links across countries. This often tends to encourage the unrealistic belief that migration is temporary and that return can easily be achieved. The governments of the sending countries often have a strong desire to encourage such beliefs, because they gain from the transmission of remittances and savings. They may also wish to retain the affection and allegiance of their citizens and future citizens.

Labour-exporting countries thus often subsidize immigrant associations and schools in the receiving countries, to strengthen national ties and consciousness among their overseas citizens and their children. Yugoslavia is a good example of a sending country that has pursued such policies, even sending teachers abroad so that the children of its overseas citizens could learn the language, traditions and culture of their parents' country. However, the divisions among the expatriate Yugoslav community, reflecting the divisions in the home country, limited the effectiveness of such policies. Many Yugoslav emigrants were recruited into political groups opposed to the Communist government of Yugoslavia and in favour of independence for Croatia and Slovenia. The recognition of Croatia and Slovenia as independent states by the European Community suggests that their aspirations may have been achieved.

The growth of a second and, in some countries, a third generation descended from immigrant workers has confronted policy-makers with the reality of settlement and the need to ensure that these young people are integrated and treated equally with their contemporaries. There are large numbers of such people in Western Europe. In West Germany in 1973 it was estimated that there were 640,000 foreign children under 16 years, and by 1983, largely as a result of family reunion, the figure had risen to 1.1 million.[4] In 1986, births to foreign parents were 11.3% of all births in Germany.[5] In France it was estimated that between 1946 and 1982 1.4 million children were born to parents both of whom were of foreign nationality, and a further 700,000 children who had one foreign parent. In 1986 some 10.4% of births were to foreign parents.[6] In Britain by 1985 over one million children had been born to ethnic minority immigrant parents.

The education of immigrant-descended children raises a number of acute policy dilemmas for decision-makers in the West European receiving countries. Should these children be educated on the assumption that they will remain in the receiving country, as is most likely, or on the assumption that they should be given the choice of returning to their parents' country if they wish? Should parents be allowed to request that their children be educated in their mother tongue, as is the case in Sweden and France, or should the children receive the normal education provided for all, in order to give them the best chance to compete for qualifications with their peers? How far can minority cultures, languages and values be recognized, respected and incorporated into national educational systems which place a high priority on transmitting a common core of beliefs and values such as patriotism and democracy? Will national cohesion be undermined if monocultural education gives way to multicultural education?

These dilemmas have been particularly acute in Germany, where the regional *Länder* or state governments have adopted three different strategies for teaching foreign children:

1 the integration of foreign children into the German educational system, by putting them straight into normal German classes;
2 the establishment of classes or schools based on nationality, with the aim of preparing the foreign children for return to their parents' country;
3 preparing the children simultaneously for integration into German society or return to their parents' country, with the aim of giving them a real choice. This strategy leads to the establishment of long-term preparatory classes.

Whichever strategy is adopted, there is a real danger that the children will not be adequately prepared for either their country of residence or their parents' country. Moreover, many of these children will have a crisis of identity, not knowing whether to accept their parents' values and national identity or those of the society in which they have grown up.[7] Interestingly, British, Swiss and German studies show that foreign or ethnic minority parents have high educational and occupational aspirations for their children, which the latter accept. A study in West Germany found that 45% of Turkish and 17% of Yugoslav children wanted to become doctors, teachers or engineers.[8] These aspirations are unrealistic to the extent that only a small percentage of working-class children achieve significant upward social mobility, but they counteract the myth that immigrant parents are not interested in their children's educational or occupational success.

The harsh reality in Europe, though, is that the majority of foreign and ethnic minority children are failing in the educational systems. In a survey in 1975 by Wilpert only 46% of young foreign men between 15 and 24 who had received their education in West Germany left with any kind of graduation certificate. Young male foreigners were concentrated in a few sectors of the labour market such as vehicle manufacture, construction, sanitation and personal services.[9] Wilpert also found that most young Turks and Yugoslavs wished to return and work in their parents' country. They felt discriminated against in Germany, and believed they would be better off in Turkey or Yugoslavia.[10] As has already been argued, however, such aspirations are unrealistic for most of these young people.

Similar problems exist for young foreigners in France. They are trapped in unskilled and semi-skilled jobs because of poor educational qualifications, poor knowledge of the French language, lack of vocational training and discrimination, especially in the labour market. French studies suggest that 60% of foreign children enter the same occupation as their parents, and 68% claim to have experienced racism. Among young Algerians, 75% claim to have experienced racism.[11] The children of foreign parents in France are members of French society and, in contrast to the German study, 60% wish to remain in France; but they feel rejected by French society and, perhaps because of this, only 20% make a positive decision to opt for French nationality – though, under the double *jus soli* provisions of the French nationality code, most receive it automatically.[12] These provisions are that if a child born in France has a French-born parent, then (s)he is automatically entitled to French citizenship at the age of majority if (s)he has spent the previous five years in France.[13]

Swedish experience suggests there is strong support among foreign parents for mother-tongue education: but special circumstances may encourage this, such as the close proximity of Finland, the major sending country, to Sweden and the absence of travel restrictions between members of the Nordic Union. In general, mother-tongue education is unrealistic and unsuccessful. The children of immigrant parents rapidly acquire the language of their country of residence, and are often less comfortable and successful in their parents' mother tongue. In Britain there is considerable concern over the lack of educational success by ethnic minorities, especially Afro-Caribbean children. There is growing pressure to reform the curriculum and allow experiments in mother-tongue education for children from the Asian communities, but developments such as the introduction of a national curriculum in the Educational Reform Act (1988) suggest that these initiatives have been unsuccessful and that the government is giving priority to the integration of the minority ethnic communities. As mentioned earlier, there is some support among Muslim groups for the introduction of Muslim schools, especially for girls, within the national educational system, but there is no consensus about the best education strategy for ethnic minority children among either educationalists or parents.[14]

Racism in Europe

As in Britain, there was little popular hostility to immigration on mainland Europe in the early period of post-war immigration. Few people appreciated that a major consequence of the long economic boom in Europe would be massive world-wide immigration. Both governments and employers encouraged immigration with an eye to the economic advantages, but gave little thought to the social and cultural consequences. These included the growth of racist attitudes among many people who were resentful about the changes in their neighbourhoods and fearful of competition for jobs and houses. More specifically European racism towards Third World peoples is a legacy of imperialism and of the enslavement and exploitation of African and Asian people in the eighteenth and nineteenth centuries. More recently, the racist theories of the Nazis, and their attempts to exterminate the Jews for reasons of 'racial purity', have left in post-war Europe and around the world a legacy of abhorrence of explicit manifestations of racism and racist ideas.

Switzerland has been more dependent on foreign labour in the post-war period than any other European country. However, despite the fact that the Swiss have not recruited non-Europeans, this has not prevented them from manifesting acute xenophobia from time to time. The labour treaty signed with Italy in 1948 began a period of massive labour recruitment, so that by 1960 there were 585,000 resident foreigners, representing 16.8% of the workforce and 10.8% of the total population. Family reunion and settlement were allowed in the 1960s, and the foreign population rose significantly. By 1987 this had risen to nearly a million foreign residents – some 15.1% of the population and 17.3% of the workforce. Opposition to foreign immigration grew in the 1960s, and in May 1969 the National Action against the Over-foreignization of People and Homeland, led by James Schwarzenbach, submitted an initiative demanding that the proportion of foreigners be reduced to 10% in four years. Despite the opposition of the political parties, employers' organizations, trade unions and Churches, this initiative was only narrowly defeated in the popular referendum.[15] The Swiss government responded to popular anxiety by introducing stricter controls, which went some way towards alleviating it. Five further proposals for reducing 'over-foreignization' were all defeated. Swiss government policy has been to create two categories of foreign worker – permanent residents who have a relatively secure and privileged position, and seasonal or temporary workers who are subject to strict controls. Two further proposals, in the early 1980s, for improving the position of foreigners in Switzerland were defeated. Naturalization procedures are very strict, and applications must be approved by the local communal and cantonal authorities as well as at the national level.

In Germany the legacy of Nazism has inhibited overt support for the extreme right and constrained anti-immigrant activity, but a right-wing party, the National Demokratische Partei Deutschlands (NPD), gained substantial support in the mid-1960s when it expanded its conventional far-right appeal to include hostility to foreign workers.[16] In the mid-1970s and the 1980s the growth of unemployment and the immigration of wives and children, which rose substantially after the halt in labour recruitment in the mid-1970s, caused a resurgence of hostility to foreigners, especially Turks. In 1982 opinion polls were reporting that 82% of West Germans thought that there were too many foreigners in the country.[17] An opinion poll in September 1989 found that 75% of West Germans felt there were too many foreigners in the Federal Republic, 69% agreed that asylum-seekers were unfairly exploiting the social welfare system, and 98% favoured reducing the number of so-called 'economic refugees'.[18] In the 1980s there was a sharp rise in violence and terrorism against immigrants, especially Turks. There had also been a sharp rise in asylum applications to West Germany, after the halt in labour recruitment in the mid-1970s and because of Germany's liberal asylum laws. This led to considerable popular resentment, as many of the refugees were from labour-exporting countries like Turkey. Most Germans felt that the asylum-seekers were in reality economic migrants trying to circumvent immigration controls.

The Conservative–Liberal coalition government which came to power in 1982 under Chancellor Helmut Kohl committed itself to reducing substantially the foreign population of Germany by maintaining strict immigration controls, encouraging voluntary repatriation and stimulating the naturalization of foreigners who had worked in the Federal Republic for over ten years. However, the refusal of many German politicians to accept that Germany is an immigration country, and the decision not to liberalize the naturalization laws in 1985 – partly at Turkey's request – suggest an emphasis on repatriation rather than on integration. Many foreign workers feel they would not be accepted as equal German citizens, and so do not apply for naturalization even though they meet all the stringent conditions.

The reunification of Germany, the collapse of the Soviet empire in Eastern Europe and the mounting economic problems of what was the Soviet Union have raised the possibility of a massive migration of Russians and other Eastern Europeans to Germany. Already before unification there was growing resentment, even against the immigration of ethnic Germans into the Federal Republic, and this seems to have played a part in the unexpected support for the right-wing Republikaner party in West Berlin in January 1989, when it polled 90,000 votes and gained 11 seats in the city parliament. The rise in support for anti-immigrant parties continued, and the neo-Nazi NPD gained seven seats in Frankfurt city parliament in March 1989. In the European Parliament elections in June 1989 the Republikaner party gained over two million

votes and six seats. The excitement of reunification and developments in Eastern Europe may overshadow concern about immigration for a time, but if substantial immigration continues then
the potential for a political backlash, as has occurred in France,
certainly exists. There has been considerable concern at the number
of racist attacks against foreigners and asylum-seekers, particularly
in the eastern part of Germany where economic insecurity and
high unemployment contribute to racism and xenophobia.[19]

In France, popular concern about immigration rose sharply in
the 1970s, as immigrants from neighbouring Southern European
countries were replaced by Muslim north Africans and West
Africans from Senegal and other countries in the French Commonwealth. Opinion polls in the 1970s showed that majorities of
respondents felt that there were too many immigrants and that the
numbers, especially of non-Europeans, should be controlled.[20] In
particular, there was very strong hostility to North Africans, which
was probably a legacy of the bitter war of independence in Algeria
coupled with the feeling that Muslims would resist assimilation
into French society and culture. In the summer of 1973 there was
a massive outburst of racial violence directed against Algerian
immigrant workers, eleven of whom were murdered between 29
August and 21 September. No one was arrested, but some immigrant leaders were expelled. Jean-Marie Le Pen and his party, the
Front National, attempted to exploit this racial tension, but without
success.

It was not until the 1980s that Le Pen and the Front National
emerged as major political actors in French politics. In 1981 Le
Pen was unable to find 500 sponsors for his presidential candidature,
but in 1983 his party achieved a spectacular success which was to
transform its prospects. It gained 17% of the vote in local elections in
Dreux, and four of its candidates were incorporated into the
united opposition list. Three of these were later appointed assistant
mayors. Between 1982 and 1986 the numbers of Front National
cantonal candidates rose from 65 to 2,000. In 1984 the party
achieved 10% of the vote in elections to the European Parliament,
and ten of its candidates were returned. In the 1986 general
election to the National Assembly, 34 Front National deputies
were elected. Virtually all of these subsequently lost their seats in
the 1988 Assembly elections, largely because of a change in the

electoral system from proportional representation to a two-stage majoritarian system. In the presidential elections of 1988 Jean-Marie Le Pen achieved 14.4% of the popular vote.[21]

In November 1989 the Front National candidates did exceptionally well in parliamentary by-elections, securing 61% of the vote in Dreux and 47% in Marseilles. The party appears to be consolidating its organizational base and its electoral support through its relentless campaigns against immigration, foreigners, and especially what Le Pen calls 'the Islamification of France'. These campaigns have had an impact on the other right-wing parties in France – namely, the Union for French Democracy (UDF) and the Gaullists, who are afraid of losing support to the Front National. In a debate on a new law to penalize employers of illegal immigrants, the usually moderate Giscard d'Estaing, a leader of the UDF, said that immigration threatened to become an invasion and called for new nationality laws and measures to encourage the birth-rate of Europeans in France.[22] This was in marked contrast to his earlier statements,[23] and was a clear attempt to win support for the UDF from the Front National in the same way as Mrs Thatcher had done with regard to the National Front in Britain in January 1978.

As in Britain, political anti-immigrant campaigns in France have encouraged racial violence, particularly against North Africans. Between 1986 and 1990 there were some 20 murders of North Africans, in at least half of which there was no other motive than a desire to kill foreigners.[24]

The European Parliament has been so concerned at manifestations of racism against indigenous minorities and immigrants that it has carried out two inquiries. The first was established in October 1984, and published its report into the rise of Fascism and racism in Europe in December 1985.[25] In June 1986 a declaration against racism, racial discrimination and xenophobia and in favour of harmonious relations among all the communities existing in Europe was signed by the presidents of the Parliament, the European Commission and the Council of Ministers, and by representatives of the member states meeting within the Council. By September 1989 the European Parliament was still not satisfied with the action taken by the Commission, the Council of Ministers and the member states to implement the 1986 joint declaration, and there were signs that racism, xenophobia and anti-Semitism were growing and even reaching 'dangerous' levels in some states. Therefore a new European Parliament committee of inquiry into racism and xenophobia was established in October 1989, and it published its report in July 1990.[26] The report is valuable in providing up-to-date information on racism in the member states, but the European Parliament has no means of ensuring that the large number of recommendations of its committees of inquiry are implemented. Moreover, support in the Parliament for the second report was significantly less than for its predecessor, and there was much criticism of its failure to support the recommendations of its committee more vigorously.

Refugees and asylum-seekers

The issue of refugees and asylum-seekers has become a major source of contemporary concern to West European governments. All European countries claim to honour their obligations under the 1951 UN Convention and the 1967 UN protocol relating to the status of refugees. Article 1 of the Convention defines a refugee as a person who is unwilling or unable to return to his or her country 'owing to a well founded fear of being persecuted for reasons of race, religion, nationality, membership of a particular social group or political opinion'. Article 33 of the Convention states: 'No contracting state shall expel or return a refugee in any manner whatsoever to the frontiers of territories where his life or freedom would be threatened on account of his race, religion, nationality, membership of a particular social group or political opinion.'[27]

However, European governments have panicked at the rising numbers of asylum applications in the 1980s. In 1972 about 13,000 people sought asylum in Western Europe; by 1988 applications had risen to nearly 234,000, and in 1991 this had leapt to some 540,000. Table 9.2 gives levels of asylum application for the major countries of Western Europe from 1989 to 1991.

The response of European governments to the rising level of applications has been to argue that most applicants are in reality 'economic migrants' who are trying to bypass the tough immigration

Table 9.2 Asylum-seekers and refugees applying to selected European countries, 1989–91 (000s)

	1989	*1990*	*1991*
Austria	21.9	22.8	27.3
Belgium	8.0	13.0	15.2
Denmark	4.6	5.3	4.6
France	61.4	54.7	50.0
Germany	121.3	193.1	256.1
Greece	6.5	4.1	----
Italy	2.2	4.7	27.0
Netherlands	13.9	21.2	21.6
Norway	4.4	4.0	3.0
Spain	4.0	8.6	8.0
Sweden	30.0	29.4	26.5
Switzerland	24.4	35.8	41.6
UK	15.5	30.0	57.7

Source: OECD, *Continuous Reporting System on Migration* (*Sopemi*), Paris, 1992

controls introduced by most West European countries in the early 1970s. The widespread existence of internal wars in Africa, and the evidence of the use of torture and forced migration in many countries, are ignored by European politicians because of concern about the rise in applications and popular resentment at home. European governments tend to view their asylum policy as part and parcel of their immigration policy, and the level of domestic unemployment is a key factor in determining how liberal or restrictive a country's asylum policy will be.[28] It is thus not surprising that European governments have been introducing more rigorous systems for screening asylum applications and imposing harsher conditions.

The number of applications to Britain has been relatively small compared with similar countries, on account of the discouraging attitude of the government. However, large increases in applications from Somalis, Ugandans and Turkish Kurds have made the number rise sharply – from 1,563 in 1979 to 5,263 in 1988 and 15,1530 in 1989. In 1991 the Home Secretary announced that applications would rise to some 50,000, despite the action the government had taken to impose mandatory visa requirements on travellers from the relevant areas, and the Immigration (Carrier's Liability) Act which penalizes airlines and shipping companies carrying passengers to the UK without the proper documentation. In 1991 the penalties on airlines and shipping companies were doubled, from £1,000 to £2,000 per undocumented passenger.

The development of a European Community immigration policy

A number of factors are converging to foster the development of a coordinated European Community policy on immigration matters, such as a common approach to asylum-seekers, visa applicants, and migrant workers. These trends are being resisted by many European politicians – the British in particular – who feel that immigration policy is too important to be left to the European Commission because of its implications for each country's security, national identity and culture. Also, Northern European countries within the EC are distrustful of the ability of southern members of the Community, such as Italy, Portugal, Spain and Greece, to control their borders efficiently. The pressures, however, to develop a coherent and consistent Community-wide policy are very great and are increasing. The agreement to establish the free internal market within the Community on 1 January 1993, when the free movement of goods, services, capital and Community nationals is due to come into operation, is a major factor. It is clearly impossible to have an integrated labour market for the European Community, if twelve different immigration regimes are in operation in the member states. This has already been recognized by the Schengen group of countries within the Community, and their discussions and agreements are likely to provide a model for the rest of the Community to follow.

The Schengen agreement was signed in 1985 by Germany, France, Belgium, the Netherlands and Luxembourg, basically to abolish their internal borders and to allow free movement of people within their territories. This involved agreeing common policies on their external borders regarding visas, asylum-seekers and the control of non-member nationals, and also on measures to control criminals and terrorists. A supplementary agreement was signed in 1990, setting out more detailed provisions concerning the exchange of information on asylum-seekers, immigrants, criminals and undesirables (defined as those refused, or likely to be refused, entry to any Schengen country) not to be admitted to 'Schengenland'. A common list of 115 countries whose nationals will require visas to enter the Schengen area has also been agreed.[29] Italy joined the Schengen group in October 1990, and Spain, Portugal and Austria have indicated that they wish to join in due course. This would result in nine of the twelve Community countries belonging to the Schengen group, making it inevitable that the Schengen agreement will become the basis for Community immigration policy.

The Schengen arrangements inevitably involve a high degree of police cooperation among the member states, and the coordination of policies to control non-citizens. Thus non-citizens who enter a Schengen country, as well as usually requiring a visa, will have to show that they have sufficient means to support themselves and will normally be admitted for only three months. If they move from one Schengen country to another they will have to register with the authorities within three days. People defined as undesirable by one state will be excluded from all, and entrants who fail to comply with their conditions of stay will be excluded from the whole area. As in Britain, airlines and shipping companies who carry aliens with inadequate or false documents will be fined. The Schengen agreement is backed up by a computerized intelligence and information system (the Schengen Information System), which is to be based in Strasbourg. This will provide data on people to be refused entry, such as asylum-seekers who have already had their applications refused, illegal immigrants, criminals and suspected terrorists.[30]

Britain already cooperates with the Schengen group and other Community countries in these matters, and the new national police computer is being planned to use the same software as the Schengen Information System. The British government seems to be against joining the Schengen group, partly because membership has implications for internal control such as identity cards, whose introduction would be controversial and would be strongly opposed by civil liberties groups, but mainly because it has greater confidence in its ability to control its borders than it has in some of the members of the Schengen group to control theirs. Italy, for example, is well known for its permeable frontiers and its liberal attitude to illegal immigrants. However, the relatively harsh response of the Italian government towards the refugees from Albania in 1991 was undoubtedly an attempt to impress the other members of the Community, and in particular the Schengen group, with its ability and determination to act toughly against illegal immigrants.[31] British politicians, who also regard immigration matters as fundamental to national sovereignty, are unwilling to relinquish control to either the Schengen group or the European Commission.

The British government is, however, involved in other European Community groups that are discussing and negotiating on similar issues. These are the Trevi group and the Ad Hoc Group on Immigration, both of which the British government was instrumental in establishing.

The Trevi group was set up in 1976 at a meeting of interior and justice ministers to consider ways in which Community countries could work together to combat terrorism ('Trevi' is an acronym for *terrorisme, radicalisme, extrémisme,* and *violence internationale*). The group has gradually expanded its remit to cover international crime, drug-trafficking, and the policing and security aspects of free movement. To deal with these matters the Trevi group has established a number of working parties in which policemen, civil servants, intelligence officers, and security and military officers are involved.[32] There is increasing concern that important policy decisions are being taken in informal groups which are accountable neither to the European Parliament, nor to national parliaments, nor to other Community institutions. The discussions of the Trevi group are confidential, and very little is reported about them in the press or other media.

The work of the Schengen group and that of the Trevi group overlap to a considerable degree, and it seems inevitable that 'Schengenland' will expand to include the whole Community, thereby making Trevi redundant. In the meantime, those EC members who do not belong to Schengen can use Trevi as the means for sharing information on matters of common concern such as immigrants, asylum-seekers, drug-smugglers, terrorists and other groups that they wish to exclude from Community territory.

The working group on immigration is yet another informal Community group concerned with the growing issue of international migration. It was formed in October 1986 under the British presidency. It is composed, like Trevi, of the interior ministers, and was initially concerned with the dramatic rise in asylum applications. In April 1987 it agreed to a common policy on applications, and to penalties on airlines and shipping companies bringing improperly documented asylum-seekers to European Community countries.[33]

The growing importance of immigration, arising from developments in Eastern Europe and continuing pressure from North Africa, led the European Council of Ministers on 8 and 9 December 1989 to request 'that an inventory of national positions on immigration be established, to provide a basis of discussion of the matter within the Council'. The Council request was divided into two areas: (1) questions relating to the entry and movement of citizens from Third World countries, and (2) the integration of non-Community nationals who have been admitted into the territories of member states. The Commission asked a group of experts to analyse the entry policy of member states — their practices with regard to residence for immigrants, the reuniting of families, access to employment, education, housing, social benefits, civic and social rights; relations between immigrants and official bodies; and facilities for repatriation.[34]

The report was greatly concerned with demographic pressures from the countries on the southern shores of the Mediterranean, arguing that of the expected population increase in Europe and the Mediterranean between 1990 and 2000, 95% will come from countries on the southern shores and only 5% from countries in the Community. Demographic pressure, the experts felt, was one of the major problems of our times, and neither increased immigrants nor relaxing immigration controls was the answer. In the long term, they argued, economic assistance and population control measures were the most likely solution.[35]

The challenge of migration

As we approach the turn of the century, international migration has become one of the most important global issues. The dramatic political events in Eastern Europe caused by the collapse of the Soviet empire and the economic crisis in the former USSR itself raise the possibility of large-scale migratory movements from Eastern to Western Europe. Population expansion in North Africa and other Third World countries like India, Pakistan, Bangladesh and Nigeria means that Third World migration to Europe will continue. Attempts to control the flow will not reduce the pressure to migrate, but will affect the composition of the migrants.

Population decline in Europe, and the huge concentration of industrial infrastructure and capital investment, mean that immigration will continue to be an essential component of European economic growth and prosperity. The crucial question is not whether immigration will continue, as it inevitably will, but how the migration flows will be managed. As already noted, most West European countries have sophisticated procedures to control immigration and can choose whom to accept and whom to reject. Will West European countries continue to recruit from the Third World on a significant scale, or will they give priority to people from Eastern Europe, as these are more skilled and, as Europeans, easier to integrate and assimilate? Xenophobic and racist pressures within Western Europe make it increasingly difficult for their politicians to allow large-scale migration from any source. Politicians have vied with each other, each claiming to be the most restrictive as far as immigration controls are concerned, or at least as restrictive as those of other political parties. Some may well favour the development of a common European Community immigration regime, to remove immigration as an internal political issue, but so far this has not materialized. Applications to join the Community from East European countries, Turkey and Morocco have considerable immigration consequences, as most of these are emigration countries.

Problems of regulation and control of international migration are thus bound to become major issues for the Community after 1 January 1993 – and can only be intensified by the growing disparities in economic, social and demographic conditions between the European Community and neighbouring areas such as North Africa and Eastern Europe.[36] Also, a common immigration regime is imperative if free movement of Community nationals is to become a reality. A common immigration regime would also allow the right of free movement to be extended to all those legally resident in the European Community, and not only to nationals of the member states. One problem with the free circulation of people within the Community is that there is bound to be greater emphasis on internal controls to monitor illegal aliens, drug-smugglers and other law-breakers – which, as already mentioned might mean the introduction of identity cards in Britain.

The challenge of political rights and citizenship

European countries have not only to decide how to respond to the external challenge of international migration, and to develop immigration policies that are fair both to Third World countries to whom they have close ties and obligations and to their neighbours in Eastern Europe. But they also have to ensure that they meet the internal challenge posed by the need to integrate post-war immigrants and their European-born descendants. The fact that the millions of permanently settled foreign migrants are often not accepted as members of West European societies, and that they are subject to routine discrimination and often racial violence, is an affront to the liberal democratic values so greatly prized in these multi-party democracies. In addition, there is the question of the exclusion of long-term residents from political participation. A substantial majority of migrant workers appear to be unwilling to follow the traditional path to political enfranchisement for foreigners – that of naturalization. This may be due to an unwillingness to compromise their national identity, the refusal of many countries to allow dual nationality, the pressure from home governments not to give up their existing citizenship, the expense and complexity of naturalization, or the fear that they would still not be accepted even if they naturalized. But should long-settled members of West European societies continue to be excluded from political participation because they lack citizenship?

The legally settled permanent immigrant population and their descendants have transformed West European societies. They are valued members of their firms and local communities, they contribute to the health and social services as well as receiving these services. Above all, they are taxpayers; but if they retain their foreign citizenship, the democratic precept of 'no taxation without representation' does not apply to them. The precept for foreign citizens is 'no representation without naturalization'.[37]

A number of countries have recognized the democratic anomaly of having large numbers of permanent residents who are in almost every way full members of society, except that they lack political rights. Increasingly, European countries are removing from foreign citizens political constraints such as bans on public employment, on political organization, on ownership of property and businesses and on the right to form associations, and the insistence on political neutrality. These constraints have become more difficult to enforce, and have been seen as increasingly unfair. Why should foreign citizens be banned from employment in the public sector or from owning businesses, when a larger and larger proportion of them are born in Western Europe? The fact that in some countries – notably, Sweden, Norway, Denmark, Ireland and the Netherlands – local voting rights have been extended to legally resident foreign citizens is partly due to a recognition that in many European cities foreign residents constitute a large proportion of the population and that they are major recipients of local services. The extension of local voting rights in these countries may be seen as a major step towards facilitating the integration of foreign residents, and perhaps towards encouraging them to naturalize. It is clearly a recognition that they are permanent members of their new societies, and that democratic states need their consent and participation to function effectively. These states hope to gain thereby greater cooperation and legitimacy among this part of their permanently settled population, and to avoid the growth of resentment and alienation that may result in future conflict.[38] The extension of the local franchise means that local politicians, at least, have to take account of the policy preferences and needs of non-citizen permanent residents, called 'denizens' by Hammar.[39] They thus become active participants in the political process, and not merely political objects to be blamed for unemployment, crime, housing shortages and poor social services, which are often associated with urban residential areas where foreign immigrants are concentrated.

The extension of political rights to non-citizens could reduce politically inspired racism, as politicians would be more wary of alienating voting groups in the population than of alienating non-voters. How far this option is taken up will depend on the size of the non-citizen population, the degree of acceptance by the general population, the role and importance of anti-immigrant parties, the role of the media, and the willingness of political leaders to exploit racist sentiments in the electorate. The fact that New Commonwealth immigrants in Britain have both local and national voting rights has greatly assisted their acceptance into the national community, even allowing for the existence of widespread racial discrimination, the prevalence of racist attacks in some areas, and the willingness of some politicians to exploit racism for political purposes. The election of four black labour members of parliament in 1987 and the selection of Mr John Taylor, an Afro-Caribbean lawyer, for the Conservative-held though marginal seat of Cheltenham in 1990, and of Mr Nirj Deva, an Asian businessman, for Conservative-held Brentford and Isleworth, are very important symbols of the gradual political integration and acceptance of black British people. In a by-election in 1991 an additional black Labour MP, Dr Ashok Kumar, was elected. In the general election on 9 April 1992 Mr Deva was elected but Mr Taylor was unsuccessful. Dr Kumar failed to retain his by-election seat but Mr Piara Khabra was elected for the Labour party in Ealing Southall. There are thus six ethnic minority MPs in the new parliament, of whom five and Labour and one is Conservative.

Ironically, despite the full political and civic rights that post-war immigrants have enjoyed in Britain, it was here that serious inner-city riots took place in 1980–1 and 1985. Although these did not exclusively involve young Afro-Caribbeans, there was a significant involvement of second-generation Afro-Caribbean Britons. Racism is an unambiguous explanation for the grievances of young Afro-Caribbeans, and has contributed to the growth of collective feelings of injustice which have led to smouldering resentment towards those in authority.[40] The British experience shows how the granting of *de jure* rights does not necessarily result in *de facto* equality of treatment. Gradually, the race relations legislation in Britain is having an effect, and procedures such as ethnic monitoring and equal opportunity policies will, it is hoped, help to combat racial discrimination. But the impact so far has been slight, even a decade and a half after the 1976 Race Relations Act.

At the European level, the focus is on managing the immigration of people from Eastern and from south of the Mediterranean rather than on legislation to combat racial discrimination. Racist and anti-immigrant sentiments are high and rising in Germany and France, and the European Commission is under intense pressure to introduce a tough immigrant regime for the whole Community. This is distracting attention from the need to introduce policies to integrate the second generation, such as allowing dual nationality, liberalizing the naturalization laws and introducing anti-discrimination legislation. In the short term, given continuing immigration flows and electoral pressures in favour of controls, stringent immigration and anti-asylum legislation is inevitable in the European Community: the official rationale of such legislation will be both to reduce indigenous European racism and to allow positive integration policies for immigrants and their descendants already permanently settled in the Community. In the longer term, immigration policies must be developed that are fair both to Eastern Europe and to the Third World, and are acceptable to European electorates. The suppression of racial attacks, discrimination and most of all political racism must become a high priority of all European governments and of the European Community as a whole.

Notes

1 France signed agreements with Italy in 1946 and 1951, with West Germany in 1950, Greece in 1954, Spain in 1961, Morocco, Mali, Mauritania, Tunisia and Portugal in 1963, Senegal in 1964, Yugoslavia and Turkey in 1965: G. Freeman, *Immigrant Labor and Racial Conflict: The French and British Experience, 1945–75* (Princeton University Press, 1979), p. 74.

2 G. Verbunt, 'France', in T. Hammar (ed.), *European Immigration Policy* (Cambridge University Press, 1985); see also Freeman, *Immigrant Labor and Racial Conflict*.

3 A number of European countries have granted local voting rights to

long-term residents. These include Ireland, Sweden, Netherlands, Norway and Denmark. See J. Rath, 'Voting rights', in Z. Layton-Henry (ed.), *The Political Rights of Migrant Workers in Western Europe* (Sage, 1990).

4   C. Wilpert, 'Structural marginality and the role of cultural identity for migrant youth', in H. Korte (ed.), *Cultural Identity and Structural Marginalisation of Migrant Workers* (European Science Foundation, 1982), pp. 117–29.

5   OECD, *Continuous Reporting System on Migration (Sopemi)*, Paris, 1988.

6   Ibid.

7   Wilpert, 'Structural marginality'.

8   Ibid.

9   Ibid.

10   Ibid.

11   H. Malewska-Peyre, 'Conflictual cultural identity of second-generation immigrants', in Korte, *Cultural Identity and Structural Marginalization*.

12   G. de Rham, 'Naturalisation: the politics of citizenship acquisition', in Layton-Henry, *Political Rights of Migrant Workers*.

13   Ibid.

14   S. Tomlinson, 'Policy dilemmas in multi-cultural education', in Z. Layton-Henry and P. B. Rich (eds), *Race, Government and Politics in Britain* (Macmillan, 1986).

15   B. S. Heisler, 'From conflict to accommodation: the "foreigners question" in Switzerland', *European Journal of Political Research*, vol. 16, no. 6 (1988), 683–700.

16   C. T. Husbands, 'The dynamics of racial exclusion and expulsion: racist politics in Western Europe', *European Journal of Political Research*, vol. 16, no. 6 (1988), 701–18.

17   *Time Magazine*, 30 August 1982.

18   European Parliament, *Report of the Committee of Inquiry into Racism and Xenophobia*, 23 July 1990, p. 53.

19   *Independent*, 4 October 1991.

20   Freeman, *Immigrant Labor and Racial Conflict*.

21   M. A. Schain, 'Immigration and changes in the French party system', *European Journal of Political Research*, vol. 16, no. 6 (1988), 597–621.

22   *Independent*, 23 and 24 September 1991.

23   See p. 218.

24   European Parliament, *Racism and Xenophobia*, p. 56.

25   European Parliament, *Report of the Committee of Inquiry into the Rise of Fascism and Racism in Europe*, December 1985.

26   European Parliament, *Racism and Xenophobia*.

27   United Nations High Commission for Refugees, *Handbook on Procedures and Criteria for Determining Refugee Status*, Geneva, 1979.

28 A. Phillips, 'Employment as a key to settlement', in D. Joly and R. Cohen (eds), *Reluctant Hosts: Europe and its Refugees* (Avebury, 1990).

29 T. Bunyan, 'Towards an authoritarian European state', *Race and Class*, vol. 32, no. 3 (1991), 19–27; M. Baldwin-Edwards, 'Immigration after 1992', *Policy and Politics*, vol. 19, no. 3 (1991), 199–211.

30 Bunyan, 'Towards an authoritarian European state'.

31 *Independent*, 13 September 1991.

32 Bunyan, 'Towards an authoritarian European state', p. 23.

33 Commission of the European Community, 'Policies on immigration and the social integration of migrants in the European Community', SEC (90), 1813, Brussels, 28 September 1990.

34 Ibid.; the experts were F. Braun, R. Böhning, J. Fernandez Corden, A. Golini, W. Hyde and P. L. Remy.

35 Ibid., pp. 11–12.

36 S. Castles, 'Migrations and minorities in Europe: perspectives for the 1990s: twelve hypotheses', paper presented at the conference on racism and migration in Europe in the 1990s, University of Warwick, 1991.

37 The case for extending political rights to foreign migrant workers and their families is made in Layton-Henry, *Political Rights of Migrant Workers*. See also T. Hammar, *Democracy and the Nation State* (Avebury, 1990).

38 Layton-Henry, *Political Rights of Migrant Workers*.

39 Hammar, *Democracy and the Nation State*.

40 J. Benyon, 'Spiral of decline: race and policing', in Layton-Henry and Rich, *Race, Government and Politics*.

Outline Chronology

1945 – Second World War ends. Government attempts to repatriate colonial workers but many settle. Substantial Irish immigration continues. Labour wins general election with landslide majority of 146.

1947 – Polish Resettlement Act; Polish Resettlement Corps established.

1948 – British Nationality Act. SS *Empire Windrush* and SS *Orbita*: first immigrant ships arrive from West Indies.

1949 – Royal Commission on Population report, arguing that immigrants should be encouraged only if they are of 'good human stock'.

1950 – Reg Sorenson introduces Private Member's Bill to outlaw racial discrimination. Not passed. General election: Labour majority reduced to 5.

1951 – General election: Conservative majority of 17.

1952 – McCarran-Walter Immigration Act restricts West Indian immigration to USA.

1954 – Immigration Control Act drafted but not presented to parliament.

1955 – Conservatives win general election, majority of 58.

1956 – Private Member's Bill to outlaw discrimination in public places introduced by Fenner Brockway: not passed.

1958 – Anti-black riots in Nottingham and Notting Hill. Labour party opposes immigration controls. Institute of Race Relations established.

1959 – Conservatives win third general election with majority of 101.

1960 – Withholding of passports from intending emigrants declared illegal by Indian Supreme Court. Birmingham Immigration

Control Association set up.

1961 – Campaign for immigration control contributes to large rise in immigration. Conservatives introduce Commonwealth Immigrants Bill.

1962 – Commonwealth Immigrants Act, making entry subject to possession of employment voucher.

1964 – Labour party wins general election with majority of 5. Peter Griffiths defeats Patrick Gordon Walker at Smethwick after anti-immigration campaign; Griffiths condones use of 'nigger neighbour' slogan. Fenner Brockway defeated at Eton and Slough. Labour government renews immigration control legislation.

1965 – Gordon Walker loses Leyton by-election. White Paper on immigration from Commonwealth reduces annual number of entry vouchers to 8,500, of which 1,000 are for Malta. Race Relations Act. Race Relations Board and National Committee for Commonwealth Immigrants set up.

1966 – Labour wins general election with majority of 96. Political and Economic Planning report on racial discrimination. Andrew Faulds captures Smethwick from Peter Griffiths.

1967 – National Front founded. Joint Council for the Welfare of Immigrants established.

1968 – Commonwealth Immigrants Act, controlling entry of East African Asians. Enoch Powell's 'river of blood' speech. Race Relations Act. NCCI replaced by Community Relations Commission. Parliamentary Select Committee on Race Relations and Immigration established.

1969 – Immigration Appeals Act. *Colour and Citizenship*: major survey of British race relations published by Institute of Race Relations.

1970 – Conservatives win general election with majority of 30. Heath Prime Minister. David Pitt loses Clapham. United Kingdom Immigrant Advisory Service set up.

1971 – Immigration Act replaces Aliens Restriction Act 1914 and Commonwealth Immigrants Acts of 1962 and 1968. Home Office sets up its own race relations research unit.

1972 – Asians expelled from Uganda; 27,000 admitted to UK.

1973 – National Front obtains 16.3% of vote at West Bromwich by-election in May. Pakistan leaves Commonwealth because of

Britain's recognition of Bangladesh. Pakistan Act passed, continuing political rights of Pakistanis in Britain.

1974 – General elections in February and October. Labour minority government returned in February; overall majority in October of only 3. Second PEP report on racial discrimination and disadvantage.

1976 – Race Relations Act. Commission for Racial Equality established. Hawley report on immigration from Indian subcontinent. Malawi Asians media panic followed by rise in support for National Front in May local elections, but they fail to win any seats. Gurdip Singh Chaggar (18) stabbed to death in Southall. David Lane, Conservative MP for Cambridge, appointed head of new Commission for Racial Equality. Notting Hill carnival involves clashes between young blacks and police.

1977 – National Front increasingly active in by-elections and confrontational marches. Gains third place at Stechford and Ladywood by-elections. Considerable publicity for National Front after violent clashes with Socialist Workers Party at Lewisham march in August. 30 August: *The Times* publishes interview with John Tyndall, leader of National Front. Clashes at Grunwick strike in East London involving Asian workers.

1978 – Mrs Thatcher's 'swamping' interview. Conservatives propose tougher immigration legislation.

1979 – Conservatives win general election with majority of 43. Mrs Thatcher becomes Prime Minister. National Front fragments after disastrous results.

1980 – Select Committee recommends repeal of 'Sus' law. Inner-city riot in Bristol after police raid on Black and White Café in St Paul's.

1981 – Nationality Act passed. Inner-city riots in Brixton, Toxteth and elsewhere. Select Committee report on racial disadvantage. Scarman report. Home Office report on racial attacks.

1983 – General election: Conservatives returned with majority of 144.

1985 – Handsworth riot: two shopkeepers die in post office fire. Broadwater Farm riot. PC Blakelock hacked to death. Visa controls imposed on visitors from Sri Lanka.

1986 – Visa controls imposed on visitors from India, Nigeria, Ghana, Pakistan and Bangladesh. Second Home Office report on racial attacks. Immigration (Carrier's Liability) Act. Immigration Act.

1987 – General election. Conservatives returned with majority of 100. Four black Labour MPs returned to parliament: Diane Abbott, Paul Boateng, Bernie Grant and Keith Vaz.

1988 – Immigration Act passed, further restricting rights of immigrants.

1989 – Viraj Mendis returned to Sri Lanka after long campaign to stay. Copy of *Satanic Verses* burned during large demonstration in Bradford. Ayatollah Khomeini passes death sentence on Salman Rushdie. Government decides to grant full British citizenship to 225,000 people from Hong Kong.

1990 – British Nationality (Hong Kong) Act. European Parliament's report on racism and xenophobia. Nottinghamshire police found guilty of racial discrimination against PC Surenda Singh, who is awarded £20,000 damages.

1991 – Home Office orders detention of 70 Iraqis and Palestinians after start of Gulf War. Bill Morris becomes first black person elected to lead a major union, the TGWU. Asylum Bill published. Dr Ashok Kumar elected at Langbaurgh by-election.

1992 – General election, Conservatives returned with overall majority of 21. At Brentford and Isleworth, Mr Nirj Deva elected as first-Asian Conservative MP since 1900. The black Conservative, Mr John Taylor, loses at Cheltenham. Five ethnic minority Labor MPs elected, including the new MP Mr Piara Khabra for Ealing Southall.

Bibliography

Anwar, M., *Votes and Policies: Ethnic Minorities and the General Election 1979*, Commission for Racial Equality, 1980.

Anwar, M., *Race and Politics: Ethnic Minorities and the British Political System*, London, Tavistock Publications, 1986.

Anwar, M., 'Ethnic minorities and the electoral process: some recent developments', in H. Goulbourne (ed.), *Black Politics in Britain*, Aldershot, Avebury, 1990.

Anwar, M., 'Ethnic minorities' representation: voting and electoral politics in Britain, and the role of leaders', in P. Werbner and M. Anwar, *Black and Ethnic Leaderships: The Cultural Dimensions of Political Action*, London, Routledge & Kegan Paul, 1991.

Baldwin-Edwards, M., 'Immigration after 1992', *Policy and Politics*, vol. 19, no. 3 (1991).

Beetham, D., *Transport and Turbans: A Comparative Study in Local Politics*, Oxford, Oxford University Press, 1970.

Benyon, J. (ed.), *Scarman and After*, Oxford, Pergamon Press, 1984.

Benyon, J., 'Spiral of decline: race and policing', in Z. Layton–Henry and P. B. Rich, *Race, Government and Politics in Britain*, London, Macmillan, 1986.

Benyon, J. and Solomos, J. (eds), *The Roots of Urban Unrest*, Oxford, Pergamon Press, 1987.

Bethnal Green and Stepney Trades Council, *Blood on the Streets: A Report on Racial Attacks in East London*, 1978.

Billig, M., *Fascists: A Social Psychological View of the National Front*, London, Academic Press, 1978.

Bochel, J., and Denver, D., 'Candidate selection in the Labour party: what the selectors seek', *British Journal of Political Science*, vol. 13 (1983).

Bradley, I., 'Why Churchill's plan to limit immigration was shelved', *The Times*, 20 March 1978.

British Nationality Bill, Session 1980–1, HMSO, 1981.

Brookes, D., *Race and Labour in London Transport*, Oxford, Oxford University Press, 1975.

Bulpitt, J., 'Continuity, autonomy and peripheralisation: the anatomy of the centre's race statecraft in England', in Z. Layton–Henry and Paul B. Rich (eds), *Race, Government and Politics in Britain*, London, Macmillan, 1986.

Bunyan, T., 'Towards an authoritarian European state', *Race and Class*, vol. 32, no. 3 (1991).

Butler, D. and Pinto-Duschinsky, M., *The British General Election of 1970*, London, Macmillan, 1971.

Butler, D. and Stokes, D., *Political Change in Britain*, Macmillan, 1974.

Cabinet Papers, 'Coloured people from British colonial territories', memorandum by Secretary of State for the Colonies, (50) 113, 18 May 1950, Public Record Office.

Cabinet Papers, 'Immigration of British subjects into the United Kingdom', 128/44, 14 February 1951, Public Record Office.

Cabinet Papers, Report of the Committee on the Social and Economic Problems arising from the Growing Influx into the United Kingdom of Coloured Workers from other Commonwealth Countries, 129/77, 3 August 1955, Public Record Office.

Cabinet Papers, 'Colonial immigrants', memorandum by Secretary of State for Commonwealth Relations, 127/77, 2 September 1955, Public Record Office.

Cabinet Papers, 'Colonial immigrants', memorandum by Secretary of State for the Colonies, 129/78, 1 November 1955, Public Record Office.

Cabinet Papers, 'Colonial immigrants', note by Prime Minister, 129/78, 20 November 1955, Public Record Office.

Cabinet Papers, 'Colonial Immigrants', report of the Committee of Ministers, 129/81, 22 June 1956, Public Record Office.

Cain, M., *Society and the Policeman's Role*, London, Routledge & Kegan Paul, 1973.

Callaghan, J., *Time and Chance*, London, Fontana, 1988.

Carmichael, S. and Hamilton, C. V., *Black Power: The Politics of Liberation in America*, Harmondsworth, Penguin Books, 1967.

Casey, J., 'One nation: the politics of race', *Salisbury Review*, no. 1 (Autum 1982).

Castells, M., 'Immigrant workers and class struggles in advanced capitalism: the West European experience', *Politics and Society*, vol. 5, no. 1 (1975),

Castles, S. and Kosack, G., *Immigrant Workers and Class Structure in Western Europe*, Oxford, Oxford University Press, 1973.

Cheetham, J., 'Immigration', in A. H. Halsey (ed.), *Trends in British Society since 1900*, London, Macmillan, 1972.

Cohen, S., *From the Jews to the Tamils: Britain's Mistreatment of Refugees*, Manchester, South Manchester Law Centre, 1988.

Commission of the European Community, 'Policies on immigration and the social integration of migrants in the European Community', SEC(90), 1813, Brussels, 28 September 1990.

Commission for Racial Equality, *Brick Lane and Beyond: An Inquiry into Racial Strife and Violence in Tower Hamlets*, 1979.

Commission for Racial Equality, *Ethnic Minorities and the 1983 General Election*, 1984.

Community Relations Commission, *The Participation of Ethnic Minorities in the General Election, October 1974*, 1975.

Conservative Central Office, *The Right Road for Britain*, 1949.

Conservative Central Office, *The Right Approach: A Statement of Conservative*

Aims, 1976.

Conservative Central Office, *Our First Eight Years: The Achievements of the Conservative Government since May 1979*, 1987.

Conservative Central Office, Conservative manifestos, 1945–87.

Conservative Political Centre, *Who Do We Think We Are?*, 1980.

Cosgrave, P., *The Lives of Enoch Powell*, London, Pan Books, 1990.

Crewe, I., 'The black, brown and green votes', *New Society*, 12 April 1979.

Crewe, I., 'Representation and ethnic minorities in Britain', in N. Glazer and K. Young (eds), *Ethnic Pluralism and Public Policy*, London, Heinemann, 1983.

Crewe, I. and Särlvik, B., 'Popular attitudes and electoral strategy', in Z. Layton–Henry (ed.), *Conservative Party Politics*, London, Macmillan, 1980.

Crossman, R., *Diaries of a Cabinet Minister*, vol. 1, London, Hamish Hamilton and Jonathan Cape, 1975.

Crossman, R., *Diaries of a Cabinet Minister*, vol. 2, London, Hamish Hamilton and Jonathan Cape, 1977.

Daniel, W. W., *Racial Discrimination in England*, Harmondsworth, Penguin Books, 1968.

Deakin, N. (ed.), *Colour and the British Electorate, 1964*, London, Pall Mall Press, 1965.

Deakin, N., 'The immigration issue in British politics', unpublished PhD thesis, University of Sussex, 1972.

Deakin, N. and Bourne, J., 'The minorities and the general election of 1970', *Race Today*, vol. 2 (July 1970).

Dear, G., *Handsworth/Lozells: September 1985*, report of the Chief Constable, West Midlands Police, Birmingham, West Midlands Police, 1985.

Defoe, D., 'The True-born Englishman', in H. Morley (ed.), *The Earlier Life and Chief Earlier Works of Daniel Defoe*, London, George Routledge & Sons, 1899.

Dominion Office, Report of the Working Party on Coloured People Seeking Employment in the United Kingdom, 35/5216, December 1953, Public Record Office.

Eade, J., 'The political construction of class and community: Bangladeshi political leadership in Tower Hamlets, East London', in P. Werbner and M. Anwar (eds), *Black and Ethnic Leaderships: The Cultural Dimensions of Political Action*, London, Routledge & Kegan Paul, 1991.

Ealing Community Relations Council, *Racialist Activity in Ealing 1979–81*, August 1981.

European Parliament, *Report of the Committee of Inquiry into the Rise of Fascism and Racism in Europe*, December 1985.

European Parliament, *Report of the Committee of Inquiry into Racism and Xenophobia*, 23 July 1990.

Fielding, N., *The National Front*, London, Routledge & Kegan Paul, 1981.

FitzGerald, M., *Political Parties and Black People*, Runnymede Trust, 1984.

FitzGerald, M., 'The parties and the "black" vote', in I. Crewe and M. Harrop (eds), *Political Communications: The General Election Campaign of 1983*, Cambridge University Press, 1986.

FitzGerald, M., *Black People and Party Politics in Britain*, Runnymede Trust, 1987.

FitzGerald, M., 'Different roads? The development of Afro-Caribbean and Asian political organisations in London', *New Community*, vol. 14, no. 3 (1988).

FitzGerald, M., 'The emergence of black councillors and MPs in Britain: some underlying questions', in H. Goulbourne (ed.), *Black Politics in Britain*, Aldershot, Avebury, 1990.

FitzGerald, M., 'Race and the criminal justice system: research issues', paper presented at the annual conference of the British Criminology Association, July 1991.

FitzGerald, M. and Layton–Henry, Z., 'Opposition parties and race policies 1979–83', in Z. Layton–Henry and P. B. Rich (eds), *Race, Government and Politics in Britain*, London, Macmillan, 1986.

Foot, P., *Immigration and Race in British Politics*, Harmondsworth, Penguin Books, 1965.

Foot, P., *The Rise of Enoch Powell*, Harmondsworth, Penguin Books, 1969.

Freeman, G., *Immigrant Labor and Racial Conflict: The French and British Experience, 1945–75*, Princeton, Princeton University Press, 1979.

Gainer, B., *The Alien Invasion: The Origins of the Aliens Act of 1905*, London, Heinemann, 1972.

Garrard, J. A., *The English and Immigration*, Oxford, Oxford University Press, 1971.

Gifford, Lord, *The Broadwater Farm Inquiry*, Karia Press, 1986.

Glass, R., *Newcomers: West Indians in London*, London, Allen & Unwin, 1960.

Gordon, P., *White Law: Racism in the Police, Courts and Prisoners*, London, Pluto Press, 1983.

Gordon, P. and Rosenberg, D., *Daily Racism: The Press and Black People in Britain*, Runnymede Trust, 1989.

Goulbourne, H. (ed.), *Black Politics in Britain*, Aldershot, Avebury, 1990.

Granada Television, verbatim report of part of an interview with Mrs Thatcher by Gordon Burns. Extract by courtesy of 'World in Action', 30 January 1978.

Hall, S., Critcher, C., Jefferson, T. and Roberts, B., *Policing the Crisis*, London, Macmillan, 1978.

Hammar, T., *Democracy and the Nation State*, Aldershot, Avebury, 1990.

Hartley-Brewer, M., 'Smethwick' in N. Deakin (ed.), *Colour and the British Electorate 1964*, London, Pall Mall Press, 1965.

Hatfield, M., *The House the Left Built: Inside Labour Policy-making, 1970–75*, London, Gollancz, 1978.

Hattersley, R., 'Immigration', in C. Cook and D. McKie (eds), *The Decade of Disillusion: British Politics in the 1960s*, London, MacMillan, 1972.

Heisler, B. S., 'From conflict to accommodation: the "foreigners question" in Switzerland', *European Journal of Political Research*, vol. 16, no. 6 (1988).

Hindell, K., 'The genesis of the Race Relations Bill', *Political Quarterly*, vol. 34, no. 4 (1965).

Hiro, D., *Black British, White British: A History of Race Relations in Britain*, London, Grafton Books, 1991.

Hirst, W., Murray, G. and Hammond, J. L. (eds), *Liberalism and the Empire*, London, Johnson, 1900.

Holmes, C., *John Bull's Island: Immigration and British Society, 1871–1971*, London, Macmillan, 1988.

Home Office, *Racial Discrimination*, Cmnd 6234, HMSO, 1975.

Home Office, *British Nationality Law: Discussion of Possible Changes*, Cmnd 6795, HMSO, 1977.

Home Office, *Proposals for Revision of the Immigration Rules*, Cmnd 7750, HMSO, 1979.

Home Office, *British Nationality Law: Outline of Proposed Legislation*, Cmnd 7987, HMSO, 1980.

Home Office, *Racial Attacks*, report of a Home Office study, HMSO, 1981.

Home Office, government reply to the fifth report from the Home Affairs Committee, Session 1981–2, *Racial Disadvantage*, HMSO, 1982.

Home Office, government reply to the third report from the Home Affairs Committe, Session 1982–3, *British Nationality Fees*, HMSO, 1984.

House of Commons, *Police–Immigrant Relations*, report by the Select Committee on Race Relations and Immigration, Session 1971–2, HMSO, 1972.

House of Commons, *The Organisation of Race Relations Administration*, second special report from the Select Committee on Race Relations and Immigration, Session 1974–6, HMSO, 1975.

House of Commons, *Commonwealth Immigration to the United Kingdom from the 1950s to 1975: A Survey of Statistical Sources*, Library Research Paper no. 56, HMSO, 1976.

House of Commons, *Race Relations and the 'Sus' Law*, second report from the Home Affairs Committee, Session 1979–80, HMSO, 1980.

House of Commons, *Racial Disadvantage*, fifth report from the Home Affairs Committee, Session 1980–1, HMSO, 1981 (Commission for Racial Equality, 1981).

House of Commons, *British Nationality Fees*, third report from the Home Affairs Committee, Session 1982–3, HMSO, 1984.

House of Commons, *Racial Attacks and Harassment*, third report from the Home Affairs Committee, Session 1985–6, HMSO, 1986.

House of Commons, *Racial Attacks and Harassment*, first report of the Home Affairs Commitee, Session 1989–90, HMSO, 1990.

House of Commons, *Administrative Delays in the Immigration and Nationality Department*, fifth report of the Home Affairs Committee, Session 1989–90, HMSO, 1990.

Humphrey, D. and Ward, M., *Passports and Politics*, Harmondsworth Penguin Books, 1974.

Husbands, C. T., *Racial Exclusionism and the City: The Urban Support of the National Front*, London, Allen & Unwin, 1983.

Husbands, C. T., 'The dynamics of racial exclusion and expulsion: racist politics in Western Europe', *European Journal of Political Research*, vol. 16, no. 6 (1988).

Immigration Act 1971, HMSO, 1971.

Immigration from the Commonwealth, Cmnd 2739, HMSO, 1965.

Joint Council for the Welfare of Immigrants, *Out of Sight: The New Visit Visa System Overseas*, October, 1987.

Joint Council for the Welfare of Immigrants, *Target Caribbean: The Rise in Visitor Refusals from the Caribbean*, July, 1990.

Joshua, H. and Wallace, T., *To Ride the Storm: The 1980 Bristol 'Riot' and the State*, London, Heinemann, 1983.

Katznelson, I., *Black Men, White Cities*, Oxford, Oxford University Press, 1973.

Kettle, M. and Hodges, L., *Uprising: The Police, the People and the Riots in Britain's Cities*, London, Pan, 1982.

Kushner, T., *The Persistence of Prejudice: Anti-Semitism in British Society during the Second World War*, Manchester, Manchester University Press, 1989.

Labour Party, *Citizenship, Immigration and Integration: A Policy for the 1970s*, 1972.

Labour Party, *Labour and the Black Electorate*, 1980.

Labour Party, *Opportunity Britain: Labour's Better Way for the 1990s*, 1991.

Labour Party, *Opportunities for All: Labour's Campaign Statement for Ethnic Minorities*, 1991.

Labour Party Race Action Group, *Don't Take Black Votes for Granted*, 1979.

Labour Party Research Department, *British Nationality Law: Our Alternative to Tory Legislation*, 1981.

Lambert, J., *Crime, Police and Race Relations*, Oxford, Oxford University Press, 1970.

Lawrence, D., *Black Migrants, White Natives*, Cambridge, Cambridge University Press, 1974.

Layton—Henry, Z., 'Labour's lost youth', *Journal of Contemporary History*, vol. 11 (July 1976).

Layton—Henry, Z., 'Race, electoral strategy and the major parties', *Parliamentary Affairs*, vol. 31, no. 3 (1978).

Layton—Henry, Z., 'The report on immigration', *Political Quarterly*, vol. 50, no. 2 (1979).

Layton—Henry, Z., (ed.), *Conservative Party Politics*, London, Macmillan, 1980.

Layton—Henry, Z., *The Politics of Race in Britain*, London, Allen & Unwin, 1984.

Layton—Henry, Z., 'The state and New Commonwealth immigration: 1951—56', *New Community*, vol. 14, nos. 1/2 (1987).

Layton—Henry, Z. (ed.), *The Political Rights of Migrant Workers in Western Europe*, London, Sage, 1990.

Layton—Henry, Z. and Studlar, D. T., 'The electoral participation of black and Asian Britons: integration or alienation?', *Parliamentary Affairs*, vol. 38, no. 3 (1985).

Layton—Henry, Z. and Taylor, S., 'Race and politics: the case of the Ladywood by-election', *New Community*, vol. 6 (1977/8).

Lebzelter, G., *Political Anti-semitism in England*, London, Macmillan, 1978.

LeLohé, M. J., 'The effects of the presence of immigrants upon the local political system in Bradford, 1945—77', in R. Miles and A. Phizacklea, *Racism and Political Action*, London, Routledge & Kegan Paul, 1979.

LeLohé, M. J., *A Study of Non-registration among Ethnic Minorities*, Commission for Racial Equality, 1987.

LeLohé, M. J., 'The Asian vote in a northern city', in H. Goulbourne (ed.), *Black Politics in Britain*, Aldershot, Avebury, 1990.

Lindley, P., 'The Merseyside task force', paper presented at the annual conference of the Political Studies Association, Oxford, August 1983.

McLellan, D. (ed.), *Karl Marx: Selected Writings, Marx to Meyer and Vogt* (9th edn. April 1870), Oxford, Oxford University Press, 1977.

Macleod, I., 'A shameful and unnecessary act', *Spectator*, 1 March 1968.

Malewska-Peyre, H., 'Conflictural cultural identity of second-generation immigrants', in H. Korte (ed.), *Cultural Identity and Structural Marginalisation of Migrant Workers*, Strasbourg, European Science Foundation, 1982.

May, R. and Cohen, R., 'The interaction between race and colonialism: a case study of the Liverpool race riots of 1919', *Race and Class*, vol. 16, no. 2 (1974).

Miles, R., *Racism and Migrant Labour*, London, Routledge & Kegan Paul, 1982.

Miles, R., 'The racialisation of British politics', *Political Studies*, vol. 38 (1990).

Miles, R. and Phizacklea, A., 'Class, race, ethnicity and political action, *Political Studies*, vol. 25, no. 4 (1977).

Miles, R. and Phizacklea, A. (eds), *Racism and Political Action*, London, Routledge & Kegan Paul, 1979.

Miles, R. and Phizacklea, A., *White Man's Country*, London, Pluto Press, 1984.

Miller, W. L., 'What was the profit in following the crowd?: aspects of Conservative and Labour strategy since 1970', *British Journal of Political Science*, vol. 10 (1980).

Ministry of Labour, Report of the Working Party on the Employment in the United Kingdom of Surplus Colonial Labour, Ministry of Labour Papers 26/226/7503, Public Record Office, 1948.

Moore, R. and Wallace, T., *Slamming the Door: The Administration of Immigration Control*, Oxford, Martin Robertson, 1975.

Morris, B., 'Time for new thinking in the black sections debate', *Tribune*, 8 January 1988.

Mullard, C., *Black Britain*, London, Allen & Unwin, 1973.

National Council for Civil Liberties, *Southall 23 April 1979*, 1980.

'National opinion polls, immigration and race relations', *Social and Economic Review*, no. 14 (1978).

Norton, P., 'Intra-party dissent in the House of Commons: a case study of the immigration Rules 1972', *Parliamentary Affairs*, vol. 29, no. 4 (1976).

OECD, *Continuous Reporting System on Migration* (*Sopemi*), 1982–90.

Osman, A., 'Blacks give ultimatum to Labour', *Observer*, 10 June 1984.

Parkinson, M. and Duffy, J., 'Government's response to inner-city riots: the Minister for Merseyside and the task', *Parliamentary Affairs*, vol. 37, no. 1 (1984).

Pearson, G., '"Paki-bashing" in a north-east Lancashire cotton town: a case study and its history', in G. Mungham and G. Pearson (eds), *Working-Class Youth Culture*, Routledge & Kegan Paul, 1976.

Phillips, A., 'Employment as a key to settlement', in D. Joly and R. Cohen (eds), *Reluctant Hosts: Europe and its Refugees*, Aldershot, Avebury, 1990.

Phizacklea, A. and Miles, R., *Labour and Racism*, London, Routledge & Kegan Paul, 1980.

Political and Economic Planning, *Population Policy in Great Britain*, 1948.

Powell, E., *Freedom and Reality*, Tadworth, Elliot Right Way Books, 1969.

Powell, E., *Still to Decide*, London, Batsford, 1972.

Ratcliffe, P., *Racism and Reaction: A Profile of Handsworth*, London, Routledge & Kegan Paul, 1981.

Rees, T., 'United Kingdom', in D. Kubat (ed.), *The Politics of Migration Policies*, New York, Centre for Migration Studies, 1979.

Rex, J., 'The race relations catastrophe', in T. Burgess (ed.), *Matters of Principle: Labour's Last Chance*, Harmondsworth, Penguin Books, 1968.

Rex, J., 'Black militancy and class conflict', in R. Miles and A. Phizacklea (eds) *Racism and Political Action*, London, Routledge & Kegan Paul, 1979.

Rex, J. and Moore, R., *Race, Community and Conflict*, Oxford, Oxford University Press, 1967.

Rex, J. and Tomlinson, S., *Colonial Immigrants in a British City*, London, Routledge & Kegan Paul, 1979.

de Rham, G., 'Naturalisation: the politics of citizenship acquisition', in Z. Layton–Henry (ed.), *The Political Rights of Migrant Workers in Western Europe*, London, Sage, 1990.

Rose, E. J. B., Deakin, N., Abrams, M., Jackson, V., Peston, M., Vanags, A., Cohen, B., Gaitskell, J. and Ward, P., *Colour and Citizenship*, Oxford, Oxford University Press, 1969.

Royal Commission on Population, Report of the, Cmnd 7695, HMSO, 1949.

Russel, T., *The Tory Party: Its Policies, Divisions and Future*, Harmondsworth, Penguin Books, 1978.

Sardar, Z. and Davies, M. W., *Distorted Imagination: Lessons from the Rushdie Affair*, London, Grey Seal Books, 1990.

Scarman, Lord, *The Brixton Disorders, 10–12 April 1981*, report of an inquiry, Cmnd 8427, HMSO, 1981.

Schoen, D., *Enoch Powell and the Powellites*, London, Macmillan, 1977.

Scott, D., 'The National Front in local politics: some interpretations', in I. Crewe (ed.), *The Politics of Race*, London, Croom Helm, 1975.

Sewell, T., *Black Tribunes: Race and Representation in British Politics, London, Lawrence & Wishart, 1992.*

Shallice, A. and Gordon, P., *Black People, White Justice? Race and the Criminal Justice System*, Runnymede Trust, 1990.

Sherman, J. A., *Island Refuge: Britain and Refugees from the Third Reich 1933–39*, London, Paul Elek, 1973.

Sherwood, M., *Many Struggles: West Indian Workers and Service Personnel in Britain, 1939–45, London, Karim Press, 1985.*

Shukra, K., 'Black sections in the Labour party', in H. Goulbourne (ed.), *Black Politics in Britain*, Aldershot, Avebury, 1990.

Sivanandan, A., *A Different Hunger*, London Pluto Press, 1982.

Smith, D., *Racial Disadvantage in Britain: The PEP Report*, Harmondsworth, Penguin Books, 1977.

Smith, D. J. and Gray, J., *Police and People in London: the PSI Report*, Aldershot, Gower, 1985.

Smith, G., *When Jim Crow met John Bull*, London, I. B. Tauris, 1987.

Smithies, B. and Fiddick, P. (eds), *Enoch Powell on Immigration*, London, Sphere Books, 1969.

Solomos, J., *Race and Racism in Contemporary Britain*, London, Macmillan, 1989.

Sooben, P. N., *The Origins of the Race Relations Act*, Research Paper in Ethnic Relations no. 12, Centre for Research in Ethnic Relations, University of Warwick, September 1990.

Spearman, D., 'Enoch Powell's postbag', *New Society*, 9 May 1968.

Steel, D., *No Entry*, London, C. Hurst, 1969.

Stevens, P. and Willis, C., *Race, Crime and Arrests*, Home Office Research Study no. 58, HMSO, 1979.

Studlar, D., 'British public opinion, colour issues and Enoch Powell: a longitudinal analysis, *British Journal of Political Science*, vol. 4 (1974).

Studlar, D. T., 'Policy voting in Britain: the coloured immigration issue in the 1964, 1966 and 1970 general elections', *American Political Science Review*, vol. 72 (1978).

Studlar, D. T., 'The ethnic vote, 1983: problems of analysis and interpretation', *New Community*, vol. 11 (1983).

Studlar, D. T., 'Non-white policy preferences, political participation and the political agenda in Britain', in Z. Layton−Henry and P. B. Rich (eds), *Race, Government and Politics in Britain*, London, Macmillan, 1986.

Studlar, D. T. and Layton−Henry, Z., 'Non-white minority access to the political agenda in Britain', *Policy Studies Review*, vol. 9, no. 2 (1990).

Tannahill, J. A., *European Volunteer Workers in Britain*, Manchester, Manchester University Press, 1958.

Taylor, S., *The National Front in English Politics*, London, Macmillan, 1982.

Tomlinson, S., 'Policy dilemmas in multi-cultural education', in Z. Layton−Henry and P. B. Rich (eds), *Race, Government and Politics in Britain*, London, Macmillan, 1986.

Tompson, K., *Under Siege: Racial Violence in Britain Today*, Harmondsworth, Penguin Books, 1988.

United Nations High Commission for Refugees, *Handbook on Procedures and Criteria for Determining Refugee Status*, Geneva, 1979.

Walker, M., *The National Front*, London, Fontana, 1977.

Wallraff, G., *Lowest of the Low*, London, Methuen, 1988.

Webber, D., 'Defusing the time bombs in Britain's inner cities', *The Times*, 14 May 1985.

Westergaard, J. and Resler, H., *Class in a Capitalist Society*, Harmondsworth, Penguin Books, 1976.

Wilpert, C., 'Structural marginality and the role of cultural identity for migrant youth', in H. Korte (ed.), *Cultural Identity and Structural Marginalisation of Migrant Workers*, Strasbourg, European Science Foundation, 1982.

Wilson, H., *The Labour Government 1964−70*, Harmondsworth, Penguin Books, 1971.

Wood, J., *Powell and the 1970 Election*, Tadworth, Elliot Right Way Books, 1970.

Zubrzycki, J., *Polish Immigrants to Britain*, The Hague, Martinus Nijhoff, 1956.

Index

All references are to immigrants/
immigration into Britain unless
it is otherwise noted.